Mama, PhD

Mama, PhD

Women Write about Motherhood and Academic Life

Edited by Elrena Evans and Caroline Grant

RUTGERS UNIVERSITY PRESS

NEW BRUNSWICK, NEW JERSEY, AND LONDON

"In Medias Res" by Sonya Huber first appeared in *Literary Mama* in 2006.

"First Day of School" by Amy Hudock first appeared in *Literary Mama* in 2003.

"On Being Phyllis's Daughter: Thoughts on Academic Intimacy" by Laura Levitt is adapted from chapter 4 of her book *American Jewish Loss after the Holocaust* (New York: New York University Press, 2007). Grateful thanks is given to New York University Press for permission to reprint some of this material.

Grateful acknowledgement is made to Big Idea for permission to use a line from "Dr. Jiggle and Mr. Sly" from *A Snoodle's Tale*, copyright © 2004. Reprinted by permission of Big Idea.

Although this is a work of nonfiction, some names and identifying details have been changed.

Library of Congress Cataloging-in-Publication Data
Mama, PhD : women write about motherhood and academic life / edited by Elrena Evans and Caroline Grant.
p. cm.
Includes bibliographical references.
ISBN 978-0-8135-4317-8 (hardcover : alk. paper)—
ISBN 978-0-8135-4318-5 (pbk. : alk. paper)
1. Women in higher education—United States—Social conditions. 2. Motherhood—United States. I. Evans, Elrena, 1978– II. Grant, Caroline, 1967–
LC1568.M35 2008
378.1′55082—dc22

2007033808

A British Cataloging-in-Publication record for this book is available from the British Library.

Visit our Web site: http://rutgerspress.rutgers.edu

Manufactured in the United States of America

Dedicated with love
to the children who lived this book

Ben, Annika, Eli, Joshua

and

Samira, Amelia Jane, Daniel, Ben, Nick, Josie, Ivan, Renn, Rory,
Rudolf, Josephine, Marian, Tania, Riley, Benjamin, Kirby, Ben, Sophie,
Sarah, Akash, William, Jacqueline, Paul, Liam, Tessa, Jordan, Noah,
Mara, Hannah, Colin, Casey, Carl, Renata, Emma, Jacob, Lucy, Mariah,
Nick, Katharine, Naphtali, Noah, Isaac, Elisha, Abraham, Micah,
Becky, Sammy, Laura, Madeline, Julia, Senna, Hannah, Ellie, Clio,
Thalia, Rachel, Henry, Mara, Eva, Hesperus, Athena, Etani, Meridian,
Arcadia, Amelia, Savannah, Ella, Finn, Linus, Griffin, Sawyer,
Jordon, Spencer, Millie, Tessa, Bo, Abby, Jesse

numbers of graduate students and graduate-degree recipients; whereas in 1966 women earned only 12 percent of doctoral degrees, by 2002 that number had risen to 42 percent.[1] But the number of women in the ranks of tenured faculty has not grown in a generation, and the number of women of color remains vanishingly small.[2] Apparently women in the academy's fabled ivory tower encounter an ivory ceiling when they try to combine careers and families.

Academic life is predominantly a man's world. Women remain on the periphery, and children are all but absent. American universities consistently publish glowing reports stating their commitment to diversity, often showing statistics of female hires as proof of success, but the facts remain: university women make up disproportionately large numbers of temporary (adjunct and non-tenure-track) faculty, while the majority of permanent, tenure-track positions are granted to men. And women who do achieve tenure-track placement tend to report slow advancement, income disparity, and lack of job satisfaction compared to their male colleagues.

The disproportion between male and female university faculty, as in other workforces, is most striking among those who choose to be both professors and parents. All working mothers, regardless of their educational level or professional status, should be entitled to on-site child care; flexible policies regarding sick and family leaves; part-time jobs that truly require only twenty hours of work per week; flextime, job-sharing, and telecommuting possibilities; private space and time to pump breast milk for their infants; health-care coverage that is independent of hours worked. In theory, working mothers in the academy could have a particular advantage in realizing such benefits; after all, schools are, by definition, places that should be at least tolerant of, if not welcoming to, children. Most university professors need only teach on campus ten to twelve hours a week, with an additional four to six hours required for advising students. Other job requirements—from committee work to research and writing—are somewhat flexible in nature, not always requiring the physical presence of the professor on campus. The academic calendar allows for generous amounts of time away from campus, and professors are eligible for periodic sabbatical leaves. Finally, many universities house undergraduate and graduate programs in child development and education from which student staffs could be drawn for excellent on-campus child-care centers. Universities, historically the most progressive of American institutions, could be a model of family-friendly workplaces.

The reality, however, is that mothers in the academy stand at a significant disadvantage to their childless peers as they try to balance the vagaries of academic life with the demands of biology and offspring. As Mary Ann Mason and Marc Goulden demonstrate in their articles "Do Babies Matter?" and "Do Babies Matter (Part 2)?" women who have at least one child within five years post doctorate are significantly less likely to achieve tenure than men who have children early in their careers.[3] Female faculty members are also more than twice as likely than men to report having fewer children than they wanted.[4] The academic structure of promotions and tenure, and the expectation that candidates will relocate for jobs, favor those who can assume a full-time helper to manage the care of children, household, and other family responsibilities. But the majority of households today have dual wage earners, and as Robert Drago and Joan Williams argue, "American women, who still do the vast majority of childcare, will not achieve equality in academia so long as the ideal academic is defined as someone who takes no time off for child-rearing."[5]

So what's a Mama, PhD, to do? Academic women who choose to embrace the body and the brain find themselves caught between the demands of their families and the demands of the academy. In a 1996 study of female assistant professors, over 40 percent reported such factors as "time required by children" to be "serious impediments to achieving tenure."[6] Despite critiques and calls for change, however, the tenure-track system continues by its very design to favor those for whom caregiving needs are not paramount. Amy Hudock, whose *Literary Mama* column first connected Caroline and Elrena, succinctly captures the problem when she writes:

> If a woman goes to graduate school fresh out of undergraduate study, she could potentially be finished with her PhD by age 28 (and few people finish that quickly). Then, if she gets a tenure-track job immediately after graduation (and fewer people do), the tenure clock starts ticking, and she has six years to do the teaching, service, and publishing demanded for tenure. Thus, if all goes perfectly, she'll come up for tenure at age 35. Then, if she is awarded tenure, she can consider having a baby at age 36. But having this baby requires she has an appropriate partner or access to genetic material at the right time, that her eggs are still viable, that her student loans don't keep her financially insecure, and that she won't fear that her faculty colleagues will see her as copping out.[7]

The picture is bleak, even in this idealized situation. A more realistic appraisal must take into account the fact that the majority of women do not

Contents

Foreword

I received my PhD in religious studies, with honors, from Duke University in May 1993. That August I joined the faculty of the University of Florida as an assistant professor. I was never more proud. Five years later I submitted my tenure portfolio, filled with articles and teaching awards, a book and an anthology. I had received several grants during that time, including one from the American Council of Learned Societies. The university itself had supported my research very generously, both with summer travel grants and grants to match those earned elsewhere, and it was because of the university's generosity that I could publish as much as I did. Tenure, too, went relatively smoothly. To all intents and purposes, I was one of academe's young success stories.

During the spring in which my tenure file left the dean's office and hovered somewhere out of my grasp between the desk of the provost and the conference table of the board of trustees, I learned I was pregnant. It wasn't something I planned; I had been working too hard during that period in my life to plan much of anything. My only goal was tenure, the job continuity and security that would allow me to continue the work for which I had been trained. I went about my life as an assistant professor diligently and fairly single-mindedly. I remember a conversation with my best friend, Laura, also an assistant professor, in which we mapped out our five-year plans, and at the top of the list, the sine qua non, was tenure. That was it. That I fell in love and married during that time is partially a blur, a series of moments that punctuated my work.

As soon as my tenure was approved by the dean's office, I asked for a year's leave of absence. The demands for tenure had been extraordinarily high, and the tenure process itself was a bear. As it turned out, I had not enjoyed my time as an assistant professor. My department's politics were bruising and petty. The normative questions of my discipline began to feel too narrow. I no longer felt compelled by the areas in which I'd been trained. I had learned during my early professorial years that writing was a passion, and that my questions and curiosities went beyond the academic. I sought leave because I wondered what else was out there, beyond the ivory tower. My leave was approved, and a month or so later, I realized I was pregnant.

I have written in *The Truth Behind the Mommy Wars* of my surprise when I learned that although my university was working hard to support women faculty—hence the generous research awards and other policies that helped me so much—they had not yet figured out how to support women who became pregnant. That was my own naiveté. In retrospect I should have been shocked, but not surprised. The lack of a leave policy for professors with young children, of family-leave policies that would keep these professors in the academy and moving ahead on their professional paths, is a story repeated at nearly every other university and college in the nation. It is a story with tremendous human fallout. For years, the academy has been experiencing a brain drain of women—women who are highly skilled and expensively trained, and whom our society needs not to lose. We also have witnessed the well-documented personal challenges that mother-professors face—the incredible and extraordinary and overwhelming exhaustion of doing their academic jobs with children, in an academic culture that doesn't recognize how much labor is entailed in either.

It's a poorly kept secret within the world of colleges and universities that parents struggle, and we've been seeing for some time now the loss that universities suffer when mother-professors take their skills elsewhere. We've recognized that this situation hurts our universities and that it hurts men who father, but that it particularly maims women, who in most families still bear the work of child raising. We know that an older generation of women academics largely kept this problem quiet, grateful to have gotten in the door at all, and that in some respects, it was perhaps easier to manage children and academic life before the ramp-up in standards for tenure. Researchers know nearly everything there is to know about the problems that currently exist.

The real question, then, is why has so little changed? Why is the brain drain not being acknowledged? Why is the loss of so many women at so many places in the doctoral and professorial pipeline not being seen, and addressed, as a truly urgent problem? Despite its progressive reputation, academe lags behind more market-driven professions in providing support for workers with children. In contrast, for example, to the worlds of business and law, academe's conversation about supporting and retaining professors with young children is moving ahead very slowly.

It must also be said that much of the impetus for change within our universities is coming from the outside, from organizations such as the Alfred P. Sloan Foundation, which created academic Centers for Working Families. The Posen Foundation funds child care for professors at the annual meetings of the Association for Jewish Studies, and at their own annual meeting. The foundation's projects in Jewish Secular Studies are filled with professors—male and female—who are parents of young children, and the foundation does not want to lose them during these years. To support their vision that professors can be parents and parents can be professors, in the past four years, the foundation has spent nearly twenty-five thousand dollars on child care.

Women in the United States have a long, storied, and hard-fought history of claiming positions in our universities, positions from which we can produce the research and new perspectives that shape our society's future, positions from which we can teach new generations of students. Women want the same opportunity that men have to produce knowledge. We want to be part of that excitement and that responsibility.

At its worst, the professoriate is a callow institution, shortsighted and heartless. At its best, though, it has a venerable history as the gateway to the production of vibrant new ideas, of empathic and rigorous education that indirectly and at times very directly shapes our nation's cultural and intellectual life. It is also an institution that comes with an incredible commitment to each professor's lifelong contributions, which makes it all the more puzzling that efforts to suggest that universities take special care of their faculty during the years of a child's new life have so slowly gained traction.

For my part, I ended up leaving my academic job. After my first child was born, I took a year or two of unpaid leave. I agreed to some adjunct work at local universities, then, a few years in, I resigned my tenure. I continued to teach, but in those years I began to find my path to a new career as an author. *The Truth Behind the Mommy Wars* was my attempt to explain the challenges and discrimination that women and mothers face in our society, the book in which I realized over and again that the work and family problem is bigger than any one of us, more than any one woman or man can solve.

The essays in this book extend that realization, documenting what happens when smart women consider motherhood in the context of institutions that have barely gotten used to the presence of women, let alone mothers who might prefer ordinary human lives where they are home for dinner, and have some time with the kids before they go to sleep. The essays question the academy's intransigence, asking why, on the whole, it's been so hard for something so humane as parenting to be taken seriously. But they also showcase glimmers of hope, as they ponder how to shift the reigning discourse so that being a parent will come to be seen as compatible with being a professor.

MIRIAM PESKOWITZ

Acknowledgments

We'd like to thank the widespread community of mothers who make up *Literary Mama*, especially Amy Hudock, for bringing us together and inspiring us with their excellent writing. We're grateful to our agent, Rachel Sussman, for her guidance, and our editor at Rutgers University Press, Adi Hovav, for her unflagging enthusiasm for this book. Our thanks to our families, particularly our parents—Christopher and Margaret Webber, and John and Gwen Prestwood—for their steadfast love and support. Caroline would also like to thank the Motherlode Writers and her sister, Libby Gruner—always her first readers—for their careful attention to her writing; Elrena would like to thank her Aunt Sharon for suggesting that she major in English rather than neonatology. Finally, we would like to thank our husbands, Tony and Bill, for making our writing lives possible with their incredible good humor, technical savvy, and love; without them, this book would not exist.

Introduction

It all started with "nursies."

Elrena was sitting at her computer, nursing her baby girl and Googling the new vocabulary of her life. If you try this, Google will ask if you really mean "nurseries," but if you're sure of your spelling, you'll still find a link to the essay Elrena found that day: Amy Hudock's column for *Literary Mama*, "First Day of School." Elrena read the piece and cried, and after several weeks of reading *Literary Mama*, writing, weeping, and nursing (often simultaneously), she was ready to submit an essay of her own. Caroline, a former academic and editor for *Literary Mama*, was still figuring out how to replace the academy's comfortably rigid structure of classes and meetings with a messy mix of playgroups and naptimes, writing and editing when Elrena's essay arrived in her inbox.

That is how we met, as words on a screen, messages e-mailed back and forth. The academy would have approved of our purely textual interaction. In this no-man's-land of black lines on white screens, we communicated, temporarily free of the physical demands of our off-line lives.

But that freedom didn't last. Elrena was a PhD student and brand-new mother, trying to find her way through this new phase in her life, trying to balance a tiny baby and a big degree. Caroline lived across the country with a toddler and another baby on the way. Our nursing, pregnant, childbearing bodies were often at the forefront of our thoughts, and soon we began to discuss our lives as more than just text. We began to discuss our lives as mothers.

Elrena's essay, "Birthing: A Process in Vignettes" went through pleasant months of gradual revisions—Caroline's baby's birth, Elrena's move to a new home, and numerous other claims on our time, our attention, and our bodies slowed us down. When the essay was finally published, Caroline wrote Elrena a congratulatory e-mail: "I hope your new year is getting off to a fine start. I kept thinking of you—well, your daughter, really—when Eli started solid food, as there were many spoon-in-eye incidents. He's getting better at the whole eating thing now. Funny to think he was still an inside baby when we first started corresponding about your essay."

In her response, Elrena mentioned other recent publication news and, for the first time outside the context of "Birthing," raised the subject of her graduate work: "What I'd really like to do is a series of essays focused around the dissertation process, and what it's like to go through a dissertation as the mother of a toddler. I know the university has made leaps and bounds in terms of being more friendly toward women, but walking the halls with a baby makes me feel like a poser at best."

Caroline, who had finished graduate work before starting a family, wrote back with enthusiasm: "There was an anthology several years ago called *On the Market* (I think) that offered people's personal reflections on the MLA job market experience; one more specifically focused on mothers dealing with academia would be really interesting. And maybe (ah, but I'm too optimistic) provoke some changes?"

And so what began as an e-mail conversation about one essay gradually grew into a larger discussion of mothering and the academy, a discussion in which we quickly found we wanted more women to participate.

As the idea for a book began to grow, we did what, as academics, we do best: research. We both had anecdotal evidence about the difficulty of raising a family in the academy; we'd both witnessed friends and family members struggle. But we wanted to know more: how many women begin advanced degree programs, and how many finish? How many have children when they start, or have children along the way? What impact do children have on women in graduate school, on the job market, or seeking tenure? How many women successfully combine family life and academic life, and what sacrifices do they make? What can universities do to make mothers' lives easier?

Our research reminded us that, originally, higher learning was not intended to accommodate women. Not until the mid-nineteenth century did colleges begin to admit women, who faced discriminatory barriers such as marriage bans (which prohibited married women from teaching) into the 1950s. Some schools refused to admit women even into the 1970s.

As the feminist movement birthed gradual changes to gender roles, discriminatory practices slowly began to change and women started participating more fully in higher education. Today, women make up increasing finish their PhD by age twenty-eight, and that academic job searches often last over two years. Many new PhDs are shunted into temporary adjunct and non-tenure-track positions, the bulk of which are occupied by women. Such appointments are usually brief, just a semester or two, requiring relocation and a continuing job search. This is a tough environment for starting a family.

For its part, the academy seems oblivious to the struggles mothers face within its walls. A *Journal of Family Issues* study by Elizabeth M. O'Laughlin and Lisa G. Bischoff measures work/family stress as a function of gender and tenure status, and the findings are abysmal: like mothers outside the academy, academic mothers are responsible for more child care and more household responsibilities than men, and as a result experience more work/family stress. Almost as distressing, the authors point out, is that so little research is being done into this disparity between men and women on the tenure tracks of our universities. Although the difficulty of combining work and family in the nonacademic sphere is currently highlighted in newspapers, dozens of books, countless Web sites, and even pending legislation, "research specifically exploring work/family conflict in academic careers is sparse," according to O'Laughlin and Bischoff despite the fact that retention and promotion of female hires surfaces again and again on universities' five- and ten-year plans. These goals operate in a vacuum, without serious consideration of the consequences of being female in a university setting.[8]

In 2001, Drago and Williams concluded a study called *The Faculty and Families Project* that reached findings sadly consistent with expectations: since women make up the majority of caregivers in this country, regardless of their employment status, the ideal worker model currently favored in academic settings is discriminatory against women. The study's recommendations are for systemwide changes that would encourage female faculty to take advantage of existing family-friendly policies without fear of reprisal, and restructure these policies to be more equitable to the academic community as a whole. One such restructuring could take the form of a half-time tenure track policy, which is a plausible solution for meeting the needs of women in the academy. Allowing half pay and half benefits along with a slowing of the tenure clock for those working half time, this proposal starts to dismantle the notion of the ideal academic as she—or more accurately, he—is currently perceived. As Drago and Williams conclude, "The time has come to expand the choices people have in structuring academic careers. We should stop measuring commitment by the ability of an academic to have a spouse ready, willing, and able to shoulder the bulk of the child-caring during the most time-consuming years of child-rearing—when the children are young. The current system is bad for women and it is inconsistent with our ideals of gender equity."[9]

Regardless, the current system is the one in which today's academic women live, work, and raise their families. With no easy solution for the struggles they encounter, women take a variety of different approaches as they attempt to reconcile family and academy. None of these solutions is perfect. An article in the education journal *Change* notes that women who attempt to take advantage of family-friendly university policies, such as an extension of the tenure clock if they have a new child, are often talked out of them by their superiors or by human resource departments; those who do use the policies often face negative consequences in terms of tenure and promotion.[10] In 2005, Princeton University became the first school to grant such tenure extensions automatically, and as a result twenty faculty members received extensions, more than three times the number granted in previous years.[11]

Even beyond the most pressing questions of how to successfully navigate pregnancy or adoption in a university setting lies the question of how then to find time to raise a child—a commitment, of course, that lasts much longer than a semester. Some women strive to keep their family lives rigidly separate from their university commitments, afraid of being taken less seriously than their cohorts.[12] Others actively resist the separation of family and academy, decorating their offices with pictures of their families, or even bringing their children to campus occasionally, despite the criticism of other faculty. Robert Drago, teaming up with Carol Colbeck, writes about a day spent shadowing an assistant professor at a major research university. Refusing to conceal her motherhood, the professor had decorated her office with photos and drawings from her preschool children—a pointed gesture in an environment that tries so determinedly to ignore families. As the professor told Drago and Colbeck, in the entire time she'd been with the university, no one had remarked on the display.

Combining work and family, of course, means much more than being comfortable decorating an office with family photos. Although the media have devoted a lot of press recently to work/family concerns, their coverage skirts the real issues as they try to stir up a newspaper-selling, ratings-earning "Mommy War" between mothers who work outside the home full time and those who do not. First, traditionalist Caitlin Flanagan claims, "When a mother works, something is lost. Children crave their mothers.

They always have and they always will."[13] Feminist critic Linda Hirschman, however, argues that "among the educated elite, who are the logical heirs of the agenda of empowering women, feminism has largely failed in its goals," a failure for which she blames women: "If these women were sticking it out in the business, law, and academic worlds, now, 30 years after feminism started filling the selective schools with women, the elite workplaces should be proportionately female."[14] With educated women under attack from critics on both sides of the political spectrum, it's no wonder that these women, let alone women with fewer educational and economic advantages, report feelings of guilt and self-doubt no matter what decision they make.

Meanwhile, in *The Truth Behind the Mommy Wars*, Miriam Peskowitz convincingly demonstrates that while judgment, envy, and anger may exist on both sides of the argument, these emotions are more properly directed at the business, government, and education leaders shaping today's work place, not the women who cycle in and out of the paid work force depending largely on the age of their children. The division between working mothers, whether they work in conference rooms or call centers, and those at home is permeable and shifting. The intractable terms of the Mommy Wars may make for good copy, but don't offer much hope for change.[15]

What's needed, Hirschman feels, is to notice that these women are leaving the work force, and ask why—and then take steps to accommodate those who want to work, "Because participation in public life allows women to use their talents and to powerfully affect society. And once they leave, they usually cannot regain the income or status they had."[16] Thus we return to the Mama, PhDs, of our title, women Hirschman would surely categorize as the "educated elite," but for whom the ivory tower continues to prove a most challenging workplace.

This is the book we needed when we entered graduate school and the academic job market. We wanted to know that blending family life with life in the ivory tower might be possible; we needed to know that others were attempting this tricky balancing act. As we sent out our call for submissions we focused specifically on women. Although men also need to combine work and family, women are the ones who bear the physical and cultural demands of parenting most heavily, and so theirs were the stories we sought. We received an overwhelming response to our call for submissions, and we were both awed and humbled by the many stories we read.

We began with the essay that brought us together, Amy Hudock's "First Day of School," and from there tried to assemble a selection of essays that represents a range of academic and mothering experiences. The submissions we received reflect the current makeup of the academy: a majority of the essays were from white women in the humanities, fewer by women in the sciences, fewer still by women of color. Making the academy more family friendly will be an important step toward improving the racial and social diversity of women within the academy, and we hope that this anthology is a step toward making the ivory tower a far less exclusionary place, one that more accurately mirrors, rather than isolates itself from, the broader world. We want the essays in this book to start a conversation that will continue to both inspire, and, more importantly, provoke change.

We've arranged the essays in this book into four sections. Part One, "The Conversation," discusses the variety of choices women make as they consider the timing of motherhood and academic work. Part Two, "That Mommy Thing," tells stories of women pursuing academic careers and motherhood concurrently. Part Three, "Recovering Academic," features essays from women who are redefining themselves and their careers after a period within the ivory tower. And Part Four, "Momifesto," offers hope for the possibility of a different future, as contributors envision changes toward family-friendly university settings.

Balance, as every working mother knows, is not a static state, perfectly still like an old-fashioned scale. The dancer in arabesque or the yogi in *vrksasana* are both perfectly balanced, every muscle aware and engaged. Their bodies are vibrantly alive as they continually assess and shift their poses, working and changing to hold a position that gives the illusion of stillness. This version of balance, this constant, alert, focused negotiation, is the lifelong process of mothers in the academy, and everywhere—working out as we go along how to be whole people.

ELRENA EVANS AND CAROLINE GRANT
Phoenixville, Pennsylvania, and San Francisco, California

Notes

1. Mary Ann Mason and Marc Goulden, "Do Babies Matter? The Effect of Family Formation on the Lifelong Careers of Academic Men and Women," *Academe* 88, no. 6 (2002): 21–27.

2. Debra Humphreys, "Faculty Recruitment in Higher Education: Research Findings on Diversity and Affirmative Action," *Diversity Web*, http://www.diversityweb.org/

diversity_innovations/faculty_staff_development/recruitment_tenure_promotion/faculty
_recruitment.cfm (accessed July 27, 2007).

3. Mason and Goulden, "Do Babies Matter?"

4. Mary Ann Mason and Marc Goulden, "Do Babies Matter (Part 2)? Closing the Baby Gap," *Academe* 90, no. 6 (2004): 1–10.

5. Robert Drago and Joan Williams, "A Half-Time Tenure Track Proposal," *Change* 32, no. 6 (2000): 46–51.

6. Susan Kolker Finkel and Steven G. Olswang, "Child Rearing as a Career Impediment to Women Assistant Professors," *Review of Higher Education* 19, no. 2 (1996): 123–139.

7. Amy Hudock, "Desiring Books Over Babies," *Literary Mama,* May 26, 2006, http://www.literarymama.com/columns/motheringintheivorytower/archives/000396.html.

8. Elizabeth M. O'Laughlin and Lisa G. Bischoff, "Balancing Parenthood and Academia: Work/Family Stress as Influenced by Gender and Tenure Status," *Journal of Family Issues* 26, no. 1 (2005): 79–106.

9. Drago and Williams, "A Half-Time Tenure Track Proposal."

10. Roberta Spalter-Roth and William Erskine, "Beyond the Fear Factor: Work/Family Policies in Academia—Resources or Rewards?" *Change* 37, no. 6 (2005): 18–25.

11. Stacy A. Teicher, "The Ivory Tower Gets More Flexible," *Christian Science Monitor,* June 29, 2006, http://www.csmonitor.com/2006/0629/p13s01-legn.html (accessed August 1, 2007).

12. Carol L. Colbeck and Robert Drago, "Accept, Avoid, Resist: How Faculty Members Respond to Bias against Caregiving . . . And How Departments Can Help," *Change* 37, no. 6 (2005): 10–17.

13. Caitlin Flanagan, "How Serfdom Saved the Women's Movement: Dispatches from the Nanny Wars," *Atlantic Monthly* (March 2004): 109–128.

14. Linda Hirschman, "Homeward Bound," *The American Prospect,* November 22, 2005, http://www.prospect.org/cs/articles?articleId=10646 (accessed August 1, 2007).

15. Miriam Peskowitz, *The Truth Behind the Mommy Wars: Who Decides What Makes a Good Mother?* (Emeryville, CA: Seal Press, 2005).

16. Linda Hirshman, "Off to Work She Should Go," *New York Times,* April 25, 2007, http://select.nytimes.com/search/restricted/article?res=F50D1EF83F5A0C768EDDAD 0894DF404482 (accessed July 27, 2007).

PART ONE

The Conversation

The Conversation

JAMIE WARNER

Well, we finally had The Conversation. It was planned for August 15, but I, of course, forced it six weeks early at an unbelievably inopportune moment. Yes, I know, I know. It's rather pathetic to have to plan a conversation. And, yes, we, or rather I, had planned this particular conversation over a year ahead of time. I had even written it on the calendar. In fact, it's in situations like this that I'm pretty sure that I deserve to be an academic. However (and also not that unusual for those with academic tendencies), all of my planning came to naught.

We had just spent the past year in what many (sane) people would consider the ideal situation: my husband, George, had defended his dissertation and, believe it or not, had gotten a job in the same town, at the same university, and even in the same department in which I currently work. After four years of living in different states, including three years of long-distance marriage, the unthinkable had happened. My department, without too much bloodshed, had actually hired my husband. Of course, moving in together after four years of living alone and mostly apart brought with it a certain level of anxiety. What if I get on his nerves with my constant chatter? And what about my cheerful early morning disposition? George is a night owl, and let's just say that he's not very cheerful in the morning, and leave it at that. Or what if, after a while, I can't stand the fact that he can't seem to close the freaking bread bag? How can someone have a PhD and not be able to get the hang of the little twisty tie thing? And speaking of the kitchen, who cares if the dishes sit in the sink for a "little while" after dinner? They're *soaking*. It seems to me that a very thorough soaking is a crucial part of the dishwashing process. (George would like me to add here that by "very thorough" I mean up to and including three days.)

Or, and this was the big concern, what if it is too weird living *and* working together? Is it possible to see each other too much? His office (my

old horrible office—sorry, babe) and my (new, windowed) office are just
down the hall from each other. What if he starts rolling his eyes and sigh-
ing loudly when we run into each other at the water fountain? "For better
or worse" seemed like a nice, rather quaint thing to say three years ago, but
what if it really, truly gets worse? What would happen then?

Luckily, however, with one year of constant on-top-of-each-otherness
under our belts, it was still much better than worse. In fact, we turned out
to be very good roommates, merging money was no problem, and I actually liked him more than I did before, which I thought was a good sign. I
guess, technically, we were still in the honeymoon phase, but I'd have to
state for the record that we were (and are) pretty happily married.

And if all this happy happy joy joy wasn't enough to make everyone
vomit, we also lucked into renting this amazing, giant, four-bedroom house
on fifteen wooded acres about eight miles from campus. The deck was bigger than our previous apartment, and the rent was cheaper. On top of all
that, I'd finally gotten a few things accepted for publication after years of
rejections. Here, at my regional state university, I would have more than
enough to go up for tenure in the fall and I even had plans for—dare I say
it?—a book. All in all, looking back I'd have to say that it was quite a year.

Thus, at thirty-eight years of age, I wouldn't quite say that I had my
dream life, but things were starting to fall into place. Living in the same
state? Check. Two tenure-track jobs with the accompanying (insultingly low
but steady) salaries? Check. Publications plus various and sundry tenure-
type items? For me—check. George still had five years before he went up
for tenure, so he would be fine. Nice house? Check—although it wasn't
ours, it was plenty big. There was *room*, if you know what I'm saying. And
thus it seemed to me that August 15 would be a perfect time to discuss
this most important topic. We'd be well rested and well fed after a summer
of light teaching, research, and gardening. We'd have plenty of time to talk.
School wouldn't start up again for at least a week.

"So are we going to have kids or what?" I blurted out as we sat on the
river wall of a beautiful island park, ten minutes before we had to be back
at his mom's house. It was June 30. This was not how I had planned to start
The Conversation. George looked pained. "Look," I said, "I'm only bringing this up now because I have to make a doctor's appointment to get more
pills, and I need to know whether I should just get a month or two or if
I should get an entire year's worth." That wasn't even a good lie. He saw
right through it. "Well, get a year's worth, and then, if we decide to have
kids, just don't use them," he said with infuriating logic. I couldn't think

of any retort, let alone a logical one, so I punched him in the thigh. He didn't respond so I punched him again. I won't regurgitate the rest of The Conversation but it followed a thirty-minute loop that went something like this:

> JAMIE: Do you think you want to have kids?
> GEORGE: I don't know. Do you think you want to have kids?
> JAMIE: I don't know either . . . And why don't you know? What else needs to happen? Is this a question of timing, or is more of an existential question?
> GEORGE: I don't know. I just don't know.

As the above snippet illustrates, I'm not sure if I want to have kids either, but his indecision pissed me off. How dare he not want to have kids with me! The nerve. The deafening noise of my biological clock was soon drowning out everything else. Like the crocodile who swallowed the clock in Peter Pan, that ticking sound in my belly was impossible to ignore as it measured out the sound of impending doom. An "I don't know" at what I now decided was an ancient thirty-eight years of age was, by fiat, a "No," and a "No" meant that he was rejecting me. He didn't want to procreate with me. He didn't want to mix his DNA with mine. Wasn't he even curious about what a child of ours would look like, act like, be like? Tick, tock, tick, tock, tick, tock.

After a couple of hours, the ticking receded, I realized that it was a tad unfair to punish him for having the same mixed feelings that I had, and we decided to call a truce. Looking back on that conversation, I think my indecision on the subject comes from different sources than his. I had actually spent a fair amount of time inside my head casually going through various procreative decisions, the same way you might think about which five CDs you'd want to have if you were stuck on a desert island: Let's see . . . Johnny Cash's *Unearthed* (yes, I know it's a boxed set, but it's my game), *Let It Bleed* by the Rolling Stones, *And All That Could Have Been* by Nine Inch Nails, *Dirt* by Alice in Chains, and Samantha, Alexandra, and Cecilia if we had triplets—because they all shorten to cool nicknames, yet they would have a formal version for when they become a famous artist, Arctic explorer, and/or President of the United States. I guess I always kind of figured that I would have kids, although technically, I really hadn't seriously considered it a possibility until George and I lived in the same state—which I think many would agree is usually a prerequisite for this kind of thing. More importantly, I had also been very well trained in the crucible known as graduate school to feel "shame" any time I wasn't prostrate in front of the altar of research, so, in all honesty, even if George and I had lived in the same state before, we probably wouldn't have discussed the possibility of having a family until at least one of us was well on our way to a successful tenure case. Like many women, I was too busy working to think much about the particle accelerator known as the fourth decade in one's life—when finishing grad school, getting a job, the tenure track, and one's aging ovaries collide at high speeds. At my graduate institution, just about every woman waited either until tenure or until almost tenure to have babies. The ones that didn't wait had a lot of trouble—officially getting an extra year on the tenure clock for a baby, but then having an extra year's worth of research expectations anyway, fewer publications, guilt for using day care and babysitters—and I learned these lessons well: Be patient and wait until you have tenure.

Being a parent, however, was always my default position, even if it was out there shrouded in the fog of a murky future. I'm a woman, after all, and women have children. It's just something we do. It was a "shame" when a woman didn't have any children. This was a different kind of shame than the shame of not publishing; it was less accusatory and condescending and much more akin to pity. Pity is hard to take. I'll probably hear it in the voices of my former classmates more than once when I attend my twentieth high school reunion this fall. Maybe I shouldn't go. And it was particularly "pitiful" for me. When I was fifteen, I signed a sworn statement in front of witnesses that I would have eight children. Yes, eight, as in *Eight Is Enough*. Even before my academic aspirations manifested themselves, my parents thought eight was a bit much and wanted proof of my position. Thus, they made me write it down so they could taunt me with it later—which they do. I guess I always thought I'd have kids. After all, why wouldn't I?

George, however, came at this from the opposite direction. He thought he'd never even get married, let alone have children. He spent no time thinking about names, or what any genetic offspring of his would look like or talk like. While I had an almost idyllic childhood, he didn't, and thus he more clearly sees all the possible ways for parents to mess up their children. He wasn't sure that he wanted that kind of power, and he had a point. I somehow got on the babysitting circuit in grad school, babysitting for many of my professors' kids, and some of those kids, to put it bluntly, were in trouble. Three-year-olds who bragged about the prestige of their respective preschools and their parents' degrees, who routinely called other kids "dumb" as if that's the worst thing a child could possibly be, and who insisted to the point of having a fit on being called an expert in dinosaurs, seemed to me to be heading for nervous breakdowns by the age of twelve. And anyway, how do children of academics rebel? Join the marines? Become televangelists? Refuse to read?

But what does it mean *not* to have children? Family-wise I'm getting no pressure to do my biological duty; my sister and brother have nicely provided very adorable grandkids and I am off the hook in that respect. My brother actively lobbies for me not to have kids, because then I could no longer be cool Aunt Jamie, the one who gets up after dinner to play with the kids so the adults can talk. My mom thinks my career is too important to me to sacrifice the time it takes to bear and raise children; I can't decide if I should be offended by that or not. George's parents know better than to pressure him with anything and they keep their opinions to themselves, for which I am grateful. I only get a little, circuitous pressure from one source, my grandmother, G. Gram. (Gram began to sign birthday cards as "G. Gram" when she became a great-grandmother. We like to think of it as her hip-hop name.) She often tells me about how sad and lonely her neighbors are, now that they are in their seventies and don't have children or grandchildren to come visit them. I always agree with her that this is very sad, and leave it at that. After all, this was the woman who bought me an electric mixer when I got my PhD.

Despite G. Gram's not-so-subtle warnings, there are quite a few items in my hypothetical "anti" column. A barren womb means that I can sleep in on weekends for the rest of my life if I want. As an academic, it means that I can work whenever I want (that shame/research thing again), wherever I want, spend whole days at the coffee shop if I want. It means that I routinely have large blocks of time. It means that I can get *more* research done during breaks than during the semester. It means that I won't feel tremendous guilt that my children are spending more hours with the day-care ladies than with me, guilt that I've seen in pandemic proportions among my colleagues in academia.

In more mundane matters, it means that George can curse whenever he wants. It means that we can take vacations to places where not one single person is dressed as a rodent and we can eat at restaurants that don't serve chicken fingers or macaroni and cheese. And we will be able to have nicer stuff all around. We could have white carpet and cream-colored furniture if we wanted. We don't, but we could, if we wanted to. We won't have to buy a minivan. We won't have to worry about what school district we live

in. We won't have to save for college. And most importantly, we won't have
to be paranoid freaks when our children are teenagers. Do you read the
news? Rapes, murders, online predators—constant danger abounds. And
we won't even have the routine worries. We won't have to stay up until two
in the morning waiting for the triplets—Sam, Alex, and Celie—to get home
from their first concert. My first concert was Judas Priest, 1984 *Defenders
of the Faith* tour. It was a very important experience in my life. Would I
want the triplets to do this kind of thing when they are sixteen? With the
exception of me, everyone in the car going to the concert was drunk, including the driver, who allayed our fears by saying that he actually drove
better drunk than sober. It made sense to me at the time. I wasn't a bad
kid growing up, but I hung out with the bad kids as much as possible.
They were much more interesting. And George *was* a bad kid. What if the
triplets had a genetic predisposition toward the dark side? Sneaking a beer
into the movie theater was rather daring in 1985, but what do kids do now
for fun? Shoot up heroin/meth cocktails between class periods while they
plan their next blow job party? (Have you read about those things??) Not
having children would save us from all of this kind of worry.

And our house is very, very quiet.

And then of course there is the long list of less selfish reasons for not
bringing any more people into this overpopulated, environmentally precarious planet. What if we took even a fraction of the money we would
spend on our own biological children and spent that on existing children
who are abused, neglected, malnourished? From this perspective, doesn't
wanting your own genetic progeny begin to sound like the supremely selfish position?

It kind of sounds like I'm trying to talk myself out of having children,
doesn't it?

But that's not necessarily the case. When I talk to academics my age with
children, some of whom try to talk me into having children (and I must say
that sometimes this gets so aggressive that I wonder if parenthood isn't
actually a cult), they talk mostly about the intangibles and I completely
understand that. It's impossible to put into words. The love that they feel
for their child—a kind of love different from anything else they thought
was possible, the joy they get from helping to mold a future person, the
intense pride they feel when their child succeeds, whether in something
big like graduating from college or something small like making their bed
without being asked. I can dig that, just based on the fact that I am in complete and total love with my niece and nephews. I call my mom and we

spend, literally, hours trading stories about them. The subject line in her e-mails to me reads, more often than not, "Funny Josie (or Nick or Ben or Daniel) story." When we all visit together, I spend more time with the kids than I do with my brother and sister.

I was talking to my sister on the phone the other day and she stopped mid-sentence and said something that I have never once uttered (and might never utter) in my life: "All right," she said wearily. "That's it. Who pulled all the leaves off the plant?" Now, I've admitted that some of George's habits aggravate me, but he has never, ever pulled all the leaves off the plant. There was a pregnant pause on the other end of the line. "And don't you dare say it was Mr. Meanie," my sister continued. Mr. Meanie is apparently a very bad man. According to my niece (three) and nephew (six), not only does he pull all the leaves off of plants, he breaks things, plays with toys and doesn't put them away, and generally makes a mess. My sister was rather annoyed, but I thought it was adorable. I even love to hear stories about other people's kids. Bill Cosby's *Himself* is one of my all time faves. So what does it mean for me to miss out on all this?

As a full-fledged feminist, I *logically* understand the pressure society puts on me to be married with children, but whether the pressure is constructed by a bunch of self-centered men or not, I still feel an emotional tug. What will I miss out on if I never experience pregnancy? Will I always feel, as I often do now, that not having experienced the rites of passage that come with parenthood I will not truly be accepted into many communities of women? Have I consigned myself to the status of the outsider within? The academy is obviously more hospitable to childlessness than many professions, but not having kids is still the minority position for women, even at the Research I institution where I earned my PhD. It's true that the academy structurally and financially rewards those who work eighty hours a week on their research, but there is still the assumption that something must be *wrong* with you if you don't have kids: you are seriously, perhaps pathologically, career driven; you are inherently selfish or obsessed with material things that you don't want to sacrifice; you are too unattractive to get laid (i.e., the sad old English prof with thirty cats); or you have biological "problems" that prevent you from fulfilling your biological destiny. Which is a "shame." Last semester, more than one colleague announced to me, happily, that they had heard I was pregnant. Okay, so I have gained a little weight recently, but I think the assumption was based on the fact that, now that my husband and I are geographically together, we would automatically start a family. After all, why *wouldn't* we?

And it gets even more complicated. What does it mean to be childless and then *not* be thin (no pregnancy weight to lose), not have a twenty-five-page CV (what am I doing with all of my time?), or not be a gourmet cook (with no little people who won't eat anything that isn't beige, covered in cheese, or deep fried)? What if my career doesn't take off? I can't blame it on soccer practice. Do I have an obligation to work every evening, serve on more committees, be a better teacher, and become a publishing machine because I don't have familial obligations? Is being "average" considered a failure in academia if one doesn't have a family?

Many women in the academy talk about the difficulties, struggles, and losses surrounding the choice to have children (with which I completely sympathize) or not have children (ditto). What about choosing not to decide? What if the choice is too difficult, too fraught with peril and danger? What if we choose incorrectly and I end up as either the frustrated Mama, PhD, whose career aspirations are thwarted by a system that doesn't support working mothers, or the sad old lady who has no children or grandchildren to come visit her in her old age? My husband and I are both paralyzed by the same skills that got us our degrees and jobs in the first place: fertile imaginations, a compulsive need to make lists, the ability to see problems from a variety of perspectives, and worst of all, the need to question societal norms. We've had The Conversation and we're still stuck in the same thirty-minute loop. *We don't know.* And we (or, more correctly, I) have not scheduled Another Conversation.

At least not yet . . .

In Medias Res

SONYA HUBER

It is the end of May, and the Goat-baby (the bubble, the little being—all these nicknames that help us both be fond and keep our distance) is eleven weeks old. Poppy dust rained in my veins this past month, and I fell asleep in lecture, blinked at my students as if I could barely see them through a thick haze. The fetus is willful, at peak intelligence before it ever speaks. Maybe we are already resisting each other.

I dipped into my previous life this morning, swallowed lovely brown coffee and jumped off the bridge of exhaustion into the traffic of words. The jagged edges and angular lines of an unfinished master's thesis shot past. I looked up to see that an hour had passed. I deleted what I'd written, ruthless with the razors of logic. A revered fiction teacher's mantra played in my head: "Kill your darlings." Hunched over the computer screen, biting my cuticles, I am the antinurturer.

I come up for air and remember that I'm pregnant. Two and a half feet down from this brain is a defenseless flesh-comma. Have I been cheating? Could I somehow make myself unpregnant? Could I break the shallow membrane between biology and fiction, inadvertently end this fragile life as I toss around the sharp-edged tools and girders needed to build hypothetical worlds? If I stop thinking about the baby, does it die? If I turn my mind toward lines of text, who reminds the baby's cells to divide, and who keeps it from getting lonely?

It's week sixteen, happy sweet sixteen, Goat-baby. I'll stop calling you "Goat" when we find out next month what you are.

I wedge the visits to my OB-GYN between classes. I struggle to finish an oral presentation in a graduate seminar, winded as if I've climbed a flight of stairs. I'm supposed to be spinning cogent thoughts about Wordsworth. "I'm pregnant," I blurt, news that leaves my classmates slack-jawed, unsure what to do with this information that has no theoretical relevance.

Goat-baby, I love you but I'm glad you're not here yet. Rather than counting down the weeks, I am banking against them, hoping for the full forty. In the coffee shop, I meet with an accomplished writer who's also the mother of an eight-year-old. "Look, you can do it," she says about my thesis and book manuscript. She glances down at her watch, timing the minutes until she has to pick up her daughter. "Just make sure you have a draft of the book done before the baby comes. You think you'll have time afterward, people always say, 'Oh, I'll write when the baby sleeps,' but that's bullshit. You're going to be sleeping or staring at the baby. So get to work and have the most productive summer of your life."

When friends ask me how I'm doing, I am honest only if I know them well. I say, "I'm panicked. I haven't ever had this kind of a deadline before." To one friend who is also a writer thinking about getting pregnant this year, I say, "You know, it feels like somehow December 2 is the date I'm going to die." Then the disclaimers: "I mean, I know that's sick, and of course I don't *really* think that . . ."

But she nods. "I know exactly what you mean. It's like, good-bye to everything."

Of course this is the opposite of a death. Even having that argument with myself makes me suspect. These are thoughts the mommy on the cover of the pregnancy manual would never entertain.

I've heard the urge for domestic completion described as a nesting instinct, a burst of furious activity before giving birth. I'm writing today in an office that's going to become your bedroom, while my future writing space waits: a tiny alcove off the bedroom, just big enough for a desk. When we looked at our limited floor plan and figured out the allotment of rooms, I had an undignified hormonal crash and spent an afternoon crying. I got up and washed off my face, feeling selfish and confused; I thought the maternal instinct would suck all of those feelings away like poison from a snakebite.

So this will become your nest, but there's no sign of a nursery. It's disgusting, actually: paper everywhere, some of it in drifts so that it's hard to tell that this room isn't rounded at the bottom like a bowl. That corner is the classes I'll be teaching, this half of the desk and the floor below it is the book, behind me is the political work I won't have time for anymore. I wonder if I'm embezzling from my maternal wellspring, burning the energy that is supposed to be used for picking out wallpaper with bunnies and lambs.

I am grateful for the blood barrier of the placenta that keeps some of my fluids separate from yours, because my mental soup is no place for a baby. I know you will develop tastes for what I ate during pregnancy, and you can have buckets of chicken tikka masala if you want. But don't soak in my thoughts.

While my belly reaches outward, my brain and my hands—resting against my swollen lap—stitch together a book about the rise of the Third Reich. Sweetheart, I hope you never read this and figure out I spent your gestation trying to close the empathy gap, to feel the fear that a German Marxist had in his throat for Hitler's brownshirts. I should be knitting booties, and instead I throw myself back in time toward horror. Do I leave you alone or take you with me? Either option sounds unforgivable.

I divert blood and nutrients from the uterus to the brain. I squirm as I listen to comments from strangers and friends about enjoying my pregnancy. Without maternity benefits, I have calculated my earning potential and academic calendar down to the day. To take three months off from teaching after giving birth, I will spend the entire pregnancy teaching at two colleges, tutoring, freelance editing, and writing for a magazine. I huff and lumber across campus, constantly late, lugging my belly along. And you in there, Sweet Pea: if you are high-strung, we will know it is because you were grown on a diet of coffee, carrot sticks, saltines, and adrenaline.

At week twenty-one, a friend tells me about a thrift store for maternity and baby clothes. Cruising the aisles, I pile up three-dollar shorts and five-dollar dresses that fit my girth. I pause in front of a huge bin filled with tiny socks and feel temporarily at rest. Moms flip through racks of T-shirts and pilot strollers through the aisles, and a clenching within my chest releases its tightened spring. Welcome to thrifting, Baby. I hope you like the pride of something twice used and comfortably broken in.

I touch a Winnie-the-Pooh lamp, a sweet swirl of color I didn't think I'd ever be able to afford. The price tag, four dollars, eases a pent-up panic about all the things I realize I want to give you. I feel the edges of a real life open up for us. Baby, you will have to meet us, and to know your dad is an artist, your mom a writer and student. We make our living as freelancers. We have flexible schedules and decidedly unimpressive incomes. You will know, as we know, the wonders of the Dollar Store, the binges at the library. I knew this—I knew all along this was how it would be.

Hanging my brand-name, slightly used dresses on hangers, I realize I've been so intimidated by you, Baby. I had this weird idea you were going to pop out of me judging and dissatisfied, like a prefab suburban child expecting a stay-at-home mom and a Lexus SUV to take her to playgroup. Baby, I have been putting myself through a revisitation of high school in my head, feeling like I'm about to transfer to a new campus where I don't know my way to class, where everyone calls me a nerd again and I don't fit in with the other moms.

I have been already ducking in shame, imagining the sneer in your liquid brown eyes when you bury your face in a receiving blanket and come up for air with the distinctive smell and imprint on your face, knowing this blankie is garage-sale worn.

It's twice loved, Baby. And it was only a dollar, I would explain. But maybe you'd already be hating me, following the North Star of your compass, waiting to escape to the life you knew you came here for, the life every Gerber baby was promised.

The thrift store—real, concrete, with helpful and harried women behind the counter not ashamed to be pushing the economical and the shared—shows me, with a surge of greedy pride and calculation, that we will get you first. Before you're able to narrow your eyes at Daddy's backyard full of sculptures and at Mommy's chaotic office and piles of books, you will be spoiled with rescued treasures, homemade toys, and the best games and on-the-spot stories two parents can invent. If we can't give you the moon and can't guarantee you much saved for college, we can at least show you the wide world, the one that exists beyond traditional opportunity. You are not even a five-month-old fetus, and you've already come along to ten demonstrations and felt the sun outside your warm womb at a New York beach where tattooed gay boys romped naked in the waves. You will be loved, but never shackled with the blinders that make real life seem frightening.

We bought your baby book on clearance, dear. It's a blank journal with a beaded cover. The pictures and collages and memories and stories that will go inside will, you can be sure, be yours alone.

➢ ⧽

Walking near the river tonight, I watch a father push a two-year-old on a swing. The boy tips back his head in ecstasy, in flagrant display of his own personality. I imagine you, Baby, and the ways you will have. We will see your twenty-one-week-old body tomorrow in ghostly grays on the ultrasound screen, and we will learn only hints about you, but I am hungry for every clue: any arch of an eyebrow or curve of a foot will be outrageous and specific. In this moment, my curiosity has eclipsed my anxiety.

My skin expands around you. It's interesting but not entirely unfamiliar to be inhabited by a strange character, to think about the spaces inside me that I don't own. This stage feels like the pre-writing of a story, that tentative, intuitive brooding where I flip through gestures and looks, searching not for a logical composite but for a foreign and fascinating whole.

Writing is the only way to replicate the feeling and privilege of being in love; those are the only two moments when staring is not impolite, when we are allowed to revel in the skin-landscape, the minute gestures, the smell and dastardly contradictions of another person. I needle together letters; I have many imaginary friends; I get lost in time. These skills, I think, will serve me well. The world out here is scary, Baby, but I want to talk with you about it. I want to see what and how you think. Last time we saw you, you were soap bubbles, semi-transparent globes scattered around a hummingbird's beating heart. I want to see you; I am hungry for the plot, for the tiny details of your story contained in the pads of your fingers, and your plans for rebellion and creation.

Scholar, Negated

JESSICA SMARTT GULLION

My sense that my status had changed was confirmed midway through the fall semester. As I sat in my office preparing a lecture on data triangulation, the department chair poked her head around my door and tapped her fingernails for a moment on the doorframe. Without looking me in the eye, she asked me to join her in her office.

I eased my large body into one of her creaky matchstick chairs, wondering if this impromptu meeting would make me late for my class. The department chair was also the chair of my dissertation committee, and had an inordinate amount of power over me.

"We need to talk about the spring," she said.

Next spring would be my last semester as a graduate student; I planned on teaching and finishing up my dissertation. I was going to give birth in February, defend my dissertation in April and graduate in May. Some of the other graduate teaching assistants had recently told me they'd already received their teaching assignments for the spring. I was currently the senior among them, and it was a general policy that seniority equated better classes. This fall I was teaching research methods and statistics, and so I assumed I would teach them again.

"I can't hire you as a GTA in the spring since you are pregnant," she said. "It would be too disruptive to have you leave in the middle of the semester." She picked some lint off of her sweater, flicked it on the floor, and stared at me.

I didn't know how to respond. I was part of a sociology department at a women's university. We had experts in feminist pedagogy, feminist epistemology, participatory research. We had activists, ecofeminists, crusaders for women's rights. The woman sitting in front of me had done pioneering work with women employed in inhumane working conditions in the *maquiladoras* along the Texas-Mexico border. This was supposed to be my feminist enclave! And this, my haven, was kicking me out, *because I was pregnant?*

My second thought was more practical than philosophical: If I lost my job, I wouldn't have my pitiful stipend, or my health insurance. And I was about to have a freaking baby.

"Well, I can understand it would be disruptive," I agreed in my trying-to-be-calm voice, the baby rolling around under my maternity top. "What about just working as an assistant to someone with a large class? That way it wouldn't be such a problem when I took off."

In our department, assistants and GTAs both made the same amount of money (not much), and had the same benefits (namely, health insurance). The primary difference was that GTAs were the teacher of record for two courses per semester, whereas an assistant just helped grade papers and tutor students in the monster-size classes, and did not have to teach.

"We generally use assistants in the beginning of the program, not at the end," the department chair said. She leaned slightly forward, elbows on the desk, her fingertips touching. "I just don't think we can use you."

Ah. I was overqualified.

"I see," I answered.

My throat burned and choked as I sat on the flimsy chair, but I wasn't going to let her see me cry. All I could do at that point was get up and leave. By the time I got down the hall to the graduate advisor's office, I was nearly hysterical. The graduate advisor closed the door behind me while I told her the story.

"What am I going to do?" I sobbed, snot attractively running down my bloated face.

"That bitch!" the graduate advisor exclaimed, slamming her hand down on her desk. "I'm not surprised. We'll support you all day long if you're a migrant transsexual teenager who needs an abortion, but God forbid you're a straight woman who wants to have a baby!" She took my hand and locked eyes with mine. "This is what we are going to do. I am going to go cancel your class right now, and you are going to go home and relax. Then I am going to have a talk with the dean. And if that doesn't go well," she said as I sniffled, "we are going to get you a lawyer." So much for data triangulation.

Fortunately, we didn't need a lawyer. The dean had actually heard of the Family Medical Leave Act, but more importantly, didn't want the publicity of a pregnant woman suing a women's university for pregnancy discrimination. To this day, I don't think the department chair thinks she

was in the wrong. Eventually she assigned me to teach one class online
(I could work from home!), and another department picked me up as a
research assistant. The class was a new prep, and the first I had taught
online, resulting in many more hours of work than my previous courses.
Five days after the birth of my son, I was online, working on my class with
him sleeping in my lap. The research assignment was completely outside
of my field, but resulted in my only peer-reviewed publication as a student.

When I got pregnant my identity changed, in the eyes of my colleagues,
from burgeoning young scholar to beached whale. Apparently my ability
to think, discuss, or write was instantly erased when my husband's sperm
penetrated my ovum. I once walked in on two fellow graduate students
discussing pregnancy in the mail room, right as one said, "I don't know
what it is, pregnant women just weird me out." She looked up and saw
me, my pregnant belly stretching through my maternity top. "Well, not
you, of course," she added hastily. Of course. I had the sense that my colleagues were avoiding me, especially as my belly grew bigger. Conversations changed from social theory and research to how I was feeling and
whether or not I planned on staying home with my baby. Even my students
treated me differently. While they had never cared much for statistics to
begin with, they now tried their best to get me to talk about my pregnancy
and about babies in general. Maternity fashions were of particular interest.
The students in my online class, however, were blessedly compassionate—
much more so than my colleagues. They kept telling me not to check the
Web site, to be with my baby; and true to their word, they continued to produce a large volume of work without my constant attention. Many of the
students in our online courses also had young children, and favored that
environment for its flexibility. Although I can't help thinking that they, too,
have been marginalized out of academia.

Prior to my pregnancy, I had not even realized how the exploration of
this fundamental fact of life is left out of the sociological curriculum. There
I was, a student of human social behavior, but pregnancy and motherhood
were considered taboo, or simply too boring to talk about. While we had a
smattering of courses on marriage and family, the general opinion among
my classmates was that these were not respected fields of study.

In the first women's studies course I took as an undergrad, the professor
explicitly told us we would not be discussing women as mothers. For too
long, she said, women and children have been lumped together as if they

were one. We were going to study women's experiences outside of that realm, with an eye toward valuing women's total experiences and not just their roles as mother or procreator. I remember this because I used it myself when I first taught courses on women's roles. It pains me now to think I could teach an entire course on women's roles and never talk about the one role that is primary to the majority of women: that of being a mother. This despite inroads women scholars have made into the field of sociology.

When I started the graduate program, the sociological theory professor gave me a list of about 250 social theory books that doctoral students were expected to know for their comprehensive exams. Of these, only one (*Black Feminist Thought* by Patricia Hill Collins) even mentioned pregnancy and motherhood. I was trained as a sociologist who could easily deconstruct the world, who could deftly spout revolutionary thought, or could speak about rationalism and bureaucracy. I could hold my own with the postmodern crowd, spewing out nihilistic criticisms of material culture. But I could not tell you anything about being a mom. Theorizing motherhood was unimportant work, and when I began to express interest in doing so, I was further devalued in the eyes of my colleagues.

I approached the feminist theory professor wanting guidance on the subject of motherhood. A strange, pained look flashed across her face. "Um. Sure," she said. But we never had that conversation, because while she was the resident expert on feminist theory, motherhood was a topic that she, like the rest of my colleagues, knew nothing about. We could all converse with passion about the right to not have a baby. But none of us could talk about what it was like to actually have one.

To triangulate data, we gather information from a variety of sources in order to draw conclusions about the subject under study. During my pregnancy, I observed how focus changed from the talents of my mind to the physicality of my body. I could see it in the way a professor would back away from me in the elevator, trying too hard not to stare at my hormonally enhanced breasts and swollen belly. I could hear it when a classmate uttered "breeder" under her breath, and it got a laugh. I resented it when I was denied my job not because of my abilities, but because I was viewed as a liability. And I felt it in the eyes that followed my heavy frame around the room. The data were there, they added up. The behaviors of my professors, my colleagues, my students, all led me to the conclusion that with pregnancy, I was a scholar, negated.

Student/Body

SHEILA SQUILLANTE

They watch my belly every Monday, Wednesday, and Friday from 11:15 to 12:05. As I lecture about active voice, clarity, and persuasion in prose, I can feel their eyes squinting, searching my middle for signs. I am three, four, five, and, finally, six months pregnant at semester's end, and I know that some of them don't believe it. Though I can feel the hard knot of my enlarging uterus pushing ever upward and outward, and can occasionally see my child's limbs poking through my skin at odd intervals and angles, I am, so far, slow to publicly show.

Sometimes I catch their stare and they blush, returning their attention to the overhead on memo writing or résumé layout and design. Sometimes the stare irritates me and I contemplate reprimand; it's no different, is it, than reading the newspaper or text messaging during class? Other times I feel myself blush beneath it, enjoying what could be admiration. Then, too, it makes me feel paranoid: I imagine them suspicious, wondering if I told the class I was expecting just so they would be nice to me, just so they would leave their eye rolls and slump-shouldered shrugs in their dorm rooms. I have yet to meet a college senior who was not resentful at being required to take Business Writing.

That first day of the spring semester, one month into my second trimester, still nauseated and nervous about teaching in the midst of this bodily chaos, I made a decision to out myself right then. After my usual read-through of the syllabus and the policies sheet, I hopped up on the desk, took off my glasses, looked out at the group and said, "Okay, now I need to let you all know that I am pregnant. This should not affect our semester in any major way, but I'm asking that you have patience with me and good humor all the same."

The applause was immediate, enthusiastic, and stunning. There were hoots and hollers, and I swear I heard a "Rock on!" I couldn't have imagined it. This class, mostly young men, looked as elated for me, their brand-new teacher of a perennially hated class, as my best girlfriends had been upon hearing my news. And that was just the first day.

I have been teaching college English for eight years, three as a graduate student, and five now as an adjunct lecturer for the same university from which I graduated. I'm a good teacher. I know how to make grammar and syntax palatable, how to drum up enthusiasm for and dedication to the résumé-writing process; how to help students develop a preference for vibrant, active language. I love writing and I know how to translate my love into practice with my students.

I am the "mom" teacher, the one students describe as "nurturing," the one about whom they write in their course evaluations, "she really *cares* about us *as people.*" I emphasize the idea of community in all of my classes. A sentence in one of my recent syllabi reads, "I expect we will all fall in love with each other and become a weird little family." During the semester, they come to my office hours to ask questions about their papers and end up telling me that they party too much because they miss their families back home on small Pennsylvania sheep farms. They tell me stories about how painful it was to come out to their parents, but how good it feels to finally feel self-acceptance. They hug me on the last day of class, and I hug them back hard, blurring the professional boundaries that many of my colleagues adhere to so carefully. I love my students openly and know that this—not my aptitude with language—is my true pedagogical strength.

But I admit that when I was first scheduled to teach Business Writing, and told that my classrooms would be populated predominantly by young men, I felt a mixture of dread and resentment. My mother was born to a family of three girls and eight boys. Her mother, my grandmother, was never shy to share her belief that "girls are sneaky and deceitful," a philosophy I admit colored my growing-up years so much that before my late twenties, I never had strong female friendships. I grew up female in the same world we all do: the one that says boys are better, stronger, and preferable in most every way. Boys had destroyed me in grammar school, picking me last for teams and chanting cruel taunts as I took a lousy swing at the softball during gym class. Boys had followed me to middle school where they circled me like a pack of drooling wolves and threatened, though I am certain that they had no idea what this really meant, to "gang bang" me right there on the playground. Boys became young men and left me in the high school band room on our three-month anniversary, giving me a key chain that said, "Never regret the things you have done; only regret the things you have never tried." One boy masqueraded as a grown man and married me in all my poufy white finery in front of family and friends, only to leave two years later so he could spend more time perfecting his dance moves and his goatee, so he could experiment with drugs and other women. The boy who finally granted our divorce was dressed like a judge when he came out of chambers to berate me in the hallway of the courtroom about how marriage is a serious matter and young people take it too lightly these days and how old was I and where was my husband anyway?

I was not, at that point, too very happy with boys.

It's fully winter now, and the trek to, from, and around campus is wearing on me, even with the welcome gift of second-trimester energy. I arrive at class bundled and sweating, out of breath. I unwrap myself like a present in front of my students. Every day I make some change to the schedule: a due date pushed back, an assignment retooled, an individual project turned into a collaborative one. I have scaled back the class requirements substantially in order to make the pacing and grading more manageable for me, and every day I feel the guilt of this. I worry that my department will reprimand me for diluting their class. I worry that my students will feel cheated, as if they are not being well prepared for a life in corporate America; that their parents will complain they are not getting their money's worth out of this Big State University. I worry that I am undoing myself as a teacher, that once I actually have this baby, I will never again be able to put my fullest self into my job.

But I really can't keep up, can't care too much about comma splices and newsletter production when I am up in the middle of the night most nights, my hands on my belly, panicking that I have not felt my baby move in x many minutes. Can't care when I am overwhelmed by feelings of terror and anticipation, when I worry every day that somehow, despite my love for and ease with other people's children, despite my great desire to have *this* child, I will not feel connected, will not love it when it is born.

The campus is slick with ice. I arrive at class, holding my teaching shoes in a plastic bag and some days not even bothering to change into them. I wear long skirts that are soft around my hard belly, and my chunky fleece snow boots. I drink bottled water, screwing and unscrewing the white plastic cap as I flounder in front of my four girls and twenty boys.

"Ms. S.," says one boy, "you look tired. We wouldn't mind if you cancelled class today. You and the baby should rest."

The class chuckles. I *am* tired and I'm sure I look it.

"Yeah, why not take the whole week off? Then you wouldn't have to come out in this cold. That can't be good for the baby."

I expect this kind of banter. These are seniors in their final semester; they would give their right arms to be out of the classroom and on to the celebratory bar tour. Still, behind the cunning smirk that delivers the suggestions, beneath the veneer of self-interest and irony, there is something tender and sincere.

"See you Friday, Ms. S.," another boy calls as I pack up after lecture. "Hey, be careful out on the ice."

We're having a boy. The ultrasound technician, a woman who wears blue eye shadow and hot pink lipstick with startling aplomb, tells us in her thick Russian accent, "Is boy. See here?" She points at the white phantom floating on the screen. Our son.

"Yes. Is penis. I am sure."

We're having a boy and for a moment I panic, imagining football injuries and fraternity parties; binge drinking and too-fast driving; sexism and insensitivity—all the terrible stereotypes, all the ugly memories.

In the classroom that week, Chris, a tall, handsome boy with Mr. Magoo glasses asks me if I know what I am having. His Japanese mother has taught him to be respectful and considerate, and his American father taught him, apparently, to mix it up with a little mischief. He is funny and smart and so consistently cheerful that when he told me during office hours earlier that week that his father had just passed away in January, I was so taken aback that I just stared at him, unable to say anything comforting or supportive. Now that I am pregnant, I can no longer bear to think of death of any kind, but to think of parentless children is especially paralyzing.

"Well," I tell him, "it appears I am going to have one of *your* kind."

"Woohoo!" comes the class cry. "Awesome!" "Do you have a name picked out?"

In fact, I do have a name picked out, but my husband and I have decided not to share it with the larger world just yet.

"Nope. Got any suggestions?"

"Adam! Justin! Marty! Sean! Mike! Joe!"

They shout their own names at me, each of them becoming my son for just a moment, and I am completely charmed, completely moved.

"Wait," says David, "I have the perfect name: *Beowulf*!"

Perfect indeed. I am a student of literature and a poet. Perfect and also perfectly ridiculous. We laugh, and I can barely contain my joy in that moment, the affection I feel for the boy growing inside of me and for these grown boys giggling in front of me. I look out at their faces and suddenly realize two things: first, that they *have* learned from me this semester—they have figured out how to read and accommodate their audience; and second, that I am, in fact, inordinately fond of boys.

On Being Phyllis's Daughter

Thoughts on Academic Intimacy

LAURA LEVITT

On the one hand, my mother adhered to the norms of mothering that defined her early 1960s generation. Although she was educated and worked as a teacher before she had children, she left her job when my brother and I were very young, and did not go back to teaching for almost five years.

But on the other hand—this is not exactly where I wanted to begin. I wanted to start by saying that my mother, like me, played with dolls. Her favorites, so she tells me, were paper dolls. She spent long days as a little girl cutting out various outfits, experimenting with how they looked. I think about my mother playing with paper dolls when I think about her accounts of what she did during her long days at home with me as a young child. For my mother, staying at home was not easy. She loved teaching, and regretted giving up her job when I was born.

I have few memories of my mother at home with my brother and me. I have memories of playing with friends and a smattering of memories of other adults, but I do not have any clear memories of my mother. What my mother tells me is that she spent a lot of her time cleaning and ironing my various outfits and dressing me up in them. I cannot help but imagine that, in part, my role was quite similar to that of her paper dolls. She did the labor in order to get my clothes ready for me to wear, and then spent her days putting them on and taking them off me. What I recall are itchy crinolines and a longing to take them off, and short, lacy socks that needed to be pulled up over my heels again and again. I think I sensed, even then, that my mother was not particularly happy staying home.

Not surprisingly, it was when my mother returned to work that my most vivid memories of her begin. My mother's passion for her work was contagious. I imbibed it. I fell in love with her students and her colleagues, their stories, their intrigues, and always my mother at the center of all of this storytelling. Over the years, my specialized knowledge of my mother and her life at school has enabled a kind of intimacy between us. It allows me to share a part of her life, as we communicate through the mediation of other people and their stories. Not unlike a beloved text, these stories have enabled my mother and me to connect in ways that seem to have foreshadowed the kinds of academic intimacy I now share with many of my own students. My mother and I have always communicated most profoundly in this way, and this is very much the kind of intimacy I know best in my own life.

When I had the chance, in my small high school, to be a student in my mother's classroom, I came to see her in her element. I watched her perform as a teacher, covering the blackboards on three sides of her classroom with her students' ideas, punning as she answered questions. She loved student renditions of scenes from Shakespeare comedies, and in those instances, her laughter was always the loudest. I learned to navigate complicated boundaries, to make distinctions between our interactions, deciding when my mother was my mother and when she was my teacher. My mother was a passionate teacher, and she loved blurring the lines between home and school. Her students could turn in assignments until midnight, and they often did, knocking on the door of our home just before twelve o'clock. No other teacher gave students her home address at the beginning of the year or allowed students to hand in their work after school hours.

My mother loved to talk about books and literature, and her students loved being part of these discussions. For almost the entire time that she taught, my mother held a Great Books class in our home once a week. Some of her students held informal reading groups over the summer after they graduated, just to continue the conversation. Others asked for reading lists that they would dutifully pursue on their own, writing or returning to visit to discuss these works with my mother.

I think of my mother and her relationship with her students as I look at my academic relationships. In my engagement with my own students, I have been most fully my mother's daughter. I have given myself over to them, helping them become scholars and teachers in their own right. With some of my graduate students, the work has been so close that we can finish each others' sentences. It is difficult to write about this without sounding self-serving or cliché, but with my students and a few of my colleagues and friends I have a kind of intimacy that I do not share with many other people. What we share is our work, especially our writing. It is at the center of what we do together: we help each other figure out what we want to say and then how to say it. This process creates a unique kind of intimacy, as we are there for each other and for our work. We often meet in my eclectic office, a hodgepodge of thrift-store finds and gifts from students. Paper in hand, the conversation starts with me deciphering my handwritten notes on the sides of the page. At various points I swivel around in my chair to take a book off the shelf or to go online for a reference. I'll meet my graduate students in local coffee shops where we hash out a new chapter outline or clarify a reading.

In part, I have been able to work so closely with my students because I was able to first share such an intellectual intimacy with my mother. Since then, I have increasingly shared this intimacy with colleagues, and many of my students. Unlike my mother, I am not a woman with children, so I do not share these connections with children of my own. For me, intellectual intimacies, my connections to my students, are where I pass on these lessons, what it means to take texts seriously, to read and write about them, or how to make them part of our everyday lives. At its very best, the back-and-forth, the ideas that we each have, make these engagements thrive. The fact that I have my own projects enables me to engage with others as they work on their own. I know the difference between what is mine and what belongs to someone else, and it is this interplay that I find compelling.

High school teachers like my mother are not often also writers in their own right. They are not required or encouraged to publish in the same way as those of us with PhDs. This is another way my life differs from my mother's. In order to work with my students, especially my graduate students, I have needed to model what it means to be a writer, to be a producer of knowledge myself. In order to help my students, I have had to take my own writing seriously. It has taken me a long time to learn how to privilege this aspect of my work. This was not something familiar; it was not the kind of thing my mother had done. And so, I have had to look elsewhere to imagine doing this part of my work. For me, finding friends and colleagues with whom to share my work has been crucial.

In many ways, writing can be lonely. Much of the time this is a solitary endeavor, and I find I am not sure of this role and my ability to claim it. The prospect that I might be joining a long legacy of writing women, women without children, remains elusive. My own life does not conform to the norms that shaped my mother's life.

For me to be a writer and a teacher and to see this as a way of being in the world is still new to me. Although there are more and more women who write and teach in colleges and universities, we remain not that far removed from the Virginia Woolf of *A Room of One's Own*. Many of us continue to yearn for some way of steadying ourselves. We want role models and reassurance that this life, a life so unlike our own mothers' lives, is possible. For me the desire is very much about wanting an inherence of writing women, ancestors I can turn to as examples for the life I lead. And even as more of us write and let our own lives be an example for our students, we feel shaky, uncertain, still unaccustomed to this way of being in the world. We want evidence of intellectual women who were engaged with each other and with other intellectuals in the past to bolster our own work, to remind us that it is possible to make a life on these terms. We want to know that there were women producing knowledges both public and private, work that was of and about their lives and their passions, and that this work had readers and that for all of these reasons their lives mattered. Such knowledge secures our own endeavors. For me, a woman who has chosen not to have children, again these efforts are critical. They define where I work and what it is that I hope to pass on as both a scholar and a teacher.

In the spring of 2005, I stumbled upon Barbara Hahn's *The Jewess Pallas Athena* and was struck by the vision of intellectual Jewish women that she describes. According to Hahn, these Jewish women who spoke and wrote in German were a critical part of modern German letters. Her book offers glimpses of not only their public writing but also of letters and journals, the intimacies behind their more public works. She shows readers, in other words, the relationships that nurtured and produced these intellectual women. As I read this book in a different register, I noticed how many of these women of letters were also women without children, women whose legacy is their writing. For these women the labor of writing and critical engagement defined their lives and, like me, they made choices to value this part of their lives. I imagine that they felt they could not do all of these things at the same time. This, too, is something I have grappled with. Knowing that these women's legacies live on in their writing is a gift. It makes me feel less anomalous and more a part of something larger than myself. This, too, is a way of being a woman in the world.

In some ways, I come to these Jewish women very much as my mother's daughter. I am improvising, looking for ways to make my life choices make sense. I now realize that it is inconceivable to me that my mother—who came from a family of pharmacists, a household without books, and who had never had a mentor of her own—would become an English teacher. I suspect that, like me, my mother was able to give to her students part of what she had wanted from her own teachers but never received. In a sense this is another lesson I learned from her. But, in turning to the Jewesses of German letters, I am also engaging in a kind of imaginative enactment; I am laying claim to an inheritance I can only embrace through an act of imagination. In reading Hahn's work I find I am not alone. I have a history of intellectual Jewish women, modern Jewish women who wrote, and whose writings reveal traces of a different kind of intimacy, a legacy of relationships that are generative, relationships that inspire writing that has both specific and broader audiences. Strangely, I find myself picking up a delicate and broken thread, the legacy of the Jewess Pallas Athena: instead of trying to re-create it, I carry it forward as inspiration in a different language, a different time, a different place. Hahn shows me that there has already been such a thing, and we can hold on to it as we continue to read and write and teach, and create all kinds of legacies in the present. And she also shows me that these German Jewish women are, like me, women without children.

I imagine my contribution to the future through my writing and teaching. More specifically, I think about how my often intimate but also quite public writing can contribute to a different future. While completing this essay, I talked to a good friend and colleague about what I was writing, and how I found myself writing about my mother. In response, she reminded me of a rabbinic dictum, a position I had not fully known before, that addresses the relationship between teacher and parent. As she explained, there is a tradition that says that when asked to choose between saving the life of his parent or his teacher, a man should choose to save his teacher. Of course my use of the masculine here is deliberate. It is clear that this rabbinic dictum was a masculine fantasy, if not an enactment; it was about fathers and male teachers. Nevertheless, I am struck that my friend thought of this dictum in relation to what I had told her about my work.

For me, the challenge is to resist such a stark choice. The contrast just does not ring true. After all, my mother was my teacher. And for me, part of the legacy of Hahn's German Jewish writers is that they offer a gendered alternative to the authority of ancient rabbis. The Jewesses Hahn writes about include women both with and without children who lived rich lives of Jewish letters. For all of these Jewish women, relationships, intimacies, and intellectual labors were intertwined. If asked to choose, they would have had to have chosen both or all of their identities; they could not have separated out the teachers and the parents. The identities of these German Jewish women, like those of contemporary Jewish feminists who also refuse to choose or to split off pieces of themselves, are rich and complicated. And I count myself among these women, knowing that this is, in part, what has enabled all of us to write.

Over the past number of years, I have watched my best friend's daughter as she has played with dolls, jumped on a trampoline, and fallen in love with baseball. And I have often done this from a distance, not always knowing exactly my role. Here again, there are few role models. Even still, I want to imagine that the very different choices my friend and I have made about our lives might someday come to matter to this young girl, and to other generations of women. In the end, I do not want these girls—or any of us—to have to choose among these things. I want there to be room for all kinds of permutations, all kinds of contradictory desires; I don't want to imagine that the decision to have or not to have children need feel so fraught.

I write in the present not knowing for whom my words will resonate. What I do know is that I have students and friends who get it. Unlike many writers with children, I am not at all sure who will bury me or in what ground I will find my final resting place. These tropes are invoked in many works of intimate public writing and performance where the addressee is the writer's or the artist's own child or children. I do not have this convention to rely on. I do not know who will ultimately receive my work, take it in, and make it her or his own. And, to be honest, I do not know who will say Kaddish for me. But this is an unknowing I am willing to live with. What I have learned from many women, and especially my own mother, is that I have some say about these things. However difficult these choices might sometimes feel, I do have some agency in these matters. I need not become the idealized rabbinic teacher to justify my role as a woman writer, a woman without children. To do that would be to refuse to appreciate the labors of all of the women who came before me, those with and those without children, as well as my contemporaries. And I refuse to do that. Instead, I want to imagine more possibilities. I want us all to be able to live more fully the lives we choose. In my case, this means being able to read and write and teach and mentor, not always having to justify my choices. In a strange way, I think that this has made me a better teacher and writer.

I am grateful to Miriam Peskowitz for thinking of me in the context of this volume. I also want to thank my mother, who, after reading this essay, reminded me that, like her, I continue to play dress-ups with all of the people I love.

Engineering Motherhood

JENNIFER EYRE WHITE

When I was in elementary school, back in the mid-1970s, my parents gave me a handheld electronic game that was like Ping-Pong. A little LED "ball" would go back and forth across the screen, and you'd have to push one of three buttons on your side (depending on where the ball "hit") to send it back to the other side. I figured there was probably a pattern to the ball's path, so I made a list showing which button the ball came to on my side after it left a button on the other side. After recording a page of data points, I found the pattern I was looking for. At which point I could play the game endlessly without losing—so I completely lost interest. My mom saw my table of data and asked me what it was. When I told her, she said, "Wow, that's a great way to play the game." Puzzled, I responded, "Well, how else would you do it?"

Grade schoolers who make data tables often have parents who make data tables. And indeed, I was the product of a mathematician mom and an engineer dad, so it was probably my destiny to do things like reverse-engineer electronic games. It apparently wasn't my destiny, however, to follow the usual path to college and learn more about the wonderful world of data, because I never made it out of high school.

I hated school and started intermittently refusing to go from the time I hit eighth grade. I was, shall we say, a troubled youth. My parents divorced when I was twelve and I stayed with my mother; she kept trying to find a high school that would suit me, but it never worked. I went to five different high schools before giving up entirely at seventeen. After I dropped out I spent most of my time working for an ice-cream store, drinking beer, wearing trampy clothes, and making bad dating choices.

My mom accepted the fact that high school and I were a match made in hell, and her response was pragmatic. "You'll need a way to support yourself," she said, and she signed me up for vocational school to become a computer operator. (Which, it turned out, mainly entailed learning how to mount tapes on gigantic tape drives and lug boxes of paper over to gigantic printers.) She was sympathetic, but the message was clear: if I wasn't going to college, then it was time for me to move along and start paying my own bills.

I finished vocational school, and went to work full time as a computer operator for a large law firm. I got my own apartment and moved out of my mother's house. After a year of incessant tape mounting and paper lugging, I weaseled my way into a position as a computer programmer. The law firm needed someone to write the software that kept track of the lawyers' billable hours, so I taught myself how to do that. Initially this was fun, but by my second year on the job I'd figured out two things: First, once you know what you're doing, writing software for a law firm is mind-numbingly boring. Second, if you work for a law firm and you're not a lawyer, your career path is likely to be a single point. I wanted out.

It was then that I decided to become an electrical engineer, convinced it would be my ticket out of intellectual petrifaction. Choosing electrical engineering wasn't a well-informed decision; in spite of having an engineer dad, I'd never actually figured out what engineers did. My dad didn't talk about his job, and my own observation was that mostly what he did was tinker on his Corvettes. When I was little—before my parents split up—I used to hang around our garage, watching him, fascinated. But he'd never tell me what he was doing and he yelled at me if I touched anything. I assumed that if I got an engineering degree, I too would learn the secrets of working on cars. I now know that this particular goal would have been better served by an auto-shop class.

I knew that engineers made reasonably good money—enough to buy Corvettes—and that they had to be good at math, which I was. In spite of my appalling high school attendance record I'd managed to get an A in calculus, though I'd accumulated plenty of Fs in other classes. I'd also heard that electrical engineering was hard. This appealed to me both because I was bored with my current job, and because I wanted to prove that I was smart. I'd dated college guys as a high school dropout and I was convinced that they were looking down on me (although considering what I was wearing, they were probably just looking down my shirt). I figured that no one would look down on an engineer.

Never mind the fact that my high school career had been a train wreck and no four-year college would take me. Never mind the fact that I had no money for college and needed to work full time to support myself. This was why God created community colleges.

I kept writing legal software during the day, and at night I took calculus, physics, and chemistry—all the engineering prereqs. It was a grueling schedule and it took forever to make any progress; I wanted to go to school full time but I couldn't yet afford it. So I hoarded my money and kept slogging along. I maintained a 4.0 GPA to make sure I'd get into the nearest engineering school—UCLA—and to convince myself that I deserved to go. It took me nearly four years before I could transfer as a junior and stop working full time. By then I was twenty-five and I had saved eighteen thousand dollars.

I had also gotten a husband.

Frank and I met in a differential equations class at community college. The class was almost exclusively male, and when I came to school one night wearing a miniskirt and high-heeled shoes (I was going out dancing afterwards) several of my fellow students were suddenly overcome by the urge to get my help with their diffEQ homework. Frank was one of them.

He was thirty-five at the time (I was twenty-three) and he was returning to school after working for years as a masseur. Like me, he planned to transfer to UCLA and get a degree in electrical engineering. We hit it off, in part, because we both had such nontraditional backgrounds. Plus, he had really blue eyes, and he said he wanted to have kids some day. He asked me to study with him a few times, and then he asked me out on a date. A year later we got married. This surprised the hell out of me.

For many years before meeting Frank, I had thought that I'd never get married or have a family. As a high school dropout and general screw-up, I did not see myself as marriage or motherhood material. In my mind, that door was shut tight. Going back to school cracked it open a notch, and when Frank and I got married it was as though the door to the whole world blew wide open. Motherhood became a real possibility for me, and I started thinking about it all the time.

Frank and I transferred into UCLA as juniors. He worked part-time as a masseur, and I lived on my savings, scholarships, and student loans. We were barely scraping by, but that didn't bother me at all; I was grateful to finally be in engineering school, and happy to be married and planning a family. We shared a beat-up old Ford Escort, we rented a grungy little apartment, and we subsisted on Kraft macaroni and cheese and beer (which we liked). The only problem was that we couldn't afford to have children. We'd written a list of baby names shortly after we got married, but we had no one to give them to.

What with us being older students and all, we agreed that we should get started on a baby as soon as possible. But it was clear (to me, at least) that one of us needed to finish school and get a job before we could afford to have a baby. So in my senior year I started working as a junior engineer. That way, I'd have a guaranteed position when I graduated, and I wouldn't have to waste precious time job hunting while my biological clock ticked.

My new employer made electronic control systems for fighter planes. This job choice was heavily influenced by the movie *Top Gun*, which stars Tom Cruise as a fighter pilot. Tom wasn't my type but I watched the movie five or six times, because those F-14s were gorgeous. My new job didn't involve sports cars, but I decided it was close enough. I planned to work for this company for a few years after I graduated, and then have a baby. That would put me in my early thirties and it was much longer than I wanted to wait, but I didn't want to piss my boss off by getting pregnant too quickly. It just didn't seem like an auspicious way to start an engineering career.

My friend Laura changed my mind. Laura was thirty-eight—a decade older than me—had a master's degree in engineering, and worked as a high-level engineering manager. While my engineering career was just getting started, hers was in full bloom. She was dark haired and olive skinned, beautiful, funny, and confident. She met me for lunch one afternoon, and we talked about engineering and babies.

She told me that she'd been trying to get pregnant for years and had undergone multiple unsuccessful fertility treatments. She spelled out what those treatments were like—the shots, the money, the stress. She said she wished she'd started trying to get pregnant much earlier.

I told her that Frank and I wanted to have several kids, but that I figured I'd have to wait a few years before getting pregnant. I was well aware that my risk of becoming infertile or having a kid with a genetic disorder was creeping up as I got older; I'd seen plenty of discouraging data tables on this topic. But I couldn't figure out how to trade off those risks against the risk of whacking my own career.

Laura listened to me closely, and then she looked me in the eye and said, "If you know you want a baby, do it now. Don't wait. There will be other jobs."

She was my catalyst—she gave me permission to put the baby first. So that's what I did. And as it turned out, grad school provided a way for me to put the baby first without leaving my career behind.

At twenty-eight, I finished my degree in electrical engineering with high honors. I didn't take a break to celebrate my graduation; that would have cost me time and money. I didn't even bother to go to my graduation ceremony. Instead, I started working full time at the fighter plane company the Monday after I graduated. Having finished my goal of getting an engineering degree, I had already moved on to my next project: the baby.

Laura had convinced me that I should compress my reproductive timeline. Instead of waiting a few years, I decided to work full time just long enough to be eligible for maternity leave (a year), have a baby, and go straight to grad school. If everything worked out, this plan would solve several problems at once.

I wouldn't have to wait to have a baby, and I wouldn't have to worry about screwing up my career because grad school would keep it moving forward. I wouldn't have to put my kid in day care (a prospect that had troubled me greatly) because Frank and I could take turns with child care. It seemed like the perfect solution. I couldn't figure out why I hadn't thought of it sooner.

Of course, there were a lot of ways the plan could go wrong; baby making is notoriously difficult to schedule, and I knew that perfectly well. But it didn't go wrong. I got into grad school, I was awarded a fellowship to pay for it, and I got pregnant the first time I tried—exactly three months after I started full-time work. It took six home pregnancy tests to convince me that I was really pregnant. I felt like I'd won the lottery, and had to keep checking my ticket.

My boss was less enthusiastic. "Did you do this on purpose?" he asked. "Yes," I said, thinking, *There will be other jobs.*

When I told Laura that I was pregnant, she hugged me close. Of all people, she understood my choice. Laura herself had finally gotten pregnant with twins, a boy and a girl. They were born shortly before I became pregnant, and they were beautiful and olive-skinned like Laura. The boy had Down's syndrome.

My daughter, Riley, was born at the UCLA Medical Center in June, right on schedule. I spent ten joyful weeks at home with her—that kid rocked my world—and then I started my master's degree.

As I'd hoped, being a mother and a graduate student turned out to be a great combination. I had plenty of time with Riley, and enough time away. I did brain things, and I did mom things. If she was sick and I needed to be home with her, no one cared that I didn't show up for class; I never had to call in sick or apologize for missing a big meeting. I didn't have to hoard my vacation and sick days like a candy bar on a desert island. I didn't have to worry whether my co-workers (or my boss) thought I was a flake. Later on, when I tried juggling an engineering career with one, then two, then three kids, I realized just how much harder it was to be a working mom than to be a student mom.

One big reason why grad school went so well was that I didn't have to worry about day care. Frank and I used an Excel spreadsheet to divide up the hours of child care fifty-fifty each week, so we'd each have time to go to our classes and do our research. Every quarter we'd arrange our classes so that the times didn't overlap. The spreadsheet governed who was taking care of Riley every hour of every day, even on weekends. This was my idea; I didn't want to be constantly wondering when I'd have a chunk of time to study or go to my research lab. It worked reasonably well as a child-care solution, but as a marriage strategy it was problematic. When I got sick with a barfing stomach bug and couldn't take care of her one day, Frank told me I'd have to make up my hours on the weekend.

There was another scheduling challenge the spreadsheet didn't solve: breastfeeding can't be split fifty-fifty. For the first six months I'd race to school for class and race home for the next feeding. Sometimes Frank would bring Riley to school to meet me, and I'd take her into the women's bathroom and sit with her on the floor while she slurped like a piggy at the trough. One of the nice things about being a female engineer is that the bathrooms are always empty and peaceful.

And I was peaceful, too. It's perhaps telling that I can remember my undergraduate GPA to two decimal places, but if you ask my what my GPA was in grad school I'd say, "Umm, I think it was three point something." Partly, this change was due to the fact that I had no intention of going on for a PhD, so I didn't need stellar grades. But mostly it was because I'd fallen in love with my baby and she didn't give a damn about my grades. Which was good, because she wasn't particularly helpful in that area.

She inevitably got some sort of virus or rash the night before I had final exams. My final exam in nonlinear control systems was preceded by hand-foot-mouth disease; my final in stochastic processes was preceded by the flu. I, too, got sick a lot, and I was tired. But grad school was still perfect, with none of those nasty work-life balance issues that would subsume my life a few years later.

I never had any women professors, much less women professors with kids. But that didn't bother me. Several of my professors were young dads (including my advisor) and these guys were totally baby friendly. They'd tell me stories about their kids and they'd ask me how Riley was doing, and when I brought her to school they made goofy faces and tried to get her to laugh. Even the professors without kids were either friendly or neutral to her. No one seemed to find it at all strange that I had a kid; hardly anyone even commented on it.

Well, one person commented. One afternoon I brought Riley with me when I went to see one of my professors during office hours. This professor was older and Indian (engineering faculties tend to include a lot of older Indian men) and he was fairly stern. He didn't look pleased when I brought her into his office. Riley was about eight months old then, built like a fireplug and wearing a pretty blue dress to match her dinner-plate eyes, and as the professor and I discussed a thorny homework problem she sat in her stroller smiling and babbling. After awhile the professor looked over at her and said grudgingly, in a thick accent emphasizing the consonants, "She's pretty well behaved, for a baby." "Yeah, she is," I agreed. We kept working on the problem. When we were finished he cocked his head and said to me, "You know, in my day, women stayed home with their babies."

Now, a statement like that could be taken several ways. It could be taken to mean that I shouldn't be there, studying engineering—or it could be taken as a simple comment on how much things have changed. I didn't detect any criticism in his tone, and I don't take offense easily, so I decided that it was the latter. I nodded and said, "Mm hmm." He said, "See you in class tomorrow." And Riley and I rolled on out.

I got an A in his class.

I finished my master's degree and my thesis was published in an engineering journal. My advisor suggested that I continue on for a PhD, but that had never been my goal. I just wanted to work as a regular engineer. And Laura was right—there have been other jobs.

Ten years later, I look back on those years in college with Riley and I can't quite believe that I did what I did. It made perfect sense to me at the time, but now it all seems like so much work. I have three young kids now and a part-time job, and mostly my goals involve napping and making the perfect mojito. Frankly, I don't know what gave me the chutzpah to try combining motherhood and grad school in the first place. Maybe it was because I'd spent so many years juggling work and school that I figured it wouldn't be much different. Or maybe it was because, at the time I made the decision, I was completely clueless about both motherhood and grad school. If so, then in cluelessness lay bliss, because that year and nine months with Riley was a magical bubble of time. Never again have motherhood and career-hood coexisted so peacefully in my life. And if I hadn't been a high school dropout—if I'd been a "good girl" and graduated from college at twenty-two instead of twenty-eight—I never would have done it.

The Wire Mother

SUSAN O'DOHERTY

On my first day of graduate school, the dean of the clinical psychology program assembled all of the new students in an airless basement classroom. "Look at the person on your left; now look to your right," he instructed us.

I felt my face go hot. I remembered this scene from *The Paper Chase*. Our dean was taking the John Houseman role, warning us as the ship steamed out of the harbor that only two-thirds of us would remain afloat to disembark when it arrived at its destination.

I knew I would be one of those jettisoned. My only real qualification for being here, I felt, was my experience as a patient. After years of juggling bill-paying but unrewarding "day jobs," stimulating but unlucrative acting pursuits, and failed attempts to write a coherent novel, I had stumbled into therapy and absorbed its language as though it were my true, but forgotten, mother tongue. Earlier, I had read Freud primarily for his astute observations on Shakespeare and Goethe; in my therapy sessions I experienced the symbolic meanings of dreams, slips of the tongue, and acting out of unconscious impulses as living, interactive poetry. I became convinced that psychology was my true vocation.

I had focused my ambition on this highly competitive program because it was the one my own therapist had attended, though she had had a baby while writing her dissertation and had never graduated. My acceptance, despite my lack of conventional qualifications, seemed like a sign from the universe that I was on the right course.

Now, though, as I sat surrounded by youth, focused intelligence, and cheery certitude, it seemed more probable that I had been taken on as ballast—providing a measure, or at least the appearance, of balance, but ultimately disposable. The poised young woman on my right, who had casually mentioned her undergraduate internship assisting a world-renowned researcher, seemed destined to thrive. So did the lanky man on my left, who had already secured a coveted, paying field placement.

The two of them even looked more legitimate than I did. She was dressed in casual but chic twill pants and a silk T-shirt; he wore perfectly tailored khakis and a soft blue shirt. They could have been illustrations in a graduate students' dress-for-success manual. My carefully chosen coral skirt and sweater, which had looked fine at home this morning, now made me feel like a giant blotch of cotton candy. I suppressed the urge to fold my arms across my chest, to make myself smaller. At least, I reflected, I was unlikely to succumb to the fate of my brilliant but uncredentialed therapist. Over the past several years, I had suffered a series of spontaneous abortions for which no medical cause had been found. One elderly male gynecologist had admonished me, "You career girls do this to yourselves. You want to do everything men do—maybe you want to be men. When you're ready to grow up and be a mother, you won't have this problem." The more enlightened woman I was seeing now had suggested that exhaustion and overwork might be contributing factors. Maybe one day I would manage to slow down enough to bring a pregnancy to term, but clearly that wasn't going to happen here. I would drown on my own demerits.

I scanned the room, wondering who was destined to sink with me, and locked eyes with a woman who seemed to be in her thirties, like me, and whose frozen face mirrored my panic.

The dean gave a hearty chortle, startling us both. "Relax, I'm joking," he said. "In our entire history, only two people have failed out, and those were extraordinary circumstances. We make our admissions process so rigorous to be sure we get the right students to begin with. Once you're in, it's smooth sailing—if you're here, it means you belong here." He paused for effect. "And one more thing—none of this 'Dr. Fishman' nonsense. It's Michael. We're all in this together."

I tried to take a deep breath, but there was still no air in the room, and as I looked into "Michael's" eyes, they weren't laughing.

When he released us, I sought out my compatriot in terror. I learned that her name was Renee. Like me, she had come to the program after a previous career—in her case, a small business she co-owned with her husband, Robert. Unlike me, she had children—two sons.

Over the next several days, I found myself reflecting that perhaps Renee's experience dealing with immature, self-centered individuals gave her a social edge here. Although her eyes registered astonishment when a professor informed us that the IQ measures we were learning were "culture neutral," because "all intelligent people know who Amelia Earhart was," or when a white classmate boasted of having been accepted "the hard way—you know, without affirmative action," she simply shrugged and went about her business. I envied her sense of proportion. I felt like a hypersensitive child myself, overstimulated and overreacting to everything, always a step away from tears, without a coherent or organized response to what I was seeing and hearing.

I invited Renee and her sons home to meet my husband, Bill. Before long, they were frequent guests at our apartment. Chris was an aspiring pianist who was so insightful and comfortable with adult conversation I sometimes forgot I was talking to a nine-year-old. Andy, at five, was bubbly and engaging and addicted to knock-knock jokes. Bill and I hoped we would be so lucky with our own kids.

We waited for a return invitation, or at least an introduction to her husband, but none were forthcoming. Instead, Renee would say things like, "We really want to have you over when things calm down," citing ongoing renovations to their house and her husband's impossible work schedule now that he was running the business on his own.

I felt vaguely insulted. I wondered whether Renee felt we just weren't important or interesting enough to meet Robert. Or perhaps, I thought, he was an antisocial loner, or a workaholic.

The semester quickly accelerated into such a haze of anxiety and exhaustion that I no longer had the mental energy to wonder about Robert. In addition to keeping up with our course work, each week we were expected to put in two full days at a field placement (mine was at an inner-city hospital a two-hour subway commute from my home); to perform a series of psychological tests on a volunteer we had recruited ourselves and to write up the results (usually entailing frantic last-minute phone calls, bribes of brownies, and all-night transcription and interpretation sessions); and to attend case conferences where more advanced students presented their clinical work and were advised by their peers and professors. The primary focus of my existence became balancing the need to imbibe enough caffeine to stay awake with the requirement that I spend more time in class and at work than in the bathroom.

In a dynamics of behavior class we studied religious cults and paramilitary groups that use sleep deprivation and inundation with propaganda to break down defenses and secure unquestioning loyalty to the groups' principles and leadership. Perhaps this phenomenon helps to explain why, at the time, I didn't connect certain experiences and incidents.

In a case conference, a third-year student presented a child client who, although bright, was a chronic underachiever. His mother was concerned that his lower-than-expected scores on standardized tests might bar him from a program for gifted children that she thought would be a good fit for him, and had inquired about assessment for possible learning disabilities. Both the presiding professor and the more advanced students immediately pounced on the "hovering" mother as the cause of the child's academic problems. "These privileged suburban moms," one student commented. "They try to live through their kids, and they end up crippling them."

A few weeks later, though, at a psychology staff meeting at the public hospital where I did my field placement, a therapist expressed frustration with mothers who "dumped" their medically ill children in the hospital and visited infrequently. "I'm supposed to be treating the kid for depression, but if the mom would just bother to show up and give her a hug once in a while, she wouldn't *be* depressed!" Another therapist pointed out that the mother in question had other young children to care for, but the first wasn't having it: "There has to be some accountability! She's the mother!" So not hovering wasn't the answer, either. No one mentioned a father, or what his accountability might be.

I asked Frank, a genial, insightful fellow student, how he handled it when his one-year-old daughter was sick. "Fortunately," he said, "my wife has a pretty flexible schedule." His wife, Mimi, was finishing up social work school. They hoped to go into practice together. "She would have liked to come here, too, but the time commitment is too great," he told me. Another classmate, Kevin, talked expansively about the joys of fatherhood. When his wife and child attended a department party, she chased their toddler around the un-childproofed house while he talked theory with professors and fellow students.

In a child development class, we read about Harry Harlow's classic "wire mother" experiments on rhesus monkeys. In one study, he separated baby monkeys from their mothers and divided them into two groups. Both groups were given "surrogate mothers"—machines that dispensed milk. One "mother" was constructed of cuddly terry cloth; the other of bare wire mesh. The monkeys with the cuddly "mothers" developed fairly normally; the ones with the wire "mothers" developed severely impaired social and attachment skills. The teacher explained that the human corollary to

Harlow's "wire mother" was the "refrigerator mother," who provides basic care and sustenance, but no emotional warmth. This maternal behavior, we learned, was thought to be responsible for most cases of childhood autism. (I did wonder what the "human corollary" was to the scientist who purposefully breaks up intact families and creates mental illness just to study it, but I couldn't think of a way to phrase my question that didn't sound disrespectful and provocative.)

At another case conference, shortly afterward, a student presented a young woman who had sought counseling to deal with depression following a miscarriage. The student noted that the client appeared anxious and laughed inappropriately. The focus of the discussion shifted to the "hysteria" that may have caused the miscarriage to begin with. It was well known, I learned, that women who are not emotionally mature enough for parenthood, or who are riddled with ambivalence, often unconsciously create a womb environment that is toxic to their fetuses.

This was essentially what the doctor who had accused me of wanting to be a man—the individual my friends and I laughingly referred to as "the misogynist gynecologist"—had said, though with a Freudian twist. Now, it seemed that he was on to something, that the joke had been on us—on me. Accommodating this idea proved even harder than staying up all night writing test reports.

When Renee started coming late to morning classes, often looking disheveled, I assumed at first that the long hours and emotionally draining material were getting to her, too. It soon became evident, though, that something more serious was going on.

She started missing class with alarming frequency. When she did show up, she was distracted and unprepared. Members of her research lab exchanged barely veiled sneers whenever her name was mentioned. At our apartment, more often than not, she would fall asleep on the couch, leaving us to entertain the boys. Chris started lodging complaints about the dryness of my brownies, the uncomfortableness of our furniture, and the fact that we didn't have cable. Andy cornered our elderly cat and pulled her ears. I wondered whether my urge to expel them all and read and work in peace was a symptom of the immaturity that had apparently driven my miscarriages.

I had always thought I loved children. I was truly fond of Chris and Andy. But it was the life of the mind, the study of the deeply symbolic and poetic language of analysis that had drawn me to graduate school and to the goal of membership in an intellectual community. Despite her first-rate mind, Renee was bogged down in a messy, earthbound existence that I had limited tolerance for, and that seemed to doom her to second-rate achievement.

Yet I also envied her. Nothing about Renee was prissy, or scared of the corporeal aspects of life. She was at home in the physical world. She had borne two children and nourished them with her body. She drove a van equipped with a child seat and Raffi tapes. She carried band-aids and dried fruit in her capacious handbag. She was a real woman. My teachers, on the other hand—all men except for one childless woman—were real intellectuals who didn't waste mental energy on such trivia as runny noses or clean socks. I was nothing, caught in the middle: ashamed of my weak-brained desire for a child, ashamed of my unwomanly inability to carry one to term.

I wanted to rescue Renee, but I felt I was drowning myself. The least I could do, I thought, was type up her overdue lab reports. It never happened, though, because she couldn't find her notes.

Another classmate, a woman named Cassie, started complaining of flu-like symptoms. Soon she was sporting outsized tops and secret smiles. Within weeks, fellow students were calling her "Little Mama" and rubbing her belly in passing. She seemed to enjoy the attention. But her complex and sometimes confusing comments, which had previously sparked probing questions and intense discussions, were now met with indulgent smiles. Or maybe that was just my imagination.

At a holiday party on the last day of the semester, I stood near a cluster of third-year students who watched as Cassie loaded her plate at the buffet table. "Classic case of self-defeating behavior," Gerard observed, and the others nodded. At my blank look, he explained, "She's afraid of success. Or she doesn't believe she has what it takes, so she found a face-saving way out."

"How do you know it didn't just happen, and now she's dealing with it?" I asked.

The group laughed. "You've been here half a year, and you still believe in accidents?"

On our first day back, as I passed Michael's open door, I saw Renee slumped across from him. She looked like she was trying not to cry. His face was unreadable.

"I'm on probation," she reported tonelessly over lunch. Out of five courses, she had received three incompletes.

"We've got to get you organized," I said.

She stood up. "Let's go for a walk."

As we traversed the running track, she told me that Robert was not running their business. The business was in bankruptcy. Robert was dying, of AIDS. He was at home, demented, running outside naked, screaming curses at the boys. A succession of home health aides had walked out with little or no notice. Chris had started pulling out his eyebrows.

I had learned the protocol for interviewing people with AIDS and their families at my field placement. It was most important, I knew, not to open with questions about how the disease had been contracted. Such a line of inquiry could suggest that the interviewer would consider and treat an active homosexual or IV drug user differently from an "innocent victim" such as a transfusion patient. I opened my mouth, intending to say something mature and comforting, and instead blurted out, "How did this happen?" Renee fixed me with the stare she usually reserved for our most clueless classmates.

"That's private," she said, "but the boys and I are all right." Which was, of course, the answer to the question I should have asked.

Michael, the dean, had urged us repeatedly to consult him about any problems, any complications that interfered with our studies. "I'm on your side," he had assured us.

"You have to tell him," I said now.

"He knows."

She went on to tell me that Robert had been diagnosed the summer before school started. Renee, feeling that she needed time to absorb the news and make plans for the business, had asked to defer entering for a year. Michael was sympathetic, but told her that the school would not be able to hold a place for her. "I decided to go ahead with it," she said. "I'm going to need a way to make money. The life insurance isn't going to put the boys through college. I have to make this work."

But "have to" wasn't translating into "can." I asked what the department was doing to help her out.

"Not kicking me out on my ass, at least not yet. Other than that . . . ?" She shrugged.

"It's the wire mother," I said. She looked at me blankly. "You know, the monkey gets just enough to stay alive, but not what it needs to be okay." But she had missed that lecture.

At home that night, Bill and I talked over the possibility of inviting Renee's boys to stay with us, at least part time. How could we just stand by and watch the family sink? On the other hand, as Bill pointed out, how could I justify jeopardizing my own academic career, which we had already gone into serious debt to finance?

I wondered what would happen if Kevin's wife, or Frank's, were to be taken ill. I imagined mothers, mothers-in-law, sisters, cousins, aunts rushing to the rescue. They wouldn't be expected to handle their children alone, especially with the pressures of graduate school. Renee's family had "other things to deal with," she told me, and Robert's was too incapacitated with shock and grief to be of much use.

In the end, I made a vague, open-ended offer to take over the boys' care "whenever you need a break." Renee thanked me, but never took me up on it. Perhaps my reluctance was too transparent, or maybe, I thought, she and the boys were all too aware of my maternal shortcomings.

In May, Cassie had her baby. I sent a stuffed bear, and she called to thank me. "So, when are you coming back?" I asked.

"I'm not sure I can," she answered. "I can make up the work from this semester, but I can't do the summer testing placement, and they won't let me register for the fall without it. Maybe next year." Despite her obvious joy in her new son, she sounded diminished to me; uncharacteristically unsure of herself.

I saw Robert for the first time that August, at his open-casket funeral. Renee was exhausted, but calm. "I'm going half time in the fall," she told me.

In our program, "half time" was a netherworld populated entirely by mothers, from which no exit was visible. In entering this limbo, Renee was dooming herself to a minimum of six more years of course work. And that was just the beginning. After fulfilling academic requirements, clinical psychology students were required to complete a strenuous year-long internship. Most of the mothers needed to do this part time, too—and so few sites offered this option that some ended up taking a year off while awaiting placement. The official line was that they would write their dissertations during this year, but that seldom happened.

After graduation came a year's supervised clinical practice (or the equivalent in part-time hours) before we could sit for the state licensing exam that, if we passed (and many didn't the first time out), would allow us to work as entry-level psychologists. It was hard to see how Renee's choice would promote her goal of feeding her family and sending the boys to college. "Crap," I said, and once again was the recipient of her stare.

Because of course it wasn't a choice. She had made up most of her first-semester incompletes, but had fallen behind again during Robert's last illness. She would not be allowed to continue in the full-time program.

A few weeks later, our first week back in class, I missed my period.

The beginning of every previous pregnancy in my married life had been imbued with joy and hope. Even with a history of losses, Bill and I had invested each occasion with the conviction that this was the "real baby," the one we were meant to have, and so this would be the one to survive. This optimism would last right up until the cramps and bleeding. Then we would admit that we had done it to ourselves again.

For the first time, though, I wasn't sure I wanted this to be happening. Or, as I told myself, I was finally bringing my internal conflicts about parenting, the ones that had destroyed the earlier fetuses, into consciousness. It wasn't just that if I had a baby I would never become a psychologist. I now doubted my ability to function as a parent. I loved reading too much. I loved ideas. I was selfish and tactless and immature and got upset when Andy wiped his nose on my sofa. Even as desperate as Renee was, she wouldn't leave me in sole charge of her children. The best I could hope for, if by some fluke I managed to deliver a live baby, would be to serve as a wire mother myself. Who would wish that on a child?

But my dreams—the pathways to the unconscious mind, I'd been taught—were imbued with baby grins, with birthday parties and bedtime stories. I woke up one morning with scratched and bloody arms and a vague memory of trying to cradle the cat. Whenever a baby appeared on television, even if I was just passing through the room, I would stop, mesmerized, completely losing track of the task I had been intent on. And when the cramping began, one Friday evening just three weeks after my period was due, I was once again swept into a whirlpool of loss, dull despair, and longing for the child whose face, whose tiny fingers, I would never see.

That Monday as I walked back into the student lounge, newly empty, and watched my fellow students chattering and studying, I felt completely alone and rudderless. My books and ideas were cold comfort against the dream smiles and hugs that now haunted my nights. Yet I couldn't deny my dread of being relegated to steerage with the other exhausted, self-sacrificing moms, and my relief at being spared. I was a mongrel, a faulty vessel, and there was no place in either world—in any world—where I was likely to find a harbor.

I thought of Harlow's motherless monkeys, frightened, alone, unable to function effectively in the world. Renee was the barrier between her children and the fate of those monkeys—but who was looking out for Renee? The stability of society, it seemed, depended on the willingness of an entire class of people to sacrifice their own needs and desires in order to nurture and comfort others.

My "misogynist gynecologist" had been right, after all. I wanted to be a man. I wanted to live a full life, to pursue my interests, and to love and enjoy my children as Freud had done, as Harry Harlow himself had done, as my male teachers did.

My classmate Kevin came in with pictures of his son's second birthday party. I hovered on the edge of the cluster of admirers, taking in the silly hats, broad grins, and ominous scowls; the handcrafted cake; the row of mothers in the background half light, poised to wipe away the tears, to kiss the boo-boos, to make it all better for everyone else.

"Parenthood," he crowed. "There's nothing like it!"

Fitting In

ELRENA EVANS

You see, Dr. Jiggle, when you know God made you special
It doesn't matter what anyone else thinks—you can just be yourself.

—VeggieTales

The weather was unseasonably warm in Pennsylvania during the fall of 2004, the semester I finished course work for my PhD and gave birth to my firstborn. The summer had been mostly mild, and as the days slipped from August into September and I traded lazy nights with my husband at the local drive-in theater for one last round with the textbooks, the weather belied this transition and stayed temperate. I was pleased; it allowed me to keep wearing most of the summer maternity clothes I'd purchased back in late spring, when I was so excited to be pregnant I ignored my still-flat belly and went out and bought an entire collection of empire-waist shirts and belly-banded pants. I was also pleased that the weather would allow me to keep wearing flip-flops—not because of the pregnancy cliché about being too big to tie my shoes, but because, through a series of careful contortions, I kept my toenails polished a bright pink right up to the day of my delivery, and I wanted to show them off. Pretty feet, for some inexplicable reason, had become very important to me as my belly finally swelled into a cute pregnancy bump and the rest of my body, not so cute, swelled right along with it.

I was admiring my toenails and their candy-pink polish when I arrived at class one day, eight months pregnant, only to discover I could no longer slide into the desk/chair combinations furnishing the classroom. I had known the day was coming; over the last month and a half I'd been sitting up straighter and straighter in my seat trying to gain additional clearance between my belly and the desk, and already my unborn daughter could make contact with the desk—through my belly—whenever she kicked. On the day I truly could no longer fit, I dragged my desk out of the line-up and back into a corner—exchanging it for the one desk in the room that allowed for about an inch more space. I could feel some of the guys in the

class watching me as I hefted and pulled, and although at first I was simply annoyed that I was starting to sweat, as I struggled with my overlarge
belly and the overlarge desk I soon refocused my annoyance on the fact
that no one offered to help me, the poor pregnant lady grown too big to sit
in her chair. But by then I should have been used to it. The desk that could
no longer accommodate my pregnant body was just one more example of
me not fitting in to the academy.

I graduated from a Christian high school where, despite my strong
Christian faith, I didn't quite fit in with the rest of the group. I was a litur-
gical Episcopalian in a largely evangelical non-denominational crowd, and
wearing ashes on Ash Wednesday and knowing when the Council of Nicaea
took place didn't win me many friends. From there I went on to attend a
small, private liberal arts college where suddenly I went from being perceived as a bit radical and left leaning to being perceived as a hard-core,
Bible-thumping conservative. Which was odd, as I hadn't changed at all;
the only thing that had changed was the context in which I lived. I sealed
my fate that first year when one of the girls on my hall casually lit up a cig-
arette while we were talking, and my face must have given away my surprise. "What?" she jokingly asked me. "Have you never seen a teenage girl
smoke before?" And I was foolish enough to answer honestly, no, I hadn't.

After graduation, I took a year off to teach at my old high school, where
I was continually in trouble with the administration for offenses like teaching barefoot. So I went to graduate school. If I thought I was at last going
to find a community of people like myself, I was sorely disappointed. In
retrospect, I should have known: I enrolled in a Master of Fine Arts program in creative writing as a nondrinking, nonsmoking, non-pot-user who
spoke readily about her faith and didn't even like coffee. I was doomed
from the word go. I was elated the first week of classes to find another nondrinking, nonsmoking, non-pot-using Christian in my department, but our
instant camaraderie somehow fizzled—perhaps I was too liberal?—and by
the time I noticed, it was too awkward to ask why.

Additionally, I'm pretty sure I horrified the graduate faculty by keeping
up my classical ballet training while working on my MFA. I figured if I
hadn't quit dancing through the body changes of middle school, the pressures of AP exams in high school, or the bemused looks of friends in college when I continually announced "I'm off to dance," there was no good
reason for me to quit in graduate school. I scheduled all of my dance
classes first thing each semester, filling in graduate seminars in the spaces
left over. It was sometimes a close fit, leaving me running to make it from

ballet lessons to seminars, arriving sweaty and disheveled with clothes haphazardly thrown over leotard and tights and hair beginning to come out of its tightly coiled bun. Both professors and peers probably thought I was odd, unconsciously pointing and flexing my pink-tights-clad feet as we read Jack Kerouac and discussed New Journalism. The rumor, as it reached my ears, was that faculty were skeptical about my commitment to the degree in light of my continued pursuit of "extracurriculars." But even if I had given up my dancing in an attempt to fit in, there was still an awful lot of booze, drugs, caffeine, and nicotine standing in my way.

After completing my MFA, I was recruited for a PhD in education by a professor with whom I'd taken a few classes. It was during the second semester of my PhD studies that I had my life-changing pee-on-a-stick moment and knew I was going to be pregnant in graduate school—the next sequence of steps in my dance of the misfit. But I figured I'd simply continue on as if I wasn't pregnant; if I could discuss Kenneth Burke's rhetoric wearing pink tights, I could discuss Burke's rhetoric behind a swollen, pregnant belly. I wouldn't fit in, but I'd manage just fine. Somehow. Like Pippi Longstocking, I had great faith in my ability to always come out on top.

What I didn't count on was a complicated pregnancy. My visions of myself sailing through nine months with no more fuss than the occasional extra bathroom trip never materialized, their gauzy idealism stamped out by the solid reality of unexplained bleeding, preterm contractions, and round after round after round of bed rest. Yet I kept on going to classes, enlisting my husband's help to drive me to campus and drop me off at the door of my classroom so I wouldn't have to walk more than a few feet and thus not technically violate my "modified bed rest" restrictions. I now scheduled ever-increasing prenatal appointments around seminars, and carted schoolbooks with me to read in the midwife's waiting room. When my complications culminated with a pulmonary embolism the week before my daughter was born, I propped my laptop up on the tray next to my hospital bed, connected to the hospital's wireless network, arranged my various IVs and fetal monitors around the piles of books I had brought to the hospital, and kept right on being a graduate student.

At the time, I never thought to do otherwise. Now, with the seasoned eyes of sixteen months of motherhood, I can look back and realize that my pregnancy marked the end of my romance with the academy. In my studies on gender and education, pre-baby and pre-embolism, one of my professors had often talked about the academy's "floating head" syndrome;

how people are expected to function as disembodied brains, not connected to bodies or families or any sort of life outside of academic pursuits. This always resonated with me on one level, as I fished my crumpled ballet shoes out from underneath Michel Foucault's *Power/Knowledge,* but I don't think I fully grasped the magnitude of what she was talking about until I experienced the academy not only pregnant, but pregnant with complications.

Looking back, all I can do is shake my head and say, "I should have known." I should have known, when I called my sympathetic advisor to ask for a restructuring of my graduate assistant duties since I had been placed on bed rest, and he suggested I might be able to do my work lying down. I should have known, when having birthed my baby and gone home to try and scrape my life back together on ungodly levels of anticoagulant, I contacted two of my professors to discuss extensions on my final papers and neither was willing to accommodate me. One of them calculated my final grade based on what I had turned in up until my hospitalization, and gave me a C. My first C. The other professor simply failed me. My first F. I should have known, when juggling a newborn and a slow recovery, somehow I ended up overseeing the duties of not one, but two separate assistantships. I should have known. I should have known.

Looking back, I want to scream. It's not about whether or not I could physically perform a task lying down instead of sitting up—it's about the fact that my every waking moment was spent communing with my unborn baby, willing her to be all right, begging her with every breath to stay inside despite the contractions, outlast my traitorous, bleeding body, *be-alive-be-alive-oh-God-please-let-her-be-alive.* It's not about the fact that a late paper was going to mess up the class curve, it's about the fact that—loath as I was to admit this to family, friends, or even myself—I could have died from the embolism. Many pregnant women, even in this great medically advanced society of ours, do. All I needed to do was Google "maternal death" while trying to work on my finals in the hospital to find out that, according to the Centers for Disease Control, embolisms are one of the primary causes of pregnancy-related deaths for women in this country. So it's not about the fact that everyone knew I would somehow rise to the challenge and continue my graduate work without interruption, while trying to recover, trying to mother, trying to nurse with bleeding nipples that couldn't heal because my blood had been thinned to the consistency of water. It's about the fact that I shouldn't have had to. I should have been afforded the dignity of being treated as a whole person, not just a floating, disembodied head.

When my daughter was six months old and I had finished (poorly) my assistantship requirements, I took a year's medical leave from the university. My little family moved to another part of Pennsylvania; I packed away all of my books with brainy titles, learned to play "This Little Piggy," and started, finally, to heal. Physically, I was able to go off the anticoagulants, and psychologically, with the help of prayer and professional counseling, the nightmares and stomachaches and panic attacks lessened, slowed, and finally stopped. Leaving the university, tearing myself out of the bad romance, left me with emotions I couldn't sort out at the time. I knew when I ended it that it needed to end, but it wasn't until time had passed and I had regained perspective that I could see just how badly it had needed to end.

My medical leave is up shortly. I'm sure I could extend it, especially since I've become pregnant for a second (and so far complication-free!) time. I'll have the summer to mull it over. If I finish my comprehensive exams I could take ABD status and then just sit on any further decisions until my PhD time clock runs out, five years from now. But the biggest question for me now is: do I want to go back? Do I really want to reenter that environment that treats people like glorified computers, and despite all assurances to the contrary, consistently treats women worse then men? Is this the legacy I want to pass on to my daughter, that Mama and so many others like her subject their personal lives, biological clocks, medical needs, and emotional health to a system that is unjust at best? Yet it is the very fact of this injustice that pulls me back so strongly. I want to go back, finish my PhD, find a university job, get tenure, and hang a huge sign on my door that says "Nursing Mothers Welcome Here." I want the entire faculty, staff, and student body to know that my office is stocked with everything from snacks to diapers, and that those who need them can help themselves. I want to cordon off a section of my office and supply it with a professional-grade breast pump, a CD player, and some really comfy chairs, so the women who need a place to pump their milk (because, despite the academy's refusal to see us, we *do* exist) have a place to go that's slightly more welcoming than the bathroom. I want to decorate my office with pictures of my family, Bible verses, and anything else I can think of that will annoy those who will have power over me. I want to be a thorn in the academy's flesh. Perhaps what I really want is to get fired.

As my daughter climbs up on the couch beside me with one of her two worn-out copies of *Pat the Bunny*, I know that I have already passed on the best of what the academy gave me. She adores books, so much so that many of hers bear the tell-tale signs of toddler love and the resulting Scotch tape. She will "read" to herself for amazing lengths of time, occasionally exchanging books with me, dragging off one of my old dug-out nerdy books and leaving me to play peek-a-boo with Paul and feel Daddy's scratchy face. She glances up from what she is "reading," making serious comments in a language that is half mine and half still her very own. She has grasped this much: we love books. We read them, we discuss them, we love them.

But that is not the only legacy I wish to pass on to her. In church, when her round eyes follow the procession of the cross and her chubby hands flip open the Book of Common Prayer, I feel a longing to bequeath to her all the parts of myself that the academy couldn't hold, all of the parts that didn't fit. *Men-men!* she calls out at the end of the prayers, and then throws her small arms around my neck to pass me the Peace of the Lord. She raises her voice and her hands to sing the Doxology, and when her song of praise vies with the soloist at Communion, I slip from my pew and take her out to the Narthex. I hold her close to my chest and whisper in her soft pink ear, not *be quiet*, but *sing, little one, sing*.

Last week my not-quite-walking daughter choreographed her first dance. Holding on to the ottoman for support, she listened intently to the music I was playing and then slowly, deliberately, began to dance. She lifted one arm purposefully over her head, then paused for a moment, thinking. She then dropped almost to the ground in a series of *grands pliés*, augmented by more arm waving. A frenetic stamping of the feet followed, and then a tentative, but proud, lifting of both arms above her head. She finished her choreography with a wild and wonderful shaking of her little backside (she definitely didn't get that bit from watching me) and then looked to me, expectantly. She probably wondered why I was crying. Something about her was so innocent, so whole. She can have her books, her faith, her dance. She doesn't need to choose between them in the world she inhabits. She is a whole person, a whole woman, and she fits in to herself just fine. Watching her I realized that, regardless of where I eventually end up with relation to the academy, that is what I want to do: I want to fit in to myself. Nothing more, and nothing less.

Motherhood after Tenure

Confessions of a Late Bloomer

AERON HAYNIE

She had been forced into prudence in her youth, she learned romance as she grew older—the natural sequel of an unnatural beginning.

—JANE AUSTEN, *Persuasion* (1818)

Like Jane Austen's *Persuasion,* my story is about waiting—and the disorienting blessing of getting what I most desire when I'd given up all hope. After years of dutiful attention to my career, at thirty-five I found myself alone in a new city, single and childless. Like Austen's novels, my own story ends happily: by forty I was tenured, married, and had a beautiful baby girl. My students read *Persuasion* as a comedy, confident that Anne Elliot, the plain and long-suffering heroine, will end up happily wed to the dashing Captain Wentworth. They skip over the waiting, forgetting that most of the novel describes the dismal plight of a single woman in the late eighteenth century. Anne Elliot seems weak to them, too easily persuaded to give up her youthful suitor for pragmatic reasons. My students believe themselves more autonomous, and a good part of this freedom is the promise of having their own careers. I forgive my students their naiveté because I've only recently begun to question my own story.

My choice to delay motherhood was based on a myriad of personal reasons; perhaps predominantly, growing up with divorced parents who had little money taught me to hedge my bets. Yet when I read recent studies that show that women are less likely to get tenure-track jobs or earn tenure if they have children,[1] I realize that decisions like mine, to delay motherhood, are part of a larger phenomenon. Academic women are often forced to choose between becoming mothers and negotiating a very rigid tenure

1. Mary Ann Mason and Marc Goulden. "Do Babies Matter? The Effect of Family Formation on the Lifelong Careers of Academic Men and Women," *Academe* 88, no. 6 (2002): 21–27.

timeline. The fact that my story ends happily should not obscure the larger picture, or the dangers of asking women to wait until they are forty to start families. Of course, not every woman wants a child; however, my experience speaks of a larger issue that goes beyond motherhood: if academia encourages women to delay having children (almost past the point of biological possibility), it discourages us all, parents and nonparents alike, from integrating our personal and professional lives.

When undergraduate women ask me for advice about graduate school, I never discuss my personal life. Perhaps that is because telling one's job story is like telling one's birth story: the details are so compelling that you feel the Ancient Mariner's compulsion to tell them over and over again. Then you realize that few people want to hear about the bucket of blood between the doctor's knees, or see the tattered manila folder that lists every job for which you applied. Instead, I explain the details of the application process, and tell them the job market is competitive so they must be willing to relocate anywhere when (and if) they are lucky enough to get jobs. Most of my first-generation college students do not apply to programs far from their homes, and many women choose graduate schools based on the career decisions of their boyfriends. If I gently suggest that graduate school and an academic life is a commitment that might preclude staying close to family and friends, these students regard me with skepticism. Perhaps they assume some failure on my part forced me to make these choices. Sometimes I wonder if they are right, if the compromises I've made are just a result of my own personal failings: if I had been smarter, things would have gone better for me. Isn't that what we all believe?

When I got pregnant during the final year of my PhD program in the midst of an intoxicating new romance, I had no health insurance and half of my dissertation still to write. Having a baby seemed as dangerous to me as marrying young Wentworth was to Austen's Anne Elliot. Perhaps this was because graduate school seemed permeated by an anxiety that went beyond the stress of writing a dissertation, grading stacks of papers, and living in poverty. Getting a PhD in English meant that very few of us graduates would land jobs at research universities, thus becoming failures in the eyes of the academic culture. It was my impression that no matter what our individual strengths, everyone felt a sense of unease. Those with teaching awards worried about publishing enough; those already published worried about proving their commitment to teaching; those who had neither felt miserable, I'm sure; and those star scholars who were also outstanding teachers worried that the fluky job market might not reward them after all. And many times it did not.

When I was in graduate school, little separation existed between school and personal life. The graduate students socialized almost exclusively with each other and dated each other (or faculty), and there was rarely a time when one felt "off the clock." Most of us arrived without families or spouses, and in retrospect I see that we tended to marginalize older students and those who had families. At the time, it seemed smarter to remain unencumbered. After all, with so few jobs, anything that claimed energy and focus made you less competitive. Being pregnant felt like punishment for allowing myself to become distracted, a consequence that I alone had to bear. Although my lover urged me to have the baby and even mentioned marriage, he was unstable; I knew that, ultimately, the baby would be my responsibility. And so I made the rational choice, one applauded by my family. I don't regret my decision, but ending a pregnancy by a man with whom you've just fallen in love is a kick in the gut.

Shortly after this, my relationship unraveling, I accepted a job at a four-year college in a small town in Montana. While many would relish the unspoiled beauty of the Rocky Mountains, I would have been happier moving to Detroit, or Cleveland, or somewhere similarly "real" to a native of Buffalo, New York. At the very least, I wanted a decent-sized city where I could have a life separate from my job, and where I could, I hoped, find another partner and begin my family. My professors counseled me to accept the job, and although they were wise in many respects, it never occurred to me to tell them that I was terrified to walk this gangplank of spinsterhood. Despite discussions of "desire" as theoretical construct, my own emotional/bodily desires were never voiced. My pregnancy hadn't seemed very intellectual, competitive, or focused. I didn't have the baby and I accepted a job I didn't want. It never occurred to me to connect these two decisions.

For the next five years I worked hard to "write myself out" of Montana: coediting a book, publishing articles out of dissertation chapters, sending out roughly one job application every day, and becoming an untenured chair of my department, all while teaching four courses a semester. As a single, childless woman living alone in a small cottage facing the mountains, I had the time to do this. The town provided little distractions: there was one movie theater, no shopping malls, and the coffee shop closed on weekends. Chastely refusing dates with students, I spent many weekends watching the snow fall in deep drifts outside my cabin.

Despite time's slow march, I was burdened with the sense that it was running out on dual fronts: I had a limited amount of time to find a second position before I went up for promotion (and hence became ineligible for most entry-level jobs) and an equally winnowing window of probable fertility. Perhaps this sounds melodramatic; after all, I was gainfully employed in Montana and I could have settled there, received tenure, and started a family. I did date a few men, including a high school English teacher who drove two hours across the Continental Divide to meet me for coffee. But despite several adventures with cowboys, I was living with one foot out the door because this place would never be my home. My parents urged me to quit my job and move to a city, someplace with a more vibrant culture and progressive politics where I could find a suitable husband and start a family. But just as accepting tenure can be a life sentence to a job and location you find intolerable, those who leave academia find it difficult to return. And in certain ways my isolation was liberating. Cut off from family, far from any urban center, and psychologically removed from the concerns of rarified Modern Language Association panels, I realized there was no one to please but myself. Unlike in a nineteenth-century novel, my patience and suffering—rejecting a compelling but unstable suitor, taking a job I didn't want, spending long hours grading, and agreeing to chair my department— would not be rewarded.

So I was thrilled when I landed another tenure-track job in a small city in the Midwest. Everything about my new position was, if not ideal, palpably better: in addition to being in a city of 150,000, the teaching load was lighter and included more upper-level courses in my research area. However, with a shortened tenure clock (I brought two years with me from my previous position), and a diminishing biological clock, I felt pressured to hit the ground running. Colleagues who had children remarked that I was lucky to have "so much time" to work, but I have never felt time's pressure so intensely. Between grading papers and starting a new book, I went on numerous blind dates, worked out regularly, and tried to maintain the upbeat personality that books like *If I'm So Wonderful, Why Am I Still Single?* suggest is vital to attracting a mate. Although I was now in a city roughly thirty times larger than where I had lived in Montana, the odds were still not great. People marry young in the Midwest, and bachelors are few. Like a Jane Austen heroine, I was marriage-and-baby minded, but trying to maintain my dignity with the fact of my singleness a glaring mark upon me. While Eliza Bennett had a meddlesome mother and the imperious

Lady Catherine to deal with, I faced endless reports about infertility in women over thirty-five and dour predictions of professional women finding mates. One local woman warned me, "There are five women to every man here!" Little did she know, 5 to 1 odds sound very good to an academic used to the 300 to 1 odds of finding a tenure-track job! Perhaps because I had read so many Jane Austen novels, I assumed that my own story would end happily, and, happily, it did.

In the end, it wasn't an old love, but a new and unexpected suitor—divorced, nonacademic, and refreshingly unneurotic—whom I married. I certainly felt like a heroine in a novel as our courtship effortlessly turned into marriage and nine months later we had a bouncing baby girl. In many ways, being tenured is an ideal time to be a new mother. No longer under such intense pressure to prove myself, I have an enviable level of job security, decent benefits, and a flexible schedule. I have less time to work, but I find that my work is better. And while I am shocked at the ways that my university does not accommodate mothers—our university has no maternity leave, no on-site day care, and no plan to extend the tenure clock for parents—I had accumulated enough sick time to spend five months at home with my baby. Compared to other professional, untenured, or working-class mothers, I know that I am fortunate. Since I was already established in my career before I married and became a mom, I was able to negotiate a more equitable parenting arrangement with my husband. However, because my academic schedule is more flexible than my husband's work schedule, I take on more child-care responsibilities.

Even with the confidence of a tenured chair, I feel anxious about the work that isn't getting done, just as I feel guilty about the hours I spend away from my daughter. In truth, I feel guiltier about my work, perhaps because I've been in academia longer than I've been a mom, and it still feels like cheating to prioritize my personal life. I think back to a similar conflict I felt when I took time off to care for my dying father, and I couldn't shake the nagging feeling that I was getting behind in my research. I knew this was irrational, but when I mentioned this anxiety to a family friend—a professor—he responded, "Can't you read articles while you sit in the hospital?" Years later, I relish the memory of the hours I spent next to my father's hospital bed, the hours I did nothing but watch him breathe. And I know that I will not begrudge the afternoons walking behind my daughter as she pumps her bike around the block, or the hours spent rolling with her down the sloping grass of our neighborhood park.

It's because of that pernicious question my family friend asked that I would not rejoice if my daughter decides to get a PhD. Unlike Lady Russell, who counsels Austen's heroine to marry safely, I will counsel my own daughter to become encumbered sooner—with failures, with a sense of herself beyond a narrowly measured standard of accomplishments, with her heart's desire.

PART TWO

That Mommy Thing

First Day of School

AMY HUDOCK

I walked down brick pathways to teach my first university class in over two years. I kept my eyes down, looking at each brick as I passed over it, trying to keep from crying. Their deep earth color reminded me of the blood that came with my daughter's birth, and it honored a new separation: returning to an academic career after being with my daughter full time since her birth. I bled fresh tears, my face frozen with the effort to stop.

I stood outside the classroom, the sun not yet fully up, and breathed the already hot and humid air. Putting my game face on. Teaching is, ultimately, a performance, and through the years, I have learned to mask my personal emotions to allow the play to start, the game to begin. But this was something different, something harder, deeper. I closed my eyes to focus on that quiet place within, finding the meditative peace I discovered while sitting for long hours nursing my daughter, Sarah. I feared the expectations.

Ask any school child to draw a professor, and you get a bearded, gray-haired, tweed-wearing, pipe-smoking gentleman. You don't get a youngish woman with a child on her hip. Rather, most people expect those who live the life of the mind to only live that life. Someone else takes care of the day-to-day activities of cooking, cleaning, shopping, and rearing children: wives. The ivory tower seems to have no room for children or grocery shopping or laundry. I remember the feeling of being caught by students in the act of grocery shopping, and they were always surprised that I eat. Imagine if they saw me breastfeeding.

That first day, my breasts were full with milk that my daughter would not drink until later. A brazen hussy of a public breastfeeder while I lived in the San Francisco Bay Area, here in South Carolina I keep my breasts covered. Many mothers here with children my daughter's age weaned long ago, though I have found a few holdouts like myself. I plan to keep on.

Experts encourage it, and most mothers I knew in the Bay Area planned to let their children wean on their own schedules.

Sarah is an enthusiastic breastfeeder. Her calls of "nursies . . . nursies . . . nursies" lure me away from grading papers, checking my e-mail, reading the literature I plan to teach the next day. And she doesn't care where she asks for "nursies." When she was a bit sick one day and particularly needing me, I brought her to class with me rather than taking her to pre-school, praying the breastfeeding issue wouldn't become important. It did. After spending most of the class drawing on the lower half of the black-board while I wrote on the top half and lectured, she started her chant. "Nursies . . . nursies . . ." I called class five minutes early and sprinted with my toddler over my shoulder to the ladies' room.

However difficult it may be, I won't give breastfeeding up until she is ready. My daughter has lost everything she knows: her home by the bay, her former family structure, a sister, a father, a full-time mother. Her father and I are getting a divorce, and this is what divorce does. She will not have to give up her favorite comfort, too; she has enough of the new. But she will need to learn to wait until just before going to bed. I know my audience.

I am a Southern girl, despite all my efforts not to be. Like many other Southern intellectuals, I both love and hate the bricks and the live oak trees and the ubiquitous columns and all the social expectations. Some women I grew up with wouldn't leave a burning house without lipstick. Because my parents were transplanted Catholic Yankees, I never felt like I fit in. My years in a northern town and my liberal politics have combined to keep me outside even while, like now, I live inside. Regardless, I know what is expected of me as a white Southern woman. And public breastfeeding isn't it. Come to think of it, neither is being a professor.

To enter the university classroom, I know I must perform childlessness, like I perform the characteristics of my gender, my ethnicity, my class, my education. Up until now, being a mother has meant actually being with my child and doing the raising myself rather than delegating her to some-one else. If I worked on a farm, my child would be strapped to my back or playing close by in the tall weeds. Or if I ran a family business, she would be playing with the money in the cash register and greeting customers with the small waves she reserves for new people. But because I teach other people's nearly grown children, I must leave my own behind. In the academy, the professional and the personal remain largely separate. While I can occasionally bring my daughter into this world, she doesn't really belong here. I feel the falseness of her absence.

Because I know it can be different. When I was out of academia, I taught freelance writing classes to mothers where we could all bring our children. A child-care provider entertained the children while we sat in a circle and did what all classes do. What was so different was that children moved into our circle and out of it without hindrance. A mother would respond to a need, then turn back to the group. I breastfed while lecturing. We were a model of how the private and the public, the personal and the professional, the family and the classroom, the emotional and the intellectual could all exist together. Despite how wonderful this was, I know university culture will not allow me to breastfeed while in front of a class. My student evaluations (written by largely childless seventeen-to-twenty-one-year-olds) would reflect a sense of me as not a professional and my peer evaluators might pretend not to see the child and the breast, but they would see them.

So, how do I live as a professor, a single mother, a liberal, and a woman in the South? Can I be both a mother all day long, and a professor all day long? Is there a place for me in the ivory tower?

For now, I stick to what I decided that first day, standing outside the columned brick portico, looking in as the students gathered: at the university I will put on my game face and perform childlessness as best I can, and at home, I will be a mother.

Two Boards and a Passion

On Theater, Academia, and the Art of Failure

ANJALEE DESHPANDE NADKARNI

I had gone to the annual conference of the Association for Theatre in Higher Education to present a paper entitled "The Maternal vs. the Paternal: Navigating the Divide in Rehearsal and in the Classroom." The paper, which explored differences between male and female directorial styles, was a bit controversial, and my department was not altogether happy. The presentation went well, but I was still on edge: somewhat preoccupied by how people would react to what they might view as sensitive subject matter, but mainly preoccupied by being away from my baby. My time at that conference was the longest I had ever been away from my son, then fifteen months old. On the last day of the conference, day ten away from the baby, I felt like I had abandoned him. I was a complete wreck.

Trying hard to maintain my professional appearance, I decided to attend a panel on motherhood, theater, and academia. As I wandered the busy halls looking for the right room, I kept thinking about meeting other theater moms. I especially hoped to meet some older moms with advice to offer, some holy-grail secret that I was desperate to hear. Just one little nugget that would make motherhood and academia symbiotic would suffice. When I finally got to the panel I was both excited and anxious.

The small conference room was filled with women ranging from their mid-twenties to mid-sixties, with just a few men sprinkled in. All the women were smiling and chatting energetically with each other, or reading a book or some literature from the conference. They all looked so confident, so together. For a moment I wondered if I was at the right panel. These women couldn't be mothers. They seemed too—happy?

A woman struggled into the back of the room with a stroller and I felt a pang of guilt: I should have been with my baby. I imagined my parents at home, nervous with my small son, and awkward at sharing responsibility with my very-soon-to-be-ex husband. The woman with the stroller lifted out a fussing infant, and for a moment I wondered how she would manage to both be a part of the discussion and watch her baby—could she really do either activity justice? The next moment a man I assumed was her husband came in, and apologetically took the stroller and the baby. He strolled out, and soon we could hear the baby cooing from the hallway. I settled in and waited for the panel to begin. Still uneasy, I smiled at these women, thinking that perhaps I wasn't the only one missing her child.

The five women on the panel began telling their stories. They all looked confident and secure—they seemed to have things figured out. And as each one began to recite her tales, I began to feel overwhelmed; the distance between myself and these wonder women, these confident, beautiful, secure-looking women, felt gigantic.

At first, the women told sweet stories of raising kids in rehearsals, making toys out of props and cribs out of set pieces. They talked about what an amazing opportunity it is to raise children in such an open and exciting atmosphere of art and higher learning. One of the attendees introduced her daughter, who claimed she had been raised running around backstage at her mother's theater department and once fell asleep in a fake pillar during a production of *Antigone*. The girl looked perfectly normal—good, even!

But soon the conversation took a turn. Women told stories of being "mommy tracked," being told they had made "career decisions" when they had kids. Some talked about giving up academia and others about knowing women who decided not to have kids so that they could make tenure. Although it was somewhat reassuring to hear these stories and know I wasn't alone, I began to wonder: Was it even possible to do this? Was it possible to raise a little person with love and grace, teach students exceptionally, direct innovative productions, and find opportunities for scholarship and service? The thought of juggling potty training and night rehearsals and daytime classes and office hours and faculty senate meetings and departmental trips and then trying to find day care for my son in a new city when offered the chance to direct there—a chance I'd have to take to meet the requirements for scholarship—provoked a small panic attack.

All the seemingly impossible requirements for being a good mother and being a success in my chosen career seemed at odds. Sitting there in the front row at the presentation, I thought about what I tell my overly ambitious students when they take on too many extracurricular activities and let their grades falter: "You can achieve anything, but not everything. If you try to do everything there is no doubt you will do everything badly. But if you choose, then you will succeed in whatever you do." Yet at that moment, I couldn't stop the voice that kept screaming in my head: I cannot choose! I cannot choose! I must do both and I must succeed!

And then I began sobbing. Quietly at first, and then with full conviction. I really couldn't stop. People tried to ignore me at first (perhaps they were embarrassed for me) but soon it was painfully obvious that I was having a very unprofessional breakdown in the middle of this academic panel. Finally I ran out of the room, found a bathroom, and cried in a stall.

Once the worst of my breakdown had subsided, I pulled out a whole bunch of toilet paper, steeled myself with a firm look in the mirror, and walked back into the panel room expecting them all to think I was completely insane. But as I sat down, one of the panelists asked me if I was okay, and what she could do. I said, "I'm sorry—it's just so hard. I mean, when do you stop feeling like a failure at everything?"

The woman leading the panel smiled and said, "I'll let you know."

Everyone laughed knowingly. The woman then went on to talk about how when she was at work she felt like she was letting her family down, and when she was home she felt as if her work was suffering for her being home. She talked about always feeling the pull, no matter where you are. Then she said, "But it gets easier. You get better at it. You find ways to laugh at it. Ways to accept it."

She asked me for my story and I told everyone about having a baby and separating from my husband in the span of fifteen months. I told them about my struggles with academia, that I was the first junior professor in my department as well as the first female in a full-time teaching position, so when I got pregnant no one knew to tell the dean, so no one advised me to stop the tenure clock. I told them about directing two shows and teaching my regular load of classes while I was pregnant, attending graduation activities and starting labor, prematurely, the next day. I told them about my baby being delivered in the spring, and spending time in the neonatal intensive care unit, and having to devote an entire summer to making sure the baby was healthy, and that summer following me, academically, for the next five years. Once I realized I'd lost a summer, I asked my department and my dean if I could stop the clock and was told that it was too late—and that if I pushed it, the tenure committee might think I was expecting special privileges for being a mother.

As I told my story, one of the conference attendees, a pregnant doctoral candidate, actually gasped. For some reason that struck me as funny. We have a saying in theater, "two boards and a passion," which is supposed to mean that all you need to create good theater is two planks of wood for a stage and a passion for acting. I think all of us disillusioned mothers in there had once thought that all we needed to live this life successfully was the baby carriage, the grade book, and the best of intentions. I looked at that grad student and smiled. Poor thing, I thought, we've just told her that the fairy tale isn't real.

I continued to share my stories, like the one about having to pump milk in a maintenance closet, and how mortified I was once when the chair of my department walked in on me. Many of the other women shared stories of similar mortification when it came to breastfeeding and talked about how most academic theater settings did not factor female faculty into the equation when designing performance centers. Brilliant, million-dollar-plus theaters, but no day-care facilities on campus. Exquisite dance studios and expensive sound equipment, but no changing tables in the bathrooms.

"But," laughed one of the panelists, "we theater folks are ingenious. We adapt." I laughed with her. It was true. My technical director was kind enough to add an armchair, a rug, and a little antique table (all props saved from past shows) to my modest maintenance/pumping closet. It was almost a homey way to pump.

We talked for another hour, and with each story told, with each fear expressed, with each knowing laugh, I felt better. Somehow this group of women seemed to express such sincere understanding that I finally felt relief. Relief in being able to share my story. Relief in knowing that I was not alone.

Looking back, the most practical pieces of advice I got out of the panel were to seek unexpected avenues for scholarship, to find mentors, and to find community. My progress so far has been slow. I hope to be more pro-active in finding an outside mentor this summer, preferably a woman, and preferably a mom. I have made attempts to find community, although it is tricky. Academics without children want to do things I generally cannot do with my child, like happy hour, or dinner parties at lovely un-baby-proofed homes. On the other hand, I don't fit in with moms outside academia. Last spring I tried to join a baby gymnastics class with my almost-two-year-old son to meet some other moms and kids; it didn't work out. During the "moms sit this one out" portion of the class, all the kids played together, and all the moms began a conversation about how one of them had to leave her two-year-old with a sitter for two hours twice a week. "Wow!" they all chimed in. "But so long! God, how can you stand it? He's sooooo little." I winced, thinking about the thirty-plus hours my baby spends in child care weekly. The next week I switched to a later class in hopes of meeting a working woman friend, and I did, but then she said, of the two-year-old swimming in the ball tub with my son, "Oh, she's not my daughter—I'm her nanny. Most of us here are nannies." Not quite what I was looking for either.

Seeking alternate avenues for scholarship has been my main focus since the conference. For a directing professor, the main forms of acceptable scholarship include directing or acting in a professionally produced play. Professional theaters are scattered across the country, and getting acquainted with a company, let alone getting booked for a show, requires a lot of travel during rehearsal and performance. This was, and is, my main anxiety about fulfilling my scholarship requirements. Courting a theater and booking a gig means considering how to care for the baby in another city—finding both day and night care, and then taking into consideration how he would adjust to unfamiliar surroundings, new bedtime routines, new caregivers, and how his eating habits (it's always a trick getting my sensitive "fourth percentile for weight category" child to eat) and upcoming potty training might be affected. Yet out-of-town productions are the primary way of achieving scholarship requirements in my discipline.

When I seek help or advice from my senior faculty members, they are at a loss. The department is not set up to support women with families. So my alternatives include options such as writing a one-woman show and courting a theater to produce it locally, writing a textbook on collaboration and finding a publisher to publish it, writing a play and finding a venue that might produce it, or, if I'm really lucky, finding a local summer stock theater that might only need me for three weeks or so as a director.

Next week I am going to an audition in another city. If I get in to the play, then I will have to take my baby to an unfamiliar place for three months in the fall, find a way to take care of him during day rehearsals and night performances, manage rent in both cities, and find other faculty willing both to take my classes and to direct the production I was slotted to direct pro bono. Yes. Well, I am hopeful. Terrified, but hopeful.

If only my department had some senior faculty members who were female, and mothers, like those wonderful panel members. The advice they had to give was invaluable. Yet the main thing that I took away from the panel that day wasn't actually the career advice. It was the moment I wept and asked the women about failure. Because they didn't speak about life becoming a success, but about letting go of the notion that success is singularly obtainable. Deciding to do this job and be a mother requires becoming not only familiar with failure, but comfortable with it. Comfortable enough to say that today, I didn't get to grade every paper, but I did get my son to poop in the potty instead of in the tub. Or that today, I didn't get him to eat anything healthy, but in rehearsal I did get a chance to work more deeply, and now the scene between Konstantine and his mother, Irina, feels much stronger and more honest. At the end of the day I realize that my experience with my son has helped me to better understand the play I am directing, and that somehow all this is interconnected in a very tangible and positive way.

I am learning to become more comfortable with both failure and success. Being comfortable with failure is knowing that the only successes that count are precarious and temporary. It is accepting that every seeming failure is the foundation for growth, and it pays to laugh at it. The papers will get graded, and my son will eat the broccoli when he is hungry. Every rehearsal I bring him to will shape him into the amazing person he will one day be. He will grow up with stories and actors, among an eclectic community of artists. Every time I take him to a faculty senate meeting or a national conference, he will understand on some level that his mother worked hard to be able to take pride in her accomplishments. Every time I carry him into class under my arm or set him up with crayons in the back of the room, he will see me with my students and watch me both teach and learn. There is no better way of sharing with my child the blessings and importance of life than by making him a part of my life. Not the perfect life, perhaps, where every day is a singular success. But my life, the one that I love, where every day is a risk and a possibility.

Living (!) A Life I Never Planned

ROSEMARIE EMANUELE

I awoke the first day of classes at my first academic job and realized that I didn't know where I was. It took me a moment to get my bearings and call my parents, several states away, who told me that I was in Cleveland. Oh, yah. I forgot for a second. Silly mistake.

But not just a mistake. As I learned in the next few days, my life was in danger from a large brain tumor. Everything else, including my life plan of teaching, marrying, having a family, and my research, had to wait. I spent the first semester of my job in a hospital. I realized throughout the trauma that I was very privileged to find myself with health insurance and access to an excellent hospital just at the point when the tumor that had been with me for many years became too large for my brain to handle. I returned to teach the next semester with a unique hairstyle and a purse loaded with the medicine I took to keep me alive and healthy enough to function day to day. Of course, I wasn't healthy—I was rather sick. I remember standing at the bottom of a flight of stairs, looking up, and not knowing how I was going to get to the top. Things did not look good, but I plodded on, hoping that this was not the end of my life, and that if I was to live, it was not the end of my academic career or my dreams for a family.

I could not look at my life as a whole, but only at the challenges that I needed to survive each day. Often the biggest challenge was focusing while taking medicine that made me very tired, and doing so while teaching classes that sometimes met both early in the morning and in the evening of the same day. I found myself taking more breaks; I was often exhausted. It felt like when I'd taken too much Sudafed back in the days before the nondrowsy formula was invented. I recall leaving work one evening after a long day of teaching and not remembering where I had parked my car; I had to call campus security to help me find it. I enjoyed my students, but didn't know what they thought of me with only half a head of hair. I do know that they sometimes played tricks on me, as when they insisted, "Don't you remember, you moved our test to next week?"

Each new day was a gift, and I greeted every Monday with a "Wow, I get to live another week!" Soon the weeks turned into months and then years, and I began to emerge from the nightmare. I was still single, but I bought my first home, experiencing a great thrill in signing a thirty-year mortgage. Would I live long enough to pay it off? I didn't know, but it sounded optimistic to make such a commitment. I knew that I would never again bemoan having another birthday.

As I started to recover, I began to talk to my colleagues about how they managed to have families and careers at the same time. What I heard was not encouraging. One woman compared her experience of having a child during her tenure-track years to my recent ordeal with a brain tumor. "In terms of their effect on one's tenure process," she said, "I think they are pretty much equal." One man told me that he felt we should not have maternity leave at all, since the men and women of his generation had made a lot of sacrifices to get where they were, so why shouldn't we? The official maternity leave was actually disability leave, which worked well if a pregnancy was extremely well timed (a child born in January, for example, would give one leave for the spring semester plus a summer to follow) but did not necessarily give any benefits to those adopting children. I did not know whether my future would include adoption, but I realized that my path to motherhood would be extra challenging.

I spent most of my tenure-track years in a fog from antiseizure medicine, and it became clear that, despite a handful of publications, I was not going to get tenure at the school that then employed me. Although I was not very successful at publishing in refereed journals, I was successful at the only thing that has mattered in the end: I met my wonderful husband when he came by to sell me textbooks one semester. We married while I was a junior faculty member, and he immediately enrolled in law school.

I stayed at that first job as long as I could. I knew that finding another academic job in Ohio would be a challenge, but I was determined to remain a college professor. One day, I found an advertisement in the local newspaper for Ursuline College, a small Catholic college near our home. Ursuline College is Ohio's last women's college, and they were looking for a mathematics professor. My PhD is in economics, but I had to take a great deal of math to get the degree, and I had been teaching business statistics for several years. I also saw that Ursuline would be a more family-friendly place to work, as it was certainly not a publish-or-perish college but one in which teaching was valued very highly. Run by and for women, it would be, I felt, an ideal place to work while raising a family. I decided to do the unthinkable and apply for a position outside of my field, ignoring warnings from fellow economists to "get back into an economics department as soon as possible." And so, while still very much an economist, I soon became the new chair of the mathematics department at Ursuline College.

My husband and I had been married about seven years when it became apparent that we were not going to have children the traditional way. We began to look into adopting a child. Conventional wisdom has it that domestic adoption is impossible, and that one must therefore travel across the globe to adopt a child. The truth is, however, that domestic adoption is very possible, but not for the faint of heart. The search for a somewhat open adoption led us to put together a book about ourselves and have it copied and bound to show to potential birth parents. I remember waiting at the printer as it was being copied and thinking, "This is not what they told me in the seventh grade about where babies come from."

Our search for our daughter included several adoptions that fell through at the last minute, one after we helped to name the baby, and many disappointments as we were scrutinized by teenage birth parents asking us questions like "What outdoor sports do you play?" Throughout the process, I recorded our experiences in a long letter to "our dearest child," describing the process, with all its twists and turns, as it unfolded. I plan to give her a copy some day, so she will know how much we wanted to find her and become her "forever family."

Our daughter eventually found us after about two years and many heartbreaks. I spent the first few weeks off campus as I got used to having a baby in our house, but while I was away, the campus was abuzz with excitement for me and my new little family. My colleagues covered my office door in pink paper, and my students brought me a congratulations balloon and baby books. I knew I was really a mom the day I caught myself slowly rocking back and forth (as I had done all day with my new baby) as I lectured about hypothesis testing in front of one of my classes.

Ursuline College had the same inadequate maternity leave policy as my previous employer, but this did not deter my husband and me from adopting our daughter. Once she was miraculously home, I decided to find a way to give myself time with her. The result was a rather unusual approach that was surprisingly well received and which has subsequently been used by other faculty members.

I chose not to take advantage of the Family and Medical Leave Act, which would have required that I write checks to the college to cover my health insurance. Instead, I made a proposal based on a clause I found in Ursuline's faculty handbook that allows up to five weeks of "paid personal leave." I noted that it was useless for a faculty member to take five weeks off, since semesters are fifteen weeks long and can't be interrupted. But five weeks is about one-sixth of the number of weeks we are expected to teach each year, so I asked the college to give me a course reduction of one-sixth of my normal load. I also moved one of my classes to the summer and another to an evening time slot, and was therefore able to stay home with my daughter during the days for the fall semester after we brought her home. This worked out well, and in the spring my husband and I found a wonderful day-care center that allowed us to enroll her part time. I continue to schedule my classes and day care to complement each other, leaving some time for my daughter and me to spend together, while continuing my academic duties as a full-time faculty member. I am conscious, as I enjoy time with my daughter, that I almost did not live to see these days.

Since my husband and I adopted our daughter, several of my colleagues at Ursuline have had children, and the issue of maternity leave has surfaced again. I have found myself sharing my story and offering advice as they negotiate the task of joining their lives as academics and as parents. In the long run, I hope to use my own experience and perhaps even my training as a labor economist to craft a workable parental leave that will be acceptable to the college and future parents.

While still not a majority on campus, quite a few faculty members at Ursuline now are parents of young children. One of the nice things about working with so many parents is that we often share parenting advice with each other. We coo over pictures of each other's children and quickly offer to hold the little ones when they come to visit. My colleagues introduced me to consignment shops, and when it was time to expand my daughter's diet, one mom suggested fruit cups while another told me about macaroni and cheese. And when the terrible twos (actually threes, but they don't tell you that) hit with a vengeance, more experienced moms were ready to top any story that made me think my child was a behavioral outlier. Since some of the students at Ursuline are parents, I found myself becoming *their* student as they taught me about raising young children. Indeed, I relied on my colleagues and my students even more than the tried-and-true parenting books during those first few years. Dr. Spock could have learned a few things from my companions.

A few years ago, I was approached at a conference by a faculty member from a nearby state college. He noted that his school would be hiring the following year, and suggested I apply for the position. Memories of the person I once thought I would become came flooding back; I thought of having the research career I had dreamed of before I grew ill, and was curious about what it would be like to teach at a more "prestigious" (according to whom? No one asked my students!) university. But I soon recalled the publish–or-perish pressure, and it only took a second for me to respond, "No, right now my family is my first priority." And for that, I am in the best place possible.

Coming to Terms at Full Term

NATALIE KERTES WEAVER

On my way back to my office the other day, I ran into a colleague accompanied by her son, a handsome, six-foot-tall high school senior. She smiled at me and said, "Mine was the size of yours just a blink ago." "A blink?" I inquired. "One blink," she nodded. I grinned in return, but the encounter left me unsettled. I wonder how I will feel a blink from now, when I am driving my boy, now seventeen months old, to his own college visits in preparation for his exodus into adulthood. Will I regret the choice I made to work when he was young? Will I be jealous of the time he spent with others while I was writing or grading or lecturing? Will he understand my reasons? Will I? These are the questions I battle nearly every day, as I remind my husband that he and the baby are my life, and ask him to please take extra care in the car. These are the questions I write about in the journal I keep for my son alongside the record of his first steps, words, and other milestones. These are the questions I struggle with at 4:00 A.M., when I wake from sleep, restless with thoughts of my own human frailty and mortality.

I question, moreover, whether I really have a choice to work or not work. I know that our family would struggle on my husband's income alone, that we need my job for health insurance, and that my work provides the possibility of a savings account. On a deeper level, I wonder whether I would work even if money were not an issue. My parents divorced when I was six and I watched my mom try to reenter the workforce with no college education and a ten-year gap in her employment history. Even as a child, I recognized that her work as a secretary was underpaid, overtaxing, and underappreciated by her employers. When she married my stepfather two years after her divorce, it must have seemed like a burden lifted. She did not know she was marrying an abuser, and in the final analysis, I think she stayed with him because she did not know how she would support my sister and me after another divorce. Her compromises and sacrifices left their marks. By the time I was ten, I believed with conviction that a woman needed her own money in order to secure her own safety and that of her children. I also knew that as an adult, I would commit myself to finding employment that engaged and rewarded me as a person. I would experience dignity in my work, while ensuring that neither I nor my children would ever be dependent upon anyone who intended us harm.

In the wake of my childhood, it is easy for me to attribute or even blame my work ethic on my experiences. Yet I would be untruthful if I did not admit that gainful employment is deeply satisfying as well as liberating. I have found not only salvation in books but also great joy. In college, I learned that my teachers were not just those in the classroom, but also St. Augustine, Plato, Immanuel Kant, Cicero, C. G. Jung, St. Paul, Ludwig Wittgenstein, and Jane Austen. In graduate school, I learned how to accept critical analysis of my ideas and writing, and I grew as a person as I learned how to see my work with increased objectivity. In completing my doctoral dissertation, I learned patience and perseverance, skills that will last me my lifetime. In interviewing for teaching positions, I learned how to have faith in myself. In teaching, I learned how important it is to have faith in others. In writing, I have learned, at long last, to listen to my voice. If I am honest with myself, I cannot but admit that I thrive on what I do. And, to the extent that I would be diminished as a person without my work, I suspect that I would be diminished as a mother apart from it as well.

I know my work has its costs. I am aware, even at an early stage in my life as Dr. Mommy, that my parenting is influenced by my schedule. I am further aware that there are effects of my choices that I cannot know until they are manifest—for good or for ill. I live with a divided heart because my life can only happen on the academic schedule. I actually checked final exam dates before I tried to conceive my son, timing his due date to coincide exactly with my last day of class. (He came one week early.) I know that I cannot manage another baby until I have completed the book for which I have contracted and submitted my tenure portfolio. I have planned my teaching and writing schedule for the next thirty-six months, so that if and when I do conceive again I will be able to stay home for a few months with my newborn.

I stumble to my computer to write after the baby falls asleep, even though I want sometimes quite badly to snuggle up next to him and to leave the professional part of my life aside for a while. Then I remember that I have deadlines to meet, papers to grade, lectures to prepare, and committee reports to write, so I get up and do it. Sometimes I find it exhilarating and sometimes it breaks my heart. Sometimes I think I have to work and sometimes I think I want to work. It is probably a little of both. I do know that I am a fortunate woman because most of what I have endeavored has worked out in my favor, and I am well supported in my vocation to teach and write. My husband is uniquely compassionate and giving. Our parents are alive and nearby. My baby is healthy. My colleagues are supportive, and the college is almost in my backyard.

To women like me who face the challenges of combining motherhood and professional life, I would like to say that I know the sensation of tension, as if you are riding on the crest of a wave that may not always support your weight. I encourage you to remember that we are not here by chance. We work with extreme dedication in order to balance academic and familial life. It is a delicate act, and one cannot do everything well all at the same time. We have to make choices, recognizing that there are costs and risks in what we do, what we postpone, and what we do not do. The key, I believe, is establishing the primacy of one's priorities, organizing life around what one cannot live without, and granting oneself the time to attend to life's goals accordingly. In the time that remains, do everything else you have to do or learn to let it go. Women often bristle at the double burden of work and family life; I bristle myself until I remember that I would not have traded breastfeeding my baby for any experience under the sun—but suckling an infant takes time. These are our choices, and they come complete with their own costs, as well as risks and rewards. Perhaps our children will celebrate us; perhaps they will feel neglected. Perhaps tenure will take longer; perhaps the child will come later. We cannot always see past the immediate value that our choices hold for us. Our only option is to pursue our choices with care and commitment. For our choices comprise our lives, and we must find the courage to meet our choices with compassion, vision, and perseverance. Blessed are we, truly blessed, who are free and able to choose to live so fully.

One *Mamá's* Dispensable Myths and Indispensable Machines

ANGELICA DURAN

Before graduate school, my favorite machine was the washing machine. My family's regular trips from California to the family ranch in Oaxaca, Mexico, no doubt helped me appreciate this common appliance, so generally (and sadly) underappreciated in the United States. The novelty of lugging laundry to the nearest (but by no means nearby) *rio* [river] to stone-wash clothes had usually worn off by the end of our long summer visits. Back home in the United States, I never complained when it was my turn to do laundry. The effort of walking down one flight of stairs to the apartment complex's laundry room and moving the clothes from hamper to washing machine to dryer then back to hamper seemed minimal in comparison.

This lovely appliance, however, lost its honored place in my heart when, as a single mother to preschooler Paul and elementary-schooler Jacqueline, I became a doctoral student in Stanford University's English Department. Then the computer became my favorite machine. I went to Stanford with two goals: be an extraordinary scholar, and be an equally extraordinary mother. I wanted to reject the myth that one goal would suffer for the sake of the other, and instead create my own story, one in which my goals were compatible and equally achievable. After all, had I heeded the prevailing story about high-risk U.S. citizens, I would never have arrived at Stanford in the first place, because I was a low-income, first-generation Chicana, raised by a single mother who had attained only a third-grade education.

Fortunately, the late 1990s were the time, Stanford the place, and the Internet-friendly computer the machine that enabled my quest. In the late 1990s, Stanford was one of the few universities in the United States with *Early English Books Online* (EEBO) and with free, in-room digital access in all its campus housing. EEBO is a fantastic, massive online archive, a digitized version of the *English Short-Title Catalog* and related microfiches. While the microfiches were great resources that provided access to rare texts, they were time intensive and difficult to view on the bulky, cantankerous viewing machines, which were usually housed in the library's dark basement. I am not overstating the case that I absolutely could not have reached my goals without EEBO. Like lab research in the sciences and on-site visits in engineering, archival research comprises the firm foundation of the high-level Renaissance literary studies that Stanford's English Department expected, much to its credit and to its students' exhaustion. EEBO's speed and its ability to display multiple books for comparison still awe me. For my dissertation, "Milton, Education, and the Scientific Revolution," I needed access to hundreds of seventeenth-century texts, by Milton, Isaac Newton, Robert Boyle, and other British writers who contributed to the founding of modern science and, by extension, modern educational institutions. My research involved finding and explaining the similarities and differences of content, and even book design, between original literary and scientific works. While I took great advantage of the stellar material archive collections at Stanford, the library's regular hours of Monday to Friday, 9:00 A.M. to 5:00 P.M., did not overlap well with my study time. A description of a typical day best demonstrates why:

- 6:30 8:00 A.M.: Drink coffee, make breakfast for the kids while they prepare their lunches, get everyone fed and dressed, and get kids to school and preschool
- 8:00 A.M.–noon: Attend or teach classes, exercise for 1 hour 3 days/week, volunteer at the preschool or in Jacqueline's classroom 1 hour/week, work part-time job 10 hours/week, research, and attempt to write a fabulous dissertation.
- Noon–3:00 P.M.: Pick up Paul from half-day preschool and enjoy time with him, often joined by my mother; run errands and do chores as "fun time."
- 3:00–8:00 P.M.: Drink coffee, pick up Jacqueline from school and enjoy time with her and Paul until kids' bedtime.
- 8:00 P.M.–1:00 A.M.: Drink coffee, research on line, and write.

You might think that my much-used coffeemaker vied for my affections with my beloved computer. Not really. I had managed to make it through the University of California, Berkeley, for my BA and MA while working twenty hours a week and even having some fun, all without coffee. But when I became a thirty-year-old single parent at the start of my second year of graduate school, coffee became my drug of choice to keep me alert and add two or three hours of wakefulness to my day.

My tight schedule demanded the rejection of another myth, that of writer's block. My working-class roots are evident in my response to colleagues' puzzled question, "How in the world do you get your work done *and* find time for your family?!" I'd answer, "A bus driver doesn't get 'driver's block,' a janitor doesn't get 'cleaner's block,' and I don't get 'writer's block.' When it's time for me to work, I work." A neat and unexpected result of getting rid of that unconstructive and all-too-pervasive myth was getting rid of my equally unconstructive personal myth of having a terrible memory. Before graduate school, I hadn't been good at remembering people's names or memorizing phone numbers. But that changed quickly. I managed to keep in mind the entire organizational structure of my (eventually 250-page) dissertation so that, in the process of copying quotes from books or taking lecture notes, I could include the page numbers or titles of the subsections where the resource or idea would best fit. Nowadays, my students are still impressed by how quickly I memorize their names at the beginning of the semester. Motherly love and professional devotion are powerful forces.

My demanding academic and family schedule had its fair share of drawbacks, though. Research and writing were made all the more difficult because I was isolated from members of my department. My fellow graduate students were a terrific bunch, who took advantage of one of the primary resources of great educational institutions: each other. But I couldn't join their regular, informal chat sessions at the coffee shop just outside of the main library, as they discussed their intriguing and important interests, traded resources, and refined their thinking through high-level discussions. They would often wave and shout a friendly "Hey, Angelica!" as I biked past on my way to work or to pick up Paul, but of course I couldn't stop and join them.

I must pause to voice my amazement, though, at the generosity of my fellow graduate students. There was Kate, who copied and brought me study notes for the qualifying exams shortly after I gave birth to Paul; Annette, who babysat chicken-poxed Jacqueline and Paul so I could take a break and enjoy Fourth of July fireworks; Brian, who encouraged me all the way through the tiring job-seeking season; and so many others. I remember, at the time, feeling that my goals of being a great researcher and great mother made me only a mediocre colleague. Now, years later, many have told me that they think of me and my good cheer when they are oppressed by the demands of earning tenure or by trying to balance work and family. They have also reminded me how conscientious I was, about bringing in a quote or e-mailing them a resource that might have been mentioned in class.

Interactions like these have led me to believe that it is important for all student-parents, but especially minorities, to realize that the disaffection they might feel with the larger graduate school population is based sometimes on personal choices that prevent cooperation and socializing, rather than on generalized unkindness or latent prejudice.

I also have to pause to acknowledge my gratitude for that time-saving, if basic, machine—the bike—for helping me stay healthy, something parents and students often overlook. Combined, graduate school and parenting create intense levels of stress, but I learned from my kids that what I call "exercise" they call "fun." Riding bikes, swimming, swinging, and such—especially when done in the company of the under-twelve crowd—created a happiness and peace that energized my other activities. And so I biked whenever and wherever I could, often with Paul strapped into the baby seat and Jacqueline pedaling alongside. Ever the scholar, as I churned the pedals, I mentally chanted a (surprisingly rhythmic) quote from one of Milton's contemporaries, the British philosopher John Locke: "A sound body for a sound mind."

There was, of course, some overlap between work life and family life. My mommy brain did not turn off when I turned on my scholar brain, or vice versa. I remember once sitting in a history class and feeling the building sway. A native Californian, I knew it was the feeling of either a small or distant earthquake. Without hesitation, I stood up, said "Excuse me," and rushed downstairs to call the kids' schools to make sure that all was well. As I walked back to class, happily reassured but slightly embarrassed for having rushed out of the room, I realized I could turn the incident into a discussion point. We had just finished looking at seventeenth-century London parish registers to track deaths within families and determine any mortality patterns. While I had come up with the appropriate empirical analysis, as had the others—history majors all—I was unique in having found the assignment emotionally grueling. Trained as a literature major to locate the human in written texts, and perhaps because I was so immersed in family life, I had read the registers' recordings of maternal deaths shortly following infant deaths as important verbal testaments to human suffering and endurance. When I shared my personal response to the tremor, I think it made my fellow students a little more willing to take seriously my comprehensive approach to historical studies.

On the flip side, my work duties provided unexpected delights in my family life. I loved picking up Paul on the days I planned to collect books from the Stanford Auxiliary Library (SAL). Holding his small hand as we shouted our good-byes to his buddies and exited the preschool, I would say, "Guess what?" He'd quickly release my hand, cup both hands over his mouth, and ask, "SAL?" I would nod, and he would then grab my hand and drag me to SAL, which lay on our short walk between the preschool and our on-campus housing. Once in the library, I would take out my list of books to be resurrected from the dead. The shelves were the space-saving, low-use kinds: closely packed with only one walkway open at a time and with control panels to access the right shelves. I've got to admit, those movable shelves came in a close second to my favorite machines. While getting the books took much, much longer, my son loved the whole thing, from the gleeful announcement of our excursion to getting a cold drink during check-out time from the water cooler near the exit (certainly not near the valuable books!). He quickly learned his letters and numbers so that he could key-pad the letter- and number-filled call numbers that set the shelves in motion. I don't know if I can attribute Paul's voracious reading habits to those trips, but they at least helped create his many good memories of books. At first, the librarians were justifiably concerned about having a toddler in the stacks. But they soon saw that my parenting style—focused on creating respectful, social beings through routine activities—ensured the safety of the books. I was proud that my time in the library with Paul reflected well on us, and I hoped it contributed to counteracting the negative images of U.S. Latinos in the media.

When I felt the often overwhelming pressure to take out loans to put my son in all-day day care or hire a babysitter for both kids during after-school hours, I urged myself to hold fast to my goals. It wasn't easy but I am glad that I did. Doing so helped my scholarship . . . in Milton studies, of all things! For one, I graduated quicker than the national average in my field—after all, I had mouths to feed. Equally importantly, I escaped the danger of making my already remote area of study irrelevant or esoteric.

In Mexican families, the *mamá* is intimately linked with the grandmother, the *abuelita*. The *mamá* serves as a bridge between generations. The process of individuals acting as bridges—a myth that deserves preserving—is beautifully represented in Virgil's Latin epic *The Aeneid*, with the hero, Aeneas, carrying his father, Anchises, on his back as he escapes the burning city of his family's past, Troy, to found Rome and establish the future of his people. For me, routine family walks were much less fraught but no less heroic. My mother often joined Paul and me on our walks to pick up Jacqueline from school, and she would usually ask me, "*¿Pues, qué hicistes hoy? ¿Qué estudias?*" ("So, what did you do today? What are you studying?") It would have been cultural anathema for me to have answered flippantly or distractedly, "Oh, you wouldn't understand," and I would have been as embarrassed with her as I would have been with my dissertation advisor if I couldn't have answered her cogently or excited her about what I was doing. Those sun-bathed, three-generational walks filtered into my nighttime research and writing in concrete ways. I often added the specific wording I had used in my conversations with my mother into my dissertation. If not for that family-time chatting, I don't think I would have lighted on those "felicitous phrasings," as they're called in the field, as quickly.

My daughter, Jacqueline, was particularly helpful in assisting my grasp of the scientific and mathematical concepts I was exploring in my research. Those early scientists were a lot like the best school kids today, studying new ideas before knowing their eventual outcomes. When Jacqueline was learning chemistry, I asked her what her favorite chemical was so that I could answer her puzzled look by telling her that mine is carbon, the chemical of life. Or I would give her a strong hug and say that I was "testing out Boyle's Law" that the product of pressure and volume is a constant. One of the main points of my dissertation is to show that the discovery of scientific facts during Milton's lifetime was the result of individuals caring, and that those findings grew because other people continued to care. So, I loved helping her care about chemistry by explaining that Mr. Boyle was a very rich man who didn't have to work as hard as he did to discover knowledge that is still useful today, and that his friend Mr. Milton cared too, even though he was a poet, not a scientist.

I am not simply being cute or nice when I tell my kids that "*we* earned a PhD" and that "*we* got the job." They knew from an early age that their job was to go to bed at 8:00 P.M. and only come downstairs if they felt sick or needed comforting from an especially bad dream. I was often surprised when I heard other student-parents complain that their kids resisted bedtime or whined about errands or chores. In turn, I think they looked upon my parental expectations—so culturally prescribed—as a bit much. I have to admit that I wondered too. Until Jacqueline took to writing kind notes—"Good job, Mom!" or "Just 8 more days until you turn in your dissertation"—and paper-airplaning those love notes down the staircase to me. She had discovered a resilient way of using written language while letting me do "our work." The first time she did this, I cried and thought, "My God, I am doing *something* right," especially because her message sounded a lot like the positive notes I would sneak into the lunch bag she packed for herself. Both kids are so good at reading and writing now that they read the draft of *this* essay and made recommendations that I incorporated—really.

Despite their cooperation, I was always pressed for time. To avoid the temptation of plopping them in front of that most ubiquitous and mesmerizing machine—the TV—we relied on a couple of other machines to fill the waking hours. We'd take the elevator up the tall Hoover Tower and look at the beautiful vistas, or we'd get on the free campus shuttle and go to the world-class campus museum. We each had our favorite works: Paul's was the very large, outdoor statue *Soft Q*; Jacqueline's the vibrant painting *Mexican Girl*; and mine the exquisite statue *Nature Unveiling Herself Before Science*. My inquisitive, energetic companions helped me learn ways to articulate the aesthetic-scientific concord of our favorites, which not haphazardly aligned with my dissertation, later published as *The Age of Milton and the Scientific Revolution*. We once looked up the materials and material engineering used for *Soft Q* to maintain its pink color in the California sun. We talked about the historical and cultural forces that might account for the disconnect between the name-plaque on the frame of Jacqueline's favorite painting, Charles Nahl's colorful portrait of a Mexican girl, and its corresponding wall plaque, which renamed it *Spanish Girl*. How integrated were my studies and those visits? The cover illustration of my first book is of the statue *Nature Unveiling Herself Before Science*. When the press approved the cover, I thought of it as one of the unexpected and positive outcomes of field trips that Milton describes so beautifully in his short prose piece *Of Education*: "In those vernal seasons of the year when the air is calm and pleasant, it were an injury and sullenness against nature not to go out and see her riches and partake in her rejoicing with heaven and earth."

My parenting experiences also strengthened the teaching aspects of my career, especially in terms of providing the combination of verbal, visual, tactile, and experiential learning so strongly promoted in pedagogical theory. Although I doubt any of my students would describe my teaching style as maternal, I always try to think of my students as someone else's kids. With that in mind, I attempt to provide them with as many engaging experiences as possible, including field trips. I've taken students to the Chicago Shakespeare Theater to see *Merry Wives of Windsor,* so they could see that Shakespeare was actually funny. We've gone to the local theater, once to see Mary Zimmerman's *Metamorphoses* to delight in the "very cool!" updating of Ovid's Latin *Metamorphoses*. More recently, I've provided students with interdisciplinary experiences by taking them to the Indianapolis Opera's dress rehearsal of *Carmen* and to the Eiteljorg Museum of American Indians and

Western Art to show how perceptions of Hispanics are conveyed through various arts. The sheer joy I have experienced in parenting ensures that I continue to fill out the extra paperwork and do the extra legwork to provide such opportunities to "someone else's kids."

I hope my story can encourage mothers pursuing graduate degrees to avoid putting life on hold, and inspire those in minority groups to find ways of merging their root cultures and contextual cultures. For example, while my mother would have been patient with me if I had used her as a baby-sitter from my Anglo-American contextual culture rather than appreciated her as an *abuelita* from my Latino root culture, I managed to be a *mamá* so that she in turn could be an *abuelita*. I am glad I did, since she died unexpectedly and quickly of pancreatic cancer the year after I graduated. Had I waited until I was less busy—and does that ever really happen?—my mother could not have passed on our precious family and cultural practices to Jacqueline and Paul. As it is, rather than looking on in awkward silence as I leave food at her grave, as is common in Mexican culture, my children lovingly participate in creating our own Mexican American family custom, selecting which of their grandmother's favorite multinational foods to leave: tamales, Chinese beef and broccoli, pizza. This is all to say that we have to act in our families in the "now, very now" (that's from Shakespeare's *Othello*—I tell you, those great authors are everywhere!).

And work doesn't necessarily have to suffer when combining it with motherhood. All the organizational skills and personal investment in my research that I honed in graduate school helped me obtain a tenure-track job at a Research I institution the first time out on the job market and, six years later, to exceed the national standards for tenure and promotion to associate professor in my field. Instead of one well-placed monograph *or* a sufficient number of well-placed articles and chapters, I had one well-placed monograph *and* an edited book *and* numerous articles and chapters. Again, though, "I" didn't do it alone: my family and my community (now at Purdue University) helped me in countless ways.

So, what is my favorite machine now? Well, it's hard to choose. I still value my computer. And with cold Indiana winters, I have learned to appreciate furnaces. I've also begun to like those airborne machines—airplanes—that take me, accompanied now by my husband, Sean, to speaking engagements, research trips, and vacations all over the Americas, Europe, and Asia. Then there's Jacqueline's iPod. Adding auditory learning to my magic hat of teaching tools, she helps me design the music CDs I play for the five to ten minutes before each of my classes. I have used Elton John's "Sorry

Seems to Be the Hardest Word" (1969) from my mental storehouse and
Natasha Bedingfield's "Unwritten" (2004) from hers, for example, to get
students thinking about free will in *Paradise Lost*. I value all the machines
in my life because I have found ways to make them bridges rather than
barriers between my root culture and my contextual culture. Whether I'm
in front of a computer, in an airplane, in a music-filled classroom, or even
in a star-filled desert that my trusty car has taken my family and me to, my
machines take me to all the right places to be because I so tenaciously cling
to the beautiful and wise directive—you knew I had to end with a quote
from Milton, didn't you?—"Wherever placed, . . . joy thou" (*Paradise Lost*).

I dedicate this essay to fellow alum Stephen Peters, for his trust and aid,
which went so far in helping me become a *Mamá*, PhD.

That Mommy Thing

ALISSA McELREATH

In December of 2004 I was invited, by a senior tenured colleague at my department, to her annual holiday party. I had only taught one semester, and felt that my inclusion was a real sign that I was becoming somebody. My colleague good-naturedly penned the words "Bring your family!" at the bottom of the invitation, and so I did. My daughter was eleven months old at the time, my son was four. My husband, also a professor, came too. The house was beautifully decorated—I think *appointed* is the right word—and the Christmas tree was hung with what appeared to be hand-blown glass ornaments. Collectibles from around the world were tastefully displayed, and the guests were a well-traveled and fascinating lot. I would have loved to have spent hours mingling and talking with any number of them. Although my husband tried valiantly to stem our daughter's destructive tide, I found it impossible to engage in any of the many conversations around me. I remember at one point trying to tell a faculty member from another university about my dissertation and becoming tongue-tied and inarticulate as I watched my daughter grab at someone's wine glass. But what sticks in my mind most about that holiday party is what the hostess— my colleague—said to me as we left. She hugged me briefly at the door, took my hand in hers and shook it firmly. She urged me to "keep up with my job" by publishing and writing, and then said, squeezing my hand for extra emphasis, "don't get *too* caught up in that mommy thing."

And there it was, right there. She had reduced my frustrating daily struggle between professional self and mothering self into one short phrase: *that mommy thing*. No matter how I look at it, my professional life and my life as a mother continue to run side by side, parallel in that tired old metaphorical way: two roads running together, and there I am on both, jumping and dashing from one to the other, always out of breath. If someone had told me when I entered graduate school back in 1996 that I would still be working on my dissertation some ten years later, through the pregnancies and births of *two* children, relocation to another state, and the first two years of a full-time teaching job, I think I would have crumpled up in disbelief right then and there.

When I was a graduate student I never felt the need to justify my desire to be a mother. My research at the time (on popular culture, women, and the history of childbirth and reproductive technology), jibed well with my own developing urge to get pregnant—to have a *baby*. I had a few graduate school friends who were newly married and also contemplating motherhood, and so there in the sheltered bubble of graduate school, I felt I could do it all. When I did become pregnant with my son (now six) I felt so proud sitting in the library, or heading off to teach a class, with my belly gently swelling under my sweater. I distinctly remember teaching a creative writing class the spring before his birth and feeling the flutters and rolls inside while I paced around the room. At home I would sit at the table in our eat-in kitchen, next to a towering stack of virtually unknown plays and novels by Upton Sinclair, my very pregnant belly pushing against the table's edge while I read, took notes, and tried fervently to get as much of my dissertation done as possible before the due date. "Push to finish before the baby comes," my father kept telling me. "Don't get too distracted." I tried, but summer heat, excitement about our first baby's arrival, and my husband's job search all kept me from making much progress.

After my son's birth, I moved from pregnant graduate student to working mom. I taught one class and managed the college writing center on campus, a job which let me bring my son to work. As I learned quickly, separating my professional self from my mothering self was almost impossible to do (anyone who has tried to nurse an unhappy baby while attempting to carry on work duties knows what I am talking about!). I also learned quickly that the academic world offers only an illusion of flexibility for women who wish to work in it and be mothers. Academia is a rat race like any other, with its own pecking orders and politics; women who are also mothers often become collateral damage in department or division disputes.

When my husband landed a tenure-track job at a small private college in North Carolina I had to redefine myself again. I was no longer any of the things I used to be: a teaching assistant, or a first-year-composition instructor, or the student manager for the writing program at my doctoral university. I was still a mother—that was a comforting constant—but I became a *trailing spouse*, a label I didn't know existed when I *was* a trailing spouse, but one I came across later, when doing some reading on the position of women in the academy. The academic side of myself proceeded to go dormant for about a year while I took care of our son, helped us all adjust to the move, tinkered (not very productively) at my dissertation, and slowly realized that I longed for something else, too—I longed to be back inside a classroom again, working with students and being a part of the world in which I felt so comfortable. One August, when my son was two, the phone rang while we were watching *Blue's Clues* and I was offered an adjunct teaching position at a local college.

In some ways I have successfully negotiated the divide between motherhood and a professional life in academia, yet in other ways I have not. I feel very much on the periphery of it all, as if the real inner circle is just out of reach. I am one of the lucky few who hit the lottery twice: I not only moved into a full-time teaching position from an adjunct job, but also did so as a candidate with no dissertation in hand—yet. Some days I tell myself proudly that I have broken the mold, that I am successfully negotiating a career in academia while not compromising my family life, that I am teaching my children that a woman *can* be a scholar, a writer, a teacher, and a mother too. Other times, though, I am caught in that classic working woman's bind: I feel spread too thin, as if I can't excel professionally or, sometimes, personally. The demands I place on myself, and the demands I feel from others, close in on me, especially on the days when I just haven't had enough time to be a mom, a teacher, a counselor, a wife, a scholar, and, well . . . *me*.

My husband's and my lives are unusually hectic and spread too thin, in large part because we "tag-team parent"—a phrase we coined early in our graduate school days, when we'd pass off our son at the bus stop like a baton. Six years later we continue our kid exchanges: three days a week I race out of class at one o'clock and meet my husband in the parking lot of the college where he teaches. My school bag takes the place of my husband's on the front seat of our van, engine idling, while we exchange a hasty kiss. Then he's off to classes while I move quickly from papers, students, and class plans to my daughter's world of *Franklin* and an afternoon in the sandbox. The wonderful upside, of course, is that we both get to share in the parenting; our marriage exemplifies teamwork at its best, for otherwise things would rapidly fall apart. The downside is obvious: this type of schedule is difficult to justify to colleagues and is emotionally and physically exhausting. Juggling teaching schedules, meetings, and the needs of two children—all with little outside help—requires a strict amount of planning and can accommodate very few fly-by-the-seat-of-your-pants changes.

Although I am in a small department in a small school, I still get late e-mails with last-minute summonses to impromptu department or division meetings, invariably at times when I simply cannot attend. Then I become the *difficult* colleague, the one who is constantly vetoing times suitable for everyone else because . . . well, I imagine the frustrated sighs between colleagues: "She has to pick up her son at car pool." When the dreaded course-calendar time of the semester arrives, I hold my breath and steel myself for the battles I must fight to keep the schedule I both like and need. In the almost three years I've been teaching full time I've fielded the whole range of comments from colleagues, from references to paying one's dues to "Why can't you just find a day-care provider?" I've had to listen to stories from older faculty women who had to make great sacrifices in the family department in order to rise up the academic ladder, and I've felt incredibly guilty that my husband and I have managed to keep it all together, to share our parenting and to use only sporadic babysitting help coupled with morning preschool time. But inside I also rage at these comments, for I know that my job is one I can—and should—be able to do regardless of whether or not I choose to also devote myself to *that mommy thing.*

I've often thought back to that comment my colleague made that December evening. I have shelved it away in my psyche and pulled it out over and over again when I feel angry or vulnerable about my job and my professional capabilities. Yet I turn to the comment as a sort of affirmation of myself, of who I am and what makes me feel whole and happy. *That mommy thing* is really what I am about. Motherhood has affected everything I do, professionally and personally, and not getting caught up in it would be not only impossible, but damaging—to my job, my writing, and my life. And I remain eternally grateful to my colleague for helping me see it this way.

Failure to Progress

What Having a Baby Taught Me about Aristotle, Advanced Degrees, Developmental Delays, and Other Natural Disasters

IRENA AUERBUCH SMITH

Jordan was conceived shortly before the 1994 Northridge earthquake, and I always wondered afterward if our first crack at conceiving a child literally caused the earth to move. The earthquake hit at 4:30 A.M. on January 17, knocking out electricity, wantonly dumping books off our shelves—Jane Austen's *Sense and Sensibility*, Slavoj Žižek's *The Sublime Object of Ideology*, *Grant's Atlas of Anatomy*, the *MLA Guide for Writers of Research Papers*— and setting off every car alarm in the greater Los Angeles area. Neither David, my husband, nor I were in the least prepared. Here we were at the University of California, Los Angeles, getting advanced degrees (David was finishing medical school, I was in my fourth year in a doctoral program in comparative literature), and we had no flashlight, no battery-operated radio, no shoes by the bed. When the shaking stopped and we ventured out of our bedroom, we cut our feet on broken glass, then lit candles to assess the damage. In our defense, it was 4:30 in the morning; we were young; we were stupid; we believed we were invulnerable. We were also lucky— for in addition to being spared from heavy falling objects, exploding gas lines, contaminated drinking water, and house fires, I got pregnant. Practically on the first try.

Nine months later, nearly to the day, Jordan entered the world via semi-emergency C-section after a twelve-hour labor during which it became manifestly apparent that my uterus was incapable of expelling him on its own. In hospital parlance, this was called "failure to progress due to fetal-pelvic disproportion," so in came my OB, trailing a battery of scalpels, spreaders, sponges, and surgical nurses in her wake, and twenty-two minutes later, Jordan, with his head still in my abdominal cavity, took his first breath and uttered his first mewling cry. The noise was so jarring in that otherwise hushed operating room, filled only with murmured requests for instruments, the soft clink of metal, and the whooshing of suction tubes, that I asked David whether that was the baby. David, seated by my head in full surgical scrubs, said, "Well, duh," with unaccustomed tenderness and squeezed my hand. "Of course it's the baby," cooed my OB as she stitched layers of muscle and skin back together and a pediatrics resident took Jordan's vital signs in the corner. "Look at that little butterball." Four days later we dressed the little butterball in a yellow onesie embroidered with ducks, slipped on a matching hat, inserted him awkwardly into a car seat, and took him home. And thus our life as new parents began.

Between Jordan's conception and birth, three things happened and one did not. David graduated from medical school, I finished my PhD qualifying exams, and we moved into a rented two-bedroom duplex on a bucolic tree-lined street in Menlo Park, California. But in spite of a substantial dissertation-year fellowship, I did not write my dissertation. While David began his psychiatry residency at Stanford Hospital, I made no progress whatsoever. I swam laps in the local community center pool, cooked chicken saltimbocca, and, in a misguided attempt at nesting, bought hideous wrought-iron candelabra at Z Gallerie. The candelabra were not returnable, and David wondered aloud why some nesting women scrub woodwork and wash windows while others feather the nest with nonreturnable wrought-iron monstrosities. The answer was simple: I didn't know what to do with myself, and the obvious solution—to get to work on the dissertation immediately, *now, this minute,* as everyone who had children suggested—was impossible, as I refused to set foot in the library.

I thought my refusal made perfect sense. Although I had practically lived at the library during my years at UCLA, I now had ample reason to avoid Stanford University's library system—ample being the operative word. Truth be told, I was embarrassed. Embarrassed to walk into the hushed, red-carpeted lobby of Cecil H. Green Library; embarrassed to squeeze through the narrow stacks; embarrassed to be seen on a college campus at all, with my belly preceding me by a good foot or so and my belly button poking through the fabric of the dowdy maternity tops like a plastic timer on a store-bought turkey. I had gone and gotten myself knocked up, and now that the evidence was in full view—well, that was pretty much it for my life as an academic.

The problem was this: when the fellowship was awarded, I was pregnant but not yet showing, skinny and smart, the darling of the Comparative Literature Department, an exemplary student without a single incomplete, a teaching assistant universally acknowledged by the comp lit faculty to be one of the finest in recent memory, admired by (most) fellow grad students, beloved by (most) undergrads, a recent Russian émigré whose dissertation—on displacement and semantic instability in the works of Henry James and Vladimir Nabokov, themselves expats and émigrés—promised to make of her own exile a thing of beauty. I was on the fast track to academic superstardom, a wunderkind, the student our chair liked to point to when asked about time-to-degree and other ticklish questions by prospective applicants. Now, however, I had grown big with child and become exiled—forever, it seemed—from the ranks of literary and literate anorexics to which I desperately wanted to belong. Without meaning to, I had internalized the unwritten rules of graduate school: academics, women in particular, were meant to lead a life of the mind. A life of the flesh, if it existed, was to be conducted elsewhere, coyly, discreetly. Excess in the form of eccentric clothing choices and unusual facial piercings—fabulous; fleshly excess, not so much. Fat people were lazy and stupid; everyone knew this, even if nobody said so. My dissertation advisor was serenely chic and rail thin; so was Ruth Yeazell, who taught the Virginia Woolf seminar; so was Virginia Woolf; so were Emily Dickinson, Charlotte Perkins Gilman, Jane Austen. Toni Morrison was a notable exception, but as an African American woman, she probably had better things to worry about. Plus, she had won the Pulitzer and the Nobel. *She* had published with steady regularity. Hers was clearly a life of the mind.

Mine, meanwhile, was fast becoming a life of the body. At barely five foot one, I was quite literally subsumed by my pregnancy. My new shape—all belly and breasts—began to attract attention from relatives, friends, acquaintances, strangers in the supermarket. Only recently, it seemed, I was in Kathy Komar's feminist theory seminar, discussing with gusto (and thinly veiled schadenfreude) ways in which the female body, in literature as in life, was objectified, fetishized, commodified, subjugated by the patriarchal gaze, and now it was happening to me. I became the object of other narratives—of conjecture, jokes, criticism, unwanted confidences, unsolicited advice. People I didn't know—or certainly didn't know well enough—asked me how much weight I had gained, remarked on my size and shape (too big, too pointy, too round, about to burst), told me not to lift heavy grocery bags, swim, take hot showers, eat sweets, bend to the side, walk too fast or too far. Get as much sleep as possible now, they said. You're not getting any when the baby comes, that's for sure. Oh, and sex too, ha ha. And finish your dissertation, finish it *now*. Because after you have that baby, it's all over. Your life will never be the same again.

I scoffed. It was painfully obvious that David and I were not like the pathetic people who pressed their advice upon us. We had advanced degrees; we had worked as summer camp counselors. Surely we would manage to lead fulfilled lives, pursuing our own interests while nurturing and molding our little one; surely we could get our child to sleep through the night. How hard could it be, for crying out loud? Everyone knew that babies slept eighteen hours a day (didn't we see that in a book somewhere?). And anyway, Jordan was going to be exceptional. He would grow up reading *Pat the Bunny* and Pushkin, speaking two languages (maybe three) with fluency and aplomb, quoting Shakespeare from memory. He would go to Harvard, or in the worst-case scenario, Princeton or Stanford or Yale. Of course it would be tough going for a few days after he was born, but then we would settle into a domestic routine in which David went off to the hospital while I, cooing baby serenely cradled against my breast, completed my dissertation and ultimately landed a plum tenure-track job somewhere in the Bay Area.

Our learning curve after we brought Jordan home was steep. We learned, among other things, that newborns never sleep and that it is impossible to write a dissertation (or anything else, up to and including a grocery list) with a newborn baby in the house. David and I spent the first three or four months of Jordan's life dazed, living from crisis to crisis. Everything leaked—diapers, breast milk, spit up, tears. I cried nonstop, because on some days my crowning achievement was a shower by 4 P.M., because there were no adults to talk to, because I was still fat and clearly getting stupider with each passing day, because I was never going to finish my dissertation, never, never, never.

We tried a nanny, Lena, who had recently arrived from St. Petersburg and was available Monday, Tuesday, and Thursday mornings (cash only, please). The arrangement was doomed from the very beginning. In our 800-square-foot duplex, I could hear every sound she and Jordan made as she gurgled to him in Russian (one of her selling points) and I stared idly at a blank computer screen, overwhelmed by guilt and inertia. The dissertation was going nowhere fast. Like Jordan's birthing process, it, and I, seemed to be suffering from a failure to progress. I also—overnight, it seemed—acquired what Henry James called "an imagination of disaster." Lena would take Jordan for a stroller walk and I would envision scenarios in which she tripped and spilled him out on the sidewalk, or he was abducted, or she dropped dead from a heart attack in the middle of the street, leaving him alone and helpless. I could see the police reports: "Abandoned infant placed in protective custody after nanny drops dead; police officers located the mother banging her head against a blank computer screen. The distraught woman assured the officers that she was 'planning to become a good mother as soon as this damn thing was finished.'" What I couldn't see—at all—was how I could care adequately for a child and at the same time produce intelligible, let alone intelligent, prose. The mind-numbing routine of feedings and diaper-changing and stroller walks and bath time and nap time and story time had done just that—numbed my mind. I could not for the life of me write without obsessing about not taking care of the baby; nor could I take care of the baby without obsessing about not writing. I felt like I had discovered nuclear fission: hey, combining a baby and work is really hard!

For all her good intentions, Lena was not helping much, which was probably my fault rather than hers. Plus, she had opinions and ideas, some of which, to put it charitably, were a little eccentric. She bundled Jordan in so many layers when they went out that it looked like they were setting off for the North Pole. Every time Jordan fussed, she claimed his stomach was bothering him. One day, she noted in passing that he never looked straight at her. "I try and try to catch his eye," she said, "and he just looks straight through me, like I'm not even there. Or he looks away. Have you had his vision checked?"

We had not had his vision checked. David was on call every third night, and his pager beeped incessantly even when he wasn't. Neither of us had had a full night's sleep for months. We were subsisting on frozen dinners and cheap takeout and having screaming fights four to five times a week. Did I mention that we were young and had had very little experience with infants? That none of our friends had yet gotten around to having children of their own, so we had no peer group, no point of comparison? That it seemed like we would never again lead a normal life?

At his wit's end, David floated the idea of placing Jordan in part-time day care, provoking our most spectacular screaming match to date. "Why even *have* children," I sobbed at the kitchen table, "if you're just going to let them be raised by other people?"

David's suggestion—"so you could finish your dissertation and move on with your life"—set off another explosion (you don't respect me now that I'm a stay-at-home mom, etc.). And on it went.

Gradually, grudgingly, I had to admit that David was right. We let Lena go and found a spot at Stanford's day-care center, where a meticulous Frenchwoman named Yvet presided beneficently over Jordan and five of his colleagues. And it turned out that Virginia Woolf was right: all I needed, really, was a room of my own. I would drop off Jordan, come home, barricade myself behind stacks of books, and write, and write, and write. I lived on a steady diet of coffee and Hershey's miniatures left over from Halloween (oddly, that and the intellectual exertion seemed to do the trick that diet and exercise could not), and as I grew slimmer, the dissertation took on shape and heft. And then it was done—done!—all 283 pages of it, not including the acknowledgments, where I thanked my parents, who had brought me to America, and David, who had brought America to me, and mentioned what a delight it was to watch Jordan grow and learn as I wrote the dissertation.

That last part was not, technically, accurate, but it seemed important to link bringing Jordan and the dissertation into the world at roughly the same time. It was a fitting end to the "How Motherhood Did Not Stop Me from Leading a Life of the Mind" narrative I had envisioned. I had finished the dissertation against long odds; that spring, I landed a part-time humanities lectureship at Stanford. I had it all: a flat belly, a baby, and a life of the mind.

But that was not the end of it at all, because while I had been blithely writing about ways in which exile impelled story making and artistic experimentation in the lives and novels of James and Nabokov, another narrative was unfolding right under our noses. It was marked by a persistent unease, a nagging sense of something out of place, something missing. It developed slowly at first, then faster and faster, with the inexorability of a train picking up speed on a downward slope. It came down to this: we were not having much fun with Jordan.

At first we thought it was us—cerebral, neurotic, overeducated parents. We would go out on date night and end up in a bookstore, in the child-development section, browsing through books with titles like *Your Fun Toddler* and *Games Babies Play*. But somehow the rousing game of peek-a-boo that was a hit with the random toddler at the supermarket left Jordan cold. While other children in his day care squealed with delight when David or I walked in, Jordan remained unmoved. And he wasn't talking—repeating, yes, but not generating words or stringing them together in meaningful, creative ways. So we would have maddening conversations along the following lines:

"Do you want a waffle?"

"Waffle."

"Say 'yes.'"

"Yes."

"Do you want a waffle?"

"Waffle."

And so on. At first it was funny. Then other children in his day care began to put two, three, four words together, and then, seemingly overnight, speak in sentences. Jordan, meanwhile, ran in circles around the playground, head tilted to one side, gaze trained on the ground. Or he would open and close doors—cabinet doors, bathroom doors, oven doors, microwave doors—or he would lie on the floor with a toy truck and watch the wheels go round and round. At first we found explanations: he was working on his gross motor skills; he was testing out cause and effect; he was befuddled by the combination of Russian and English he heard every day.

But then he turned two, and he still wasn't talking, or holding a crayon, or calling us "Mommy" or "Daddy," and one day one of his preschool teachers cautiously mentioned the phrase "developmental delay." So we took him to a developmental specialist, who told us what we already knew, but with numbers and percentiles attached: that he showed a significant delay in expressive and receptive language ability without an attempt to compensate through gesture or other nonverbal communication; impaired eye contact; lack of imaginative play; delayed fine motor skills. The office was sunny and spacious, as offices where bad news is delivered often are. Jordan met eight of the ten major criteria for autism. He would, in all likelihood, eventually acquire language, although it was too early to tell if he would ever use it in a meaningful way. We got a long list of speech therapists, occupational therapists, behavioral therapists, parent support groups (everything, David said later, except for some good tips about how to commit suicide) and went outside, into the bright May morning. Jordan was two years and seven months old.

All at once, the things I had prized as a graduate student (aside from a low body mass index)—indeterminacy, ambiguity, open-endedness—receded, and I wanted clarity and closure. How autistic was Jordan? Was autism permanent? Would he ever be normal? Would he ever have meaningful speech? Would he go to kindergarten, to college, to the bathroom unattended? Would he fall in love? Would he ever love us? Would he ever hug us spontaneously, without one of us holding his hands together behind the neck of the other?

Clearly, the earthquake accompanying Jordan's conception, the very one that knocked our books into a jumbled heap on the floor, had been trying to tell us something. Having children was unpredictable, messy, and

dangerous. Unlike books, children did not come with informative labels—
"This One Will Break Your Heart"; "This One Will Cry for Three Months
Straight When You Bring Her Home"; "This One Will Steal Candy from
7–11"; "This One Will Be Funny, Engaging, Smart, and Beloved by All until
He's Killed by a Drunk Driver at Seventeen." We were on our own with this
one. As David put it, "It's like all the other parents got on the fun train to
Disneyland and here we are at the station."

"Kicked off at Bakersfield is more like it," I said.

We went to Lane Medical Library and checked out all the books on
Applied Behavioral Analysis, the only approach to teaching autistic children that had shown consistent and validated results. At its core, this was
operant conditioning, a way of breaking any task, no matter how complex,
into small, manageable steps, and rewarding successful completion of each
step with praise (which was secondary to the autistic child) and the much
more motivating "reinforcers" (Cheerios, M&Ms, pretzels, dime-store toys,
etc.). Apparently, anything could be taught this way, from tying shoelaces
to imaginative play ("Move the truck forward. Now say 'vroom.' Great job.
Have a Cheerio!").

A lifetime ago, it seemed, I had debated with undergrads if Aristotle
was on to something in *Ethics,* if virtue really could be acquired through
mechanical repetition of virtuous acts. We were about to find out. We
bought a small table and two tiny yellow chairs at a school supply store and
got to work—an hour in the early morning, an hour in the evening, and
lots of what the books called "incidental teaching" in between. My life, like
Humbert's in Nabokov's *Lolita,* became "monstrously two-fold." By day, I
taught precocious first-year students at Stanford; by night, I was a behav-
iorist to a recalcitrant two-year-old who didn't talk, deliberately avoided eye
contact, and arched his back when I tried to hold him. Unlike my Stanford
students, however, Jordan was not argumentative. He sat in his little yellow chair, his feet not touching the floor, and (for the most part) did what
we asked of him. "Touch blue," we would say, and he would, and we would
feed him a Cheerio and say "Good job!" and repeat the whole process and
then switch to expressive language and then to fine motor skills and then
play skills and then repeat the whole thing all over again the next morning. Ten attempts in every drill, with 80 percent mastery the goal (since
no self-respecting two-year-old, normal or not, would ever comply with a
request ten out of ten times), until he achieved consistent mastery of a task
regardless of prompter or setting. It was a tedious, repetitive, and frustrating process; it felt completely counterintuitive.

But it worked. Within three months, Jordan had gained close to a year across all domains—language, cognition, motor skills, play skills—and within a year, it was difficult to distinguish him in a roomful of kids in nursery school. While we were nowhere near finished with the project David had taken to calling "making Jordan into a human being," Jordan was, with lots of help from us and hordes of professionals and paraprofessionals, catching up and blending in. So is this, then, the happy ending? Yes and no. In fact, there is no ending, and that, kind of, is the whole point.

Jordan is twelve now. He just started middle school, where he's on the cross-country team. He swims competitively. He has friends—not many, but enough. He makes consistent eye contact; he tries to tell jokes (with mixed success) and laughs in the right places; he rides his bike to school; he makes a passable peanut–butter-and-jelly sandwich and knows how to microwave a frozen burrito. He also throws gargantuan tantrums, often for no reason, which involve flying barstools, broken pencils, and high decibels. He has comprehension, processing, and behavioral problems, which is why he is in a social-cognitive class with what he calls "a bunch of freaking weirdos." To compound the irony further, he wants more than anything to be like everyone else. All this calls to mind the accusation Caliban hurls at Prospero in *The Tempest*: "You taught me language, and my profit on't / Is I know how to curse." We did try to teach him not only language, but also—broken down into component parts, reinforced by pretzels and Cheerios—what it is to be human. But how do you teach reciprocity, imagination, kindness, humor, tenderness, spontaneity? To a small degree, Jordan possesses all of these; they are poor and paltry things, but they are his—taught to him and perceived by him as a second language, with an alien vocabulary and grammar. He may become fluent one day, or he may not.

This is supposed to be the part where I talk about how much we learned, how we revised our assumptions and expectations, how humbled we were by having a special-needs child, how we realized what was truly important—or, alternatively, how Jordan was miraculously cured, how we got on that train to Disneyland with the other parents after all. We're south of Bakersfield, but certainly not at Anaheim; Jordan has good days and bad days, and David and I occasionally fantasize about sending him to boarding school, where he can tantrum at leisure about math problems that don't work out or recalcitrant Ziploc bags. So here, instead, is a partial list of all the things I got as a result of giving birth to a dissertation and an autistic child in the same year. They are, in no particular order: a no longer quite

concave belly-button; a nearly encyclopedic knowledge of Applied Behavioral Analysis, speech acquisition, and play therapy; a deeper appreciation
of cosmic irony and Aristotle's *Ethics*; an ability to quote from memory
from most of James's and Nabokov's canonical works; unexpected insights
into *The Tempest* and *Frankenstein*; a series of part-time, dead-end academic
lectureships that fit into Jordan's school and therapy schedule; and a new-
found sympathy for my graduate school colleagues who took incompletes
rather than finishing seminar papers—even toward those who couldn't
get their act together and received threatening "failure to progress toward
degree" letters from the Graduate Division. I know all about failure to progress now—the kind that no amount of pushing can overcome, and the kind
that imperceptibly, painfully inches forward. For that reason I prefer to
think of Jordan—and of my patched-together, part-time academic life—as
an outstanding incomplete, not a lapsed one—a work in progress, in fact.

Infinite Calculations

DELLA FENSTER

The airmail letter arrived five months after the birth of my third child. I had just begun a year-long leave of absence, ostensibly to adjust to motherhood in a family of five. I hoped to keep my research moving along by writing one short article that year, but that was the full extent of my professional plans. The letter with the Oberwolfach, Germany, postmark changed all of that for me.

"Upon the recommendation of the organizers," the letter from the director of the Mathematisches Forschungsinstitut Oberwolfach (MFO) began, "I am pleased to invite you to participate in a Number Theory conference at Oberwolfach." Designed to facilitate the crucial exchange of ideas between mathematicians, the MFO invites "leading representatives" of significant research areas from across the globe to meet for an intense week of discussion and interaction. I read the words once, then twice, even a third time, to make sure I actually held an invitation to this math institute I had only dreamed of visiting one day. But it had arrived at the most inopportune time in my career. I had a baby who depended primarily on my body for his physical sustenance, just as surely as I had a tenure case on the horizon that would benefit from a talk given at an Oberwolfach conference.

I had always claimed I would find a balance between my professional and personal lives. But what did balance mean when the predictable world of mathematics met the unpredictable world of children? Since the birth of my first child I had been defining and redefining *balance* constantly, depending on circumstances at home and at school. Over time, that balance seemed to hinge on sleepless nights more than anything else. What did balance mean now with three children, an upcoming tenure decision, and the professional opportunity of a lifetime? That confluence of events deserved some thought.

I started negotiating with myself that same day. I had ten months to prepare a talk. I could manage that. Casey, the baby, would have blown out
his first birthday candle a few months before the conference convened. I
could leave him for a week. I could even leave him for a week guiltlessly.
My husband could handle seven days with three kids. It might even be
"good for him."

I accepted the invitation. In the 279 days between the arrival of the invitation and the conference itself, I tended to an infant, his three-year-
old brother, and his first-grader sister. I invested the waning hours of the
night in my research. Ironically, the early-twentieth-century mathematician I study produced his best mathematics from 8:30 P.M. to 1:30 A.M.
Never mind that he had a wife to awaken the kids and send them off to
school the next morning. Or that he typically arrived at his office at 10:00
A.M. He and I had the night in common.

I finished my talk a week before I left. That left me with only one thing
to do before my departure: cry. So I did. I cried when I changed the baby's
diaper. I cried when I read to my three-year-old. I cried when I circled
around the car-pool loop. I cried when my husband carried my suitcase to
the car and the three kids clung to my neck.

And then I drove away.

I read a novel on the airplane. I watched a movie. Not *Thomas the Tank
Engine* or *Thumbelina*. No. I watched Hugh Grant and Julia Roberts in *Not-
ting Hill*. In fact, I watched it twice. When the flight attendant inquired
"Chicken or pasta?" I felt sure I had a tiara on my head.

Any lingering traces of guilt left me as the train rumbled along from
the airport in Frankfurt, Germany, to the tiny town of Wolfach. I had forgotten what it was like to travel with a book bag and without a diaper bag.
I ordered hot tea from the food cart and didn't worry about it spilling on
anyone. I put in lots of sugar, since no one was looking. I took in the Black
Forest landscape like I had as a college student sixteen years earlier.

I departed the train in Wolfach with one other passenger. He had a long
beard and tousled hair, sure signs of a mathematician. We rode in silence
to the institute. For reasons I cannot explain, many of the best math insti-
tutes in the world are located in stunningly beautiful areas, and Oberwolfach
is no exception. Situated halfway up a small mountain, the institute offered
an unparalleled opportunity for stillness and reflection, particularly for a
mother of three. With its Spartan decor of a bed, a desk, and a bedside
table, my room overlooked the lush, green valley below. As a first-time visitor to the institute, I was given a tour of the dining room, the wine closet,

and the chocolate cabinet. Mathematicians understand the quintessential aspects of life. The institute served three (gourmet) meals a day, along with tea at 4:00 P.M. and evening snacks at 10:00. It had been at least seven years since I had enjoyed this sort of quiet luxury.

Even so, the first twenty-four hours of the conference I felt anxious and uneasy. What was I doing here with all these "experts"? Why had I left my children halfway around the world to spend a week discussing mathematics? On Monday night, in one of the common areas specifically designed for conversation, I shared a bottle of wine with the conference organizers. On Tuesday, after my talk on how a historical study of number theory led to the proof of a significant result in pure mathematics, I began to feel more a part of the group. By Wednesday, I felt comfortable enough to ask questions and by Thursday, I offered my insights without reservation. On Saturday, I boarded the train back to Frankfurt with a tiny twinge of regret. The focused week of discussions had not only introduced me to an entirely new community of scholars and their ideas, but it had bolstered my confidence. I could hold my own on an international stage. I could even hold my own as a scholar with three children.

By tenure time, two years later, the Oberwolfach experience had led to invitations in Pisa and Vienna. I felt confident that my portfolio contained convincing evidence of an "international reputation." While my colleagues at the University of Richmond debated my tenure decision, I began pursuing the possibility of a sabbatical in Vienna.

I had first articulated the idea to my husband, Michael, at a candlelit dinner ostensibly celebrating our seventeenth anniversary. Much to my surprise, he met my proposition with several mouthfuls of silence. He was not at all enthusiastic. How could he possibly leave his academic position for six months or a year? We could only agree he would ask his dean and move forward from there.

A week later, Michael tentatively approached his dean. Much to his surprise, the dean did not let him finish his query. "Of course we will make this happen," the dean assured him. "This is a once-in-a-lifetime opportunity for you and your family." And so it was done. Or it had just begun.

Were we crazy or courageous? When the ball dropped in Times Square in 2005, we had three seasons of clothes for five people tucked in to seven suitcases and scholarly materials stashed in two. At the airport, my four-year-old's hands activated the sensor under the faucet in the bathroom. "It's a miracle," he celebrated. If he only knew. Shortly before dinner on New Year's Day, the five of us boarded an Airbus bound for Vienna.

We traded our house with its expansive yard for a glorified student apartment. If we had focused on the bare white walls, worn carpet, and tattered furniture, we would have headed back home. Instead, we delighted in the minuscule window in the apartment door with its own shutter for peeking out at a potential visitor and the red crescent moon that appeared above the door handle when the bathroom was occupied. The Austrian neighbor across the courtyard, who exercised in his boxer shorts in sub-zero temperatures, kept us entertained under the gray skies of winter.

We began to establish a rhythm in our lives. On weekday mornings, our "big kids," Hannah (eleven), and Colin (eight), traveled to bilingual schools via subway and train *on their own*. They discovered they liked independent living. My husband made his way to an office in the Geology Department at the University of Vienna via a neighborhood coffeehouse.

I walked hand in hand with our four-year-old, Casey, to a small school around the corner from our apartment. His teachers, Daniela and Doris, cared for Casey *and* me, exchanging a few minutes of conversation each morning about practical aspects of life in Vienna. They taught me about the essential ski underwear for children to survive an Austrian winter, the one bakery in Vienna open twenty-four hours a day, and the critical importance of fresh flowers on a regular basis. Daniela later admitted that they looked forward to teaching the "maths" professor some quotidian lesson each morning. Although nearly two decades separated us, Daniela and Doris quickly became my first women friends in Vienna.

I continued on toward the Erwin Schrödinger International Institute for Mathematical Physics (ESI) by way of the Anker bakery. Evaline patiently helped me find the right words to place my order every morning except Wednesdays (her day off). The walk up the Strudlhofstiege, an elegant outdoor staircase designed by the sculptor and painter Peter Strudel, brought an inspired focus to my morning even with a book bag and computer on my shoulder and ice beneath my feet.

At the top of the stairs, I walked to the first right, Boltzmanngasse, named after the Austrian physicist. I climbed seventy more stairs to the third floor of a sixteenth-century abbey, which gave way to the ESI. If I arrived early, I punched in the secret code—a certain prime number less than 10,000. My office overlooked the rooftops of the ninth district of Vienna and served as an impossibly perfect conduit for afternoon sun. The full-length chalkboards in the bathrooms reflected the overall emphasis on capturing original thoughts.

The ESI was an oasis for me. The physical setting alone encouraged the thoughtful atmosphere so essential to academic scholarship, particularly in mathematics. I no longer measured stillness in small portions parceled out throughout the day and, mostly, night. Instead, I came to savor stillness as part and parcel of my life in Vienna. A certain contemplative spirit returned to me in those months. I wrote professional manuscripts, I found new ideas with ease, and I filled pages of moleskins with personal and professional thoughts. I recaptured the life of the mind—until late afternoon and weekends. But that was enough.

We spent our weekends exploring the Austrian countryside and relaxing in thermal baths. We discovered we liked expansive pools of warm water with therapeutic bubbles. We found truffle torte and tea could cure just about any malady. Without a car, going anywhere—even the grocery, library, or pharmacy—quickly escalated to the status of an adventure.

All the while, of course, I gave considerable thought to my children and their Vienna experiences. Had this foray into the unknown asked too much of them? Shortly before we returned to the States, my daughter assuaged my concerns with one of those conversations you never plan and never forget. Since the summer sun set close to 10:00 P.M., Hannah went to bed at the equivalent of dusk. One night I found Hannah with her elbows propped up on her windowsill. The pink sky was just noticeable over the rooftops of a row of apartment buildings. Each building had its own jagged roofline that gave a definite shape to the nighttime sky. Hannah described her "favorite" neighbors inside various apartment windows. There was the woman who liked to read in a red chair, the family with children who ate at a counter like ours at home in Virginia, and the man who worked expansive puzzles on an equally expansive table. Her descriptions seemed to introduce me to characters in a novel, all bound together by their close living quarters.

As we cast our gaze out the window at these people we knew but had never met, Hannah made a query I will always remember. "Do you think you've helped women gain respect in mathematics?" she asked quietly, as easily as she would have asked if we could put milk on the grocery list. "I'm not sure if I've done that," I replied, "but I hope I've shown people you can be a thoughtful, attentive parent and a successful college professor at the same time." "Of course you've done that!" Hannah assured me.

There it was, a spontaneous evaluation I had not asked for, an evaluation that did not require seven binders of material to document and fifteen letters to support, an evaluation far more critical than the one that had made this windowsill conversation possible in the first place. In that single moment, the precarious balance I had carefully pursued for more than a decade overwhelmingly fell in my favor.

Now back in the classroom, in and among the mathematics, I continue to emphasize pursuing what you love and listening to the silent, inner voice that speaks to you in the more still moments of life. Only now, although I don't mention it to my students, I know that voice can whisper to you on windowsills in foreign countries when you least expect it.

I Stand Here Teaching

Tillie Olsen and Maternity in the Classroom

JULIA LISELLA

"I Stand Here Ironing," written in 1961, is Tillie Olsen's landmark story about the conflicted feelings of a mother who works outside the home and wonders, as she stands ironing her daughter's dress, what effect her crowded, overburdened life of scrambling to put food on the table has had on her talented but troubled daughter, Emily. I have taught this story in almost all my writing classes, and in some literature seminars, too. It could be said, I suppose, that teaching is half obsession, half stubborn determination, and it's hard to say how the halves differ very much. Though I find the story moving and fascinating, up until recently the story did very little to aid my teaching objectives. In a first-year writing class, that objective is, mainly, to spark provocative conversation, which in turn ought to spark strong writing. And yet, each semester as I doggedly presented the story, I was struck by how miserably the story failed to engage my students in class discussion. Why could I not find an inroad to my students and their writing by using it? Why did I feel so attached to it? And why did I keep teaching it? Over time, I've discovered that I could not let this story go because it held for me essential and intrinsic links to my work as a teacher, a scholar, a poet, and a mother, all roles I inhabit simultaneously, though at times begrudgingly, stingily favoring one over another in the classroom.

When I first read the story, as a college student, I related most to the daughter, Emily. I wanted to be Emily with all her pain and difficulty; I wanted, simply, to be part of Olsen's magic. I wanted someone's prayers to be with me that I might be "more than this dress on the ironing board, helpless before the iron," as Olsen's narrator prays in the final lines of the story. It might have been easy, too, to see the mother as my own mother. Like this narrator, my mother was shaped by Depression America. Like this narrator, my mother had had limited traditional education, and because, like

Olsen's narrator, my mother worked and kept house and relied on relatives
for child care, she too must have worried in an obsessive way about her
children and about her own mothering skills. But I rarely thought about
my mother while reading this story in college. What I related to, what I
really saw as the main character of the story, was the lyricism of the writing itself. The story's language engaged me, pulled me in, and it made me
want to be a writer, too, to be able to do that to someone else.

When it was my turn to play teacher, however, as a graduate student
teaching first-year writing courses, I forgot that I might not be faced with
a dozen future writers, but with students trying to place out of a second
term of expository writing by getting a decent grade and moving on. So in
all my naiveté, the first time I taught the story, I hadn't prepared much for
discussion; I was convinced that the power of the story would be sufficient
to keep the class lively and engaged. This speaks as much to my inexperience at that point as a teacher as to my own enthusiasm for Olsen. Perhaps,
I reflected later, it was difficult for my comfortably middle-class students
to relate to a story set during the hard times of the Depression. And even
the few working-class students in my class seemed embarrassed by Olsen's
use of poverty as an "excuse" for average parenting. Slightly more experienced as a teacher, I next taught the story against the backdrop of 1930s
Depression America; I discussed the role of the social worker in the lives
of the poor; I asked students to imagine Tillie Olsen's voice as a minority
voice in Nebraska; and so on. Still, I met with silence or with disregard for
the mother and impatience with the writing style, which some of my students described as undisciplined, fuzzy, too impressionistic. One student
felt I must have assigned it to demonstrate writing with no thesis.

So the next time I taught the story I came equipped with a question that
another, more experienced teacher had generously offered to me. He had
told me that a fascinating discussion ensued in his class around the idea of
whether the mother was a good mother. Hmm, I thought, this could spark
controversy; this idea could get to the heart of things. So I initiated the discussion (sometimes we writing teachers are willing to sell our souls for a
good discussion and an essay with a position). It was a starting place, but
it took us down an awful road. Whether the mother in the story is a good
mother or not is an argument that can only break down along partisan lines:
if you're a good liberal (like your teacher) you'll realize the narrator was
trapped by her circumstances; if you're conservative and believe the welfare
fraud arguments waged against poor people in this country you'll believe
this is a bad mother who can't make it on her own. Such a discussion was

a pedagogical dead end that led to many unbearably moralistic or simplistic student essays.

Despite my own misgivings, I stuck with this approach to the story because it entailed a question I believed required some level of analysis. Meanwhile, my personal situation was changing. In the spring of my last term of course work I was pregnant. Oddly, through some fluke of the registration system, my students were all women. So when I used this question about whether the mother was good or not, I felt some queasiness, some discomfort that I could not attribute to the pregnancy.

In fact, the most telling experience of teaching this story happened when I returned to teaching from maternity leave. My daughter was four months old. I left her with a babysitter. But my daughter had had stranger anxiety from the time she was three weeks old—something I was told was scientifically, developmentally impossible. The babysitter would arrive at 11:00; I would leave at 11:15 with my baby's small shrieking and howling following me down the stairs. She would cry until I returned at about 12:30. I had no babysitter for my prep time or grading, so I did all of that at night, along with some freelance proofreading and copyediting. I was exhausted most of the time, and grouchy, and, let me say it, angry. I was beginning to feel I *was* the mother in Tillie Olsen's story. There were times when I just had to leave my daughter crying in the crib and go into the next room and howl in despair. She had to be held—by me—constantly.

In my daughter's first year of life I taught, freelanced, and finished off two graduate course incompletes (which I had acquired while drugged up on terbutaline—a remedy for pre-labor contractions that makes your tummy calm but your heart race—and half mad from four months of bed rest!). I finally gave in to paying for twenty hours of day care a week so that I could cram a year's worth of studying into three months to pass my orals, slogging through one more century of British literature or literary theory. I always felt a one-to-one correlation between babysitters and work—if you're working, you ought to be earning money. And here I was, just studying. Lots of friends lectured me about the importance of finishing the degree, getting that PhD. And I wanted it, badly. But my roots were deep and thick in that relationship between work/labor and money. In retrospect, what a funny profession for me to have chosen—one in which there is no correlation between hours spent on an effort and the money awarded for it. At any rate, though Olsen and I were talking about different kinds of labor, and though during the early part of Emily's upbringing, Olsen's mother-narrator was single, there was no question in my mind that that harassed, guilt-ridden mother from the 1930s and I had a lot more in common than I had been owning up to. My parents may have left their working-class roots behind as they ventured out to the suburbs of Queens for more middle-class trappings, but I had inherited their working-class sensibilities. The thing that had made it possible for me to teach Olsen from the position of a self-satisfied, educated, middle-class reader had also allowed me to fool myself about the academic life in general: I could no more replicate the erudite-nineteenth-century-gentleman model of intellectual pursuit than I could hide the spit-up stains on my favorite teaching outfit.

And yet, for one more year of my daughter's young life, I continued to teach from a kind of untouchable class-less and perhaps even gender-less position, one I imagined as objective. I felt I had no claim or right to identify so closely with Olsen's narrator. She was a young mother. I was experienced and in my mid-thirties. She had a life of manual labor. I had the life of the intellect. She had to rely on social services. I had private help: first, seven hours a week from two lovely college girls, and then later, a family day-care center. The college students would look into my face as I returned home from teaching to say, "It wasn't too bad today, she stopped crying for fifteen minutes to take her bottle"; or "When we stood in front of the window she would only whimper instead of cry." The caretaker at the day-care center was someone I trusted, loved, and respected. So who was I to lay claim to this narrator's experience? And further, what use would it be to me as a teacher to say, "Yeah, me too, me too?" Hadn't I been taught that encouraging students to identify with a character without any analysis led to a literary stalemate? How could I, or to what end could I, use the same method to teach this story?

In class I would still dutifully ask the question, "Is the narrator of this story a good mother?" I listened, full of patience, to the arguments against her. In addition, I offered an introduction to the story that explained both Olsen's background as a leftist radical, a writer, and a mother, and the social and political backdrop of the 1930s and the realities of the Great Depression. I believed that arming my students with solid information about the struggles all working-class families faced at the time would make it more difficult for them to argue against the mother's decisions to have another child despite the difficulties of caring for the first and to leave her child in the care of the state for a brief time and with her husband's relatives another time. Rather than seeing the average single parent of the Depression era, who had to rely on less-than-perfect social services and limited family assistance, though, they still insisted on reading this narrator through the lens of their own present. This mother was the welfare mother their parents railed against at the dinner table, the woman who couldn't stop having children whether she had a husband or not. And certainly, Olsen did not make my job any easier. She does not humanize her narrator. The writing instead complicates this mother by infusing the story with her sense of guilt, which in turn infused my students' proud moral positions with authority. So though I was still asking them if she was a good or a bad mother, I would also sometimes mention that my own child, as we spoke, was being cared for by someone else. Did it matter to them? If I made that aspect of my mothering present did it make it harder for them, and for me, to judge this narrator?

One year into parenting, with my doctoral exam behind me, my confidence in my writing boosted by my selection of a dissertation topic, and all my incompletes completed, I approached the story anew. I had asked more students than I cared to think about whether the mother in Olsen's story was a good mother. My acumen as a reader, a teacher, and a parent seemed to be growing exponentially despite my loss of sleep and my tendency to cram my scholarship and prep time into those tiny lulls between my daughter's mini "power" naps and Playmobil rug play. I began to understand that whether the narrator is a good mother has as little to do with the story as controversy has to do with good writing. In fact, it was that tipsy daydream play between mothering, researching, reading, and writing that led me to my deeper feelings about that other question I always asked (and still do ask) my writing students, "What is good writing?"

Did I have to become a mother myself to teach this story or to understand it? I'm not sure. Such a theory would certainly counter all my poststructuralist theoretical training that railed against any kind of essentialist discourse: one need not be a woman to write in a woman's voice; one need not be white to write from a white perspective; one need not be a mother to understand Olsen's writing. My training, however, did not rail against experience; and what I had now as a teacher and a writer and a mother was experience. What else could I do but bring all I had of myself to my teaching? How else to reach my students but to bring the whole package of me to the classroom?

Many may argue against the poststructuralist theoretical practices English majors are currently mired in, but one thing such training brought us at the height of the 1990s was that the best way to know anything was to accept that it was fairly impossible to know anything. What we could bring to a discussion were good questions. Similarly, I have come to feel that the only way to teach writing is to teach students how to repeat their inner questions out loud, not to argue a controversial point, but to care about what they don't know or don't understand, to ask questions about what outrages them, or just bothers them, just a little. So when I teach Olsen's story now, I don't care to ask those questions anymore, who is good? who is bad? What do such questions mean in the scheme of things? And finally, how artfully Olsen's story itself frustrates and resists such reading performances! Olsen's narrator calls for one thing only, an audience to listen, to consider the difficulty of what she is trying to tell us about guilt, limitations, potential, power, writing. Now I try to teach to the difficulty of this story. "Whom is the narrator speaking to?" I ask. "Is the 'you' the same throughout the story? Does any aspect of the story resonate in your own life? Why or why not?"

There never would be a golden time for me, a time when I could sit alone to contemplate my literary studies and my writing. Class preparation, reading, writing, revising, research—for me they are all still done in a commotion between domestic tradeoffs with my husband, pickups, children's band concerts and dance performances, making lunches, quelling nightmare fears, cleaning up vomit. It is all work. It is all my life. And there aren't any excuses for what I have or haven't accomplished. The story Olsen tells, and learning to teach the story to my students, both replicates and honors my own struggles and the struggles most Americans face.

By the end of the story, the narrator's focus seems to change: the explanation of Emily's behavior to a hypothetical school counselor is replaced with a kind of prayer. It has always been a troubling shift to understand. The narrator seems in love with her own prayer/song/story/request and there is a connection between the words and their music that offers solace not to Emily, the possibly neglected daughter, but to the narrator, the mother. This is a very unmotherly gesture; indeed *Tell Me a Riddle,* the collection in which "I Stand Here Ironing" appears, is guided by a series of gentle revelations of unmotherly gestures. This is not something my students say or understand right off. But I do think they feel it, and it's an uncomfortable feeling. Being able to name this feeling is what has kept me connected to this story. Most critics like to note that during this narrative shift, the mother is no longer at the ironing board. She is at the desk. She is making this offering for the salvation of her own mind. That triumph isn't only about Emily. It's about language and survival; it's about how one can't have one without the other. As a young would-be writer, single and without children to care for or to complicate my feelings about this story,

I could appreciate one aspect of this narrative—its lyric pull and tug. But as a teacher now with children of my own, I enjoy listening to my students find their way through it. I like asking, finally, what they think the mother thinks of herself. Surely, some still reject this story or simply don't enjoy Olsen's writing. But others read the effort and have an interesting change of heart. They come to see the mother as working-class hero; the daughter as heiress of that frustration and hope. It is not just that writing triumphs, or that the writing individual survives; in fact, I like to sidestep that reading because most college students don't really understand the contested nature of writing. Instead, for me, what is important is that the narrator succumbs only to her own judgment—she was both good and bad at what she did, but nevertheless her children remained intact. Mothering itself survives the telling of truths about mothering. Could students relate to that; do they have the ability to tell truths about their own lives and survive the telling?

As I have unfolded the years it took me to allow my life experience to help me read and teach "I Stand Here Ironing," it has occurred to me how frightening it is to bring my whole self to my academic tasks—and how rewarding, too. Bringing one's whole self to the project of teaching seems essential. It's a long and difficult walk away from concepts of good and bad (good and bad mothering, good and bad literature, good and bad teaching) toward some more complicated picture that includes the grays, the distractions, the kinds of prayers that help break down my own and my students' silences and resistances. But ultimately, it's certainly a walk worth taking. I once read about a photographer who had a long-range photo project involving his son: he would place him in the same adult outfit every year and take a picture of him. Each year the child would fit more nearly into the outfit, until at his twenty-first birthday he fit into the outfit exactly right. It would be sheer delusion for me to suggest that my teaching style now fits perfectly into the arms and legs of "I Stand Here Ironing." No, I think we are all both the narrator, the one who believes we have the control and power to change things, and the daughter, the one who is both helpless like the dress before the iron, and somewhat evasive of and oblivious to such constrictions. But it is appropriate, I think, that I end this essay about teaching Tillie Olsen's complex and idiosyncratic story with the image of a parent trying to capture the growth and development of his child, even if only to reveal the surreal and comical edges of that story of parenting, of teaching, and of making art.

The Facts, the Stories

LEAH BRADSHAW

I am fifty-three years old. I have three children: Emma (twenty-two), Jacob (seventeen), and Lucy (thirteen). I have had two academic husbands, one with whom I had my two oldest children, and one with whom I had my youngest at the age of forty. I no longer have the husbands. They have moved on to new partners and more children. One of them left me with a five-year-old and a three-month-old baby. I left the other, taking three kids with me as I bolted at Christmas time, in the break between semesters. I have a PhD in political philosophy; I have had a teaching position (tenured) in a university for twenty years. I have an award-winning book, many articles, and a slew of conference papers. I have chaired my department, run national meetings, served on book juries, and done my time as a referee on manuscripts, tenure applications, and department reviews. I have been named three years in a row in a national magazine as one of my university's most popular professors. I have nursed a dying sister, younger than I. I own an old house in a working-class district of the city where I live, and I spend a lot of time foraging in other people's garbage for furniture that I scrape and paint in the colors of Mexico and southern France. I love high-heeled shoes and nail polish and red lipstick and I am widely known among my friends and acquaintances for my open-door hospitality.

Those are the facts. Here are some stories.

My first child is born in Toronto. I have just finished three years of full-time teaching in sessional appointments at a university in rural Quebec, while my husband was pursuing a PhD at another university. During those three years I filled in for three different sabbaticant professors, meaning that every course I taught was a new course. I was also writing my PhD thesis on Hannah Arendt, which I finished the year before my daughter was born. My pregnancy is unexpected, as my husband and I barely saw each other in our commuter marriage, and some quick planning has to be done. My husband finishes his comprehensive examinations, my sessional teaching train comes to a stop, and we move to Toronto with no jobs and a very pregnant me. We spend the summer fixing up an old apartment, and my daughter arrives in September, perfect and very, very loud.

Two things stick in my mind from the first few months of Emma's life. One, I am in a dreadful state of fear that I will never be able to read or write, or even think, again. My mind goes into a kind of amorphous sludge and I feel like an engorged piece of fruit. My postpartum, lactating body feels different to me, as if my skin is thinly stretched over a pulp that could burst at any moment. Scholarly work takes discipline, rigor, and a certain amount of ascetic remove, and the care of a child requires practically the opposite of these things: openness, flexibility, and porous affection. The birth of my first child absolutely shakes my academic resolve to the very core of my being. It is the first time in my life that I begin to seriously doubt the equality of the sexes. Everything about this experience, the bulging abdomen of pregnancy, the swollen breasts and enlarged nipples, the pain and mess of the birth itself, the post-birth leaking breasts, the bleeding uterus, and the small, warm bundle that is my daughter, seem to militate against my image of myself as a cerebral force. I had honestly never given much thought to my body before the birth of this child. I had been blessed with a smoothly functioning physical organism: no monthly cramps, small breasts, agile limbs. I had always experienced my body as a kind of vessel for carrying my mind and my desires. Pregnancy, birth, recovery, and nursing are mostly about the body and I can no longer treat it as a vehicle for larger aspirations. René Descartes's famous line, "I think, therefore I am," for the first time strikes me as absurd, as a line that could only have been penned by a man whose body has never harbored another life force.

The second thing that sticks with me is a memory of waking up in the living room of our apartment, on a cold November night. My daughter has developed colic, and the only thing that soothes her is latching on to the breast, so I spend hours and hours, day and night, sitting with a bare chest and stroking Emma's small blonde head. This particular November night, I wake up to find Emma and myself covered with a fine blanket of snow. The door has blown open and the two of us are so exhausted that we are not disturbed. I look down at my daughter and am dumbstruck at how much I love her. She has been in the world only two months, yet I feel a rush of love unlike *anything* I have ever felt before. I would die for her, I think, and I have never consciously thought that about anyone in my life. Years later I will still think about this revelation, and what it means about mothers. For someone who has spent her life devoted to inquiry into truth, justice, and beauty, the realization that I would throw over every-thing for twelve pounds of human existence whom I barely know, who can't speak, let alone make moral judgments . . . well, it comes as some-thing of a shock.

Emma is now twenty-two, in her final year of an undergraduate degree in philosophy and literature, living on her own in an inner-city slum with a bunch of other girls, and slinging beer and food to pay her tuition.

More stories. Unfortunately, the most vivid ones are horror stories. My son Jacob is born. He, like his older sister, is born perfect, and he does not have colic. This child is a planned child. I did manage to return to my scholarly work after Emma's arrival, and things have unfolded wonderfully (so I think). My husband has his PhD, my book is out, and we both have tenure-track jobs within reasonable commuting distance of the house we bought in an upscale neighborhood where lots of professionals border each other. My combination of research grant and sabbatical will allow me to stay home with my son for a year and a half. I am healthy and happy, and by the second go-round, I am content with my fecund condition, even rev-eling in it. Jacob is born just before Christmas, and five-year-old Emma is delighted with him. But his father appears to be depressed, and in March, when Jacob is three months old, announces sadly that he is leaving us, that he cannot do this anymore. He packs up and moves to a neighboring city, and I am left in the sprawling house (that I did not choose) with pitying neighbors, two kids, and a cat. On the upside, however, I have just secured a driving license, at the age of thirty-six.

It gets worse. When my son is nine months old, he develops a high fever and I am worried. A friend has just arrived for dinner, and I ask him to stay with my daughter briefly while I run Jacob to the hospital. The doctor on duty cannot find a location of infection and she is worried. She suspects meningitis, and her hunch is right. I am weeping with a grief so intense that I cannot speak, and I know that this is grief for all of us, my sick son, my failed marriage, and our botched lives. I spend the night in isolation with my baby boy attached to my breast, staring at the tubes running out of his head. I find myself praying, which for someone who has spent a lifetime sorting out the difference between reason and revelation, and who errs on the side of reason, is a new tactic. I am like Faust, pledging my fortune, my life for that of my son. The doctor stays all night and keeps coming in to reassure me. There is a good chance that Jacob will be brain-damaged, or deaf, or that he may even die, but none of these things happens. My son survives and thrives.

Now, Jacob is six foot three and a top-scoring basketball player.

Then there is child number three. After living on my own with Emma and Jacob for less than two years, I get married again, again to an academic, this time in my own department. He has had wives, but no children, and is desperate for progeny. I agree to have another child. Husband number two has spent much of his academic career floating back and forth across the Atlantic for his studies, so I ask that he stay close to home in our child's early years. After all, I am forty years old, and I have already borne and raised two children largely on my own, a lot to ask of any scholar and university teacher. I gain sixty-five pounds in this last pregnancy, and am so front heavy that I fall and break my ankle; I spend the next two months in a cast. We need a bigger house to accommodate two academics and three children, so we are moving. I find the perfect house, with three floors, the top floor being one vast open expanse sealed off from the rest of the house. This will be husband number two's study, where he will park his thousands of books, his numerous computers and telephones, away from the continuous din of domestic mayhem below. I will work at a desk on the open landing at the top of the staircase to the second floor, in clear view down the hall from the bedrooms of my three children. After we leave that house (this will be known afterward as the Christmas bolting), my youngest daughter will lament for months how she misses looking out from her dark room late at night and seeing me hunched over my books and papers.

When Lucy finally arrives, the day after her sister's ninth birthday, she emerges looking like a three-month-old, with fat rolls descending down her thighs and a head the size of a late autumn melon. Another year of breastfeeding. I should say that after the initial earthquake-type awakening I experienced with my firstborn, I came to love breastfeeding my babies. It awes me that the female body can sustain *two* lives. As I did with Emma and Jacob, I love the physical sensation of breastfeeding Lucy, the smell of her close to my skin, and the feeling of bloated satiation that comes over her as she drinks her fill and falls off the breast in sleep. This may be one of the few things that Jean-Jacques Rousseau got right: that the bond between mother and child may be the only *truly* natural bond among human beings because it is a bond cemented by mutual need. The mother seeks relief from a body engorged with milk, and the child seeks sustenance. It is a perfect pairing, and from this physical imperative grows a natural affection. It is not easy, though, to breastfeed infants and sustain an intellectual life at the same time. When I look back, I marvel at the dexterity and ingenuity required to balance these things. When Lucy is two months old, I have to deliver a conference paper, and I cut a sanitary napkin in half and plaster the two wads to my nipples so as to avoid large wet patches flowering out onto my blouse as I stand before my (mostly male) colleagues, holding forth on some phenomenological train of thought.

Lucy flourishes in infancy, but there are bouts of croup, long nights in the bathroom with the door closed and the hot water on full blast, followed by the two of us with our heads plunged in the freezer. Once, I call an ambulance because she is turning blue. I have had three children, and I absolutely know that I cannot manage this one on my own. Lucy and I spend two days and nights in the hospital with her in an oxygen tent, and on the way back home I am so exhausted that, stopping for gas, I drive straight into a concrete pylon and implode the side of my van. When Lucy is three, husband number two is offered a two-year government position over six thousand miles away from our home. He accepts, and I spend the next two years traveling back and forth to see him, sometimes with all three children, sometimes with two, sometimes with just Lucy. End to end, the flight takes twenty-three hours, with a five-hour stopover. Forty-six hours of air time (return calculated here) requires a lot of juice boxes, coloring books, dollar-store plastic toys, and changes of clothes. Not to speak of all the immunizations with which I had to shoot up my kids before our departures. People say to me "what a wonderful experience for your children," and these are invariably people without small children. When we rendezvous with husband number two, I move into the role of diplomatic wife, and am expected to turn up at interminable banquets with three well-turned-out and impeccably behaved children who eat the food. Once I get up from the banquet table with my seriously stressed son and move him to a corner of the room where I build him a cave out of chairs and coats and let him retire for the remainder of the evening.

During the time that husband number two is away, I become chair of my department. The husband returns in the summer, my younger sister is dying of ovarian cancer, and the husband is away eight weekends between September and December. I count them. He informs me that he is leaving again as soon as his lectures are over in early December, and will be back Christmas Eve. Even though we are not zealous Christians, we celebrate the holiday and that means that presents have to be purchased and wrapped, three kids have concerts and end-of-the-year parties, teachers have to be given gifts, relatives have to be visited. Also, there are exams and papers to be marked and course preparations to think about for the next term, plus administrative duties as department chair. When husband number two leaves, I am reading the local paper one morning and my eyes fall upon an advertisement. Four-bedroom house for rent. In my neighborhood. I call my oldest daughter at her school (she is fifteen at the time), and we agree immediately on the move. I rent the house, I call the movers, and we are out. I pack up the kids and what is mine and just leave. Three weeks later my sister, my best friend, dies. Lucy thinks that her aunt has become an angel and claims that my sister now visits her.

Lucy is thirteen, beautiful and ethereal now, bearing little resemblance to her infant corpulence.

I tell these stories to give a real sense of what my life as an academic mother has been like. I look back at these years in my thirties and forties, typically the time when one builds a career, establishes a reputation, and solidifies one's scholarly sense of self. Instead, I see a random patchwork of crises, readjustments, and regrouping. The birth of each child is a mountain in this landscape. Whatever else I may do in my life, especially as a scholar and a writer, I know that my first job is to keep the kids alive and love them. I *am* a mother. There is no choice about that now, and the irretrievability of unencumbered freedom has been an unanticipated gift.

I think a lot about varying kinds of attachments—erotic, filial, familial, friendly—and I write about them too. It is hard when you have made a life of studying political philosophy to get away from the thread first spun by Plato in the *Symposium* that the highest attachments are those of shared intellectual virtue. In the crowning speech of that dialogue, Diotima (a goddess) proclaims that the best life is one that leaves behind the imperfection of corporal bodies and beholds ideas in their pure, uncorrupted state. As a woman who both loves ideas and has borne children, I cannot accept this. Grappling with the foundations of Western philosophy in this mind/ body tension has become, over the last decade, the principal focus in my academic work. I have written about varying accounts of love in the Western tradition, on early modern constructions of the divided female, on the relationship between emotions and reasons in making judgments, and on tyranny and the womanish soul. I am trying to understand myself as someone who loves philosophy, and her children.

Fierce loves compete for one's loyalty, and I see no way out of the tension that characterizes the life of a woman who feels these twin passions. We are, as Aristotle says, a combination of what we are given by nature, the way in which we are habituated, and what we choose. I try to remember this, even though the insurmountability of the combination sometimes discourages me. I chose to pursue an academic career and to have three children. I love clothes and I cook and sew, I read voraciously and write, and I am a mother. My life is messy and highly unprofessional, and I am a scholar. If someone were to ask me point blank who I am, I would have to say all these things. I am a woman. I am a mother. I am a scholar.

I Am Not a Head on a Stick

On Being a Teacher and a Doctor and a Mommy

ELISABETH ROSE GRUNER

I walked into the history professor's office with my two-and-a-half-year-old on my hip and the signature page in my hand. My dissertation was done. The history professor was the last to sign off.

I'd first met this professor three years earlier, when I was six months pregnant, and about to take my orals. My director had recommended her for the fifth person on the exam committee so I had given her a prospectus to read, but I'm not sure we'd really met before the exam itself. I had, however, had a dream about her. In it my qualifying exam had turned, improbably, into a garden party. We all wore floral dresses and hats. My director was grilling me over the cucumber sandwiches and the history professor came to my defense. I awoke from the dream bemused by the images—the hats! the dresses!—and looking forward to meeting my imagined savior.

The actual exam didn't go quite like that, but she had been pleasant. My committee comprised four women and one man, and everyone in the room was a parent except my female director. They gave me a break halfway through, in deference to my "delicate condition." They asked tough questions, but I passed, and then I went on dissertation fellowship. About six weeks later I had my appendix out—not a surgery one looks for, seven months pregnant—and my daughter was born uneventfully right after Christmas.

I'd been surprised when the history professor volunteered to be my outside reader, since I'd never met her before my orals. I don't recall running chapters by her along the way, though it's possible I did. I wrote the first one through my daughter's colic, the others in whatever time I could afford to pay a sitter. After that first-year dissertation fellowship—"the best maternity leave in the state," a fellow grad student called it—I had gone back to trying to write through my teaching assistantship, around the baby's nap time, sending chapters to a director who had taken a job across the country. Frankly, those three years are a blur; photos prove that we held birthday parties for our daughter, enrolled her in preschool, occasionally had dinner with friends, but it's hard to remember many details other than an overwhelming sense of never, not once, being quite ready for anything.

And now here I was in the history professor's office. I was a bit flustered; it felt unprofessional to bring my daughter with me to gather this last signature. But we'd had a babysitting breakdown so I was on my own with my daughter for the day. As usual, I'd forgotten to bring along any toys, crayons, paper—any of the useful entertainment that some mothers seem naturally to carry with them everywhere. Once we'd passed the toilet-training milestone and ditched the diaper bag, I traveled light—often too light. Knowing I had a pretty limited window of good behavior, then, I thrust the paper toward the history professor for her signature. But she looked straight at my daughter.

"Do you know what your mommy's doing today?" she asked. My daughter shook her head. "Your mommy's doing something very important," she said. "She's finished a big piece of work. You should be very proud of her. She's a doctor now." She made sure my daughter heard her, looking into her blue eyes and ignoring the paper I still awkwardly held. Finally, when she knew she'd gotten through, she signed my page and congratulated me. As we left the office, though, Mariah objected to my professor's words: "You're not a doctor, you're a mommy." So I reminded her that I was already a teacher, and that people could be more than one thing. For months afterward, when my husband and I asked my daughter what she wanted to be when she grew up, she'd answer, "A teacher and a doctor and a mommy," that being the formulation that made sense to her.

I think that may be the best moment I've ever had in trying to balance academe and family: baby on my hip, signature page in my hand. Friends of mine without kids thought balancing school and family would be easy: "Can't you just put the baby in the Snugli while you teach?" But that never worked for me. Books and babies stopped mixing for me just about the time of my oral exams, in fact; my daughter, still in utero, used to kick books off my belly when I'd rest them there to read. My husband and I joked that she knew they were competition. Maybe it wasn't a joke.

I've often wondered why it was the history professor who was able to make that connection to my daughter, to engage her at that moment and make me feel as if the two halves of my life really did come together. Maybe it's because of the field she's in: historians, after all, know the importance of bodies in the world. While literature professors can often lose themselves in the abstractions of language (and at many times during my life as a parent that's been an appealing possibility), historians always know there's something outside the text, even if (as so often happens in contemporary historiography) it's a shadowy figure best represented by yet another text. By bringing my daughter with me that day, I made my own body visible, my own life a (tenuously) unified whole. There she was, unignorable evidence that I'd had other things than my dissertation on my mind for the past three years. For whatever reason, this historian made a connection that I've spent much of the rest of my career trying to get back to.

After I finished my degree I took a one-year lectureship in my department, and the following year began a tenure-track job. And for the next few years I did my best to be that bodiless intellectual the academy seemed to want while also balancing the demands of a husband finishing his dissertation and a daughter making an awkward transition to a new child-care situation. My schedule was relatively flexible, my pay was more than adequate, and I was encouraged to explore new areas of intellectual interest while consolidating the work I'd done in graduate school. I even had colleagues with children—it began to seem that I wasn't alone in the world, that some kind of balance was possible.

And it was possible, of course, but it was damned hard. Every day I could see things that could be better, and isn't that seeing what becoming an academic is all about? I entered the academy because it was a place I could see myself growing old, reading and writing books, teaching students, changing the world—albeit incrementally. Well, I'm an Episcopalian: the only kind of change I really believe in is incremental. Even I have been impatient, though; the change has been slower than I like.

While there are certainly more women in the profession now than when I started my graduate program (when I counted only seven women among the ranks of the seventy-plus tenured and tenure-track faculty in my department), and there must be more parents as well, I don't see the academy shifting to accommodate them in anything like the ways that some sectors of corporate America have been making the change. Work part time? Lengthen the tenure clock? Shift responsibilities during busy periods? Institute on-site child care, breaks for nursing mothers, subsidized child care, flextime for new parents? Outside the academy and the tenure system, these are the kinds of accommodations that some workplaces have been able to make; mine, like many other universities, has not. This goes back to the problem of minds and bodies: we are, after all, valued for our particular expertise, our particular knowledge—our own particular minds. This makes it hard for us to imagine that anyone else could fill in for us, that we could share a job, that we are, in fact, not uniquely indispensable. Doctors, lawyers, and accountants, too, are valued for their knowledge and expertise; yet I know lawyers who job share, doctors whose office hours always end before school pickup time, accountants who work part time from home. The academy, bound by tradition and, it must be said, oversupplied with qualified workers, has been slower to come up with innovative acknowledgments of the fact that minds are inextricable from bodies.

Amy Hudock notes in her essay for this anthology that academics who are also mothers are required to "perform childlessness" on the job, and that's something I've never been willing—or, indeed, able—to do. When I announced my second pregnancy to the chair of my department, he blanched visibly, doing all he could to keep from staring at my already-prominent belly. Then he told me the story of a female colleague who had hidden two pregnancies, timing them so each child was born during the summer, returning to work (with a two-hour commute) the following fall. Maybe he didn't mean it to be, but the story felt like a rebuke. Why hadn't I planned better, figured out a way that he wouldn't have to deal with me and my baby? We joked, my husband and I, that what he really wanted in the classroom was a head on a stick, a bodiless intellectual who could simply perform as required in the classroom. I couldn't do it. My child would be born late enough in the summer that I'd need some maternity leave before I returned to teaching. The university complied with, indeed surpassed, the Family and Medical Leave Act by offering six weeks *with* pay—which meant that I would return to work three weeks into the semester, brain dead and sleep deprived. I remember little from that fall other than the constant fear that I'd forget to lock my office door while pumping. I'm pretty sure my student evaluations tanked. In addition to a newborn, after all, we had a seven-year-old at home, who was making the transition to older-siblinghood with little grace and serious sleep problems. While my second born was a relatively "easy" baby, no amount of ease compensates for disrupted sleep and the pure physical exhaustion of new motherhood and the early days of nursing.

So why didn't I just take the semester off without pay? That was the other option my university offered, after all. Put simply, I couldn't afford to. My husband, who had already given up his aspirations to a full-fledged academic career when we moved for my job with a three-year-old in tow, was out of work and my income paid the mortgage. The fact that he was out of work, of course, meant that we could sidestep the child-care issue for the first few months: he stayed home, taking our daughter to school in the mornings and picking her up in the afternoons, the newborn strapped onto his chest like a baby monkey. That's right: in the early days of parenting (and many other times) I had a "traditional wife," but one who knew how to change the oil and put up drywall, too. His career sacrifice enabled my success, and I profoundly regret the loss to both him and the academy, even as I am grateful for the benefits that accrued to me.

It wasn't easy. We often wondered if we should have done it differently: chosen different fields, found my husband a job before I got pregnant, prepared our daughter better? In the end, though, I wanted my job to accommodate me, to recognize that I was an asset even with—indeed especially with—two children.

As a mother I have finished a dissertation; found an academic job; written academic articles; and coedited an academic journal. Like many of my colleagues, I have also chaired committees, written reports, served on endless boards, committees, commissions, subcommittees, and the like. I've taught roughly one thousand students. Along the way, I've earned tenure.

In addition to the baseline requirements of my position, however, I've added two subspecialties to my teaching that arise directly out of parenting: children's literature and creative nonfiction writing, a genre I discovered first in Anne Lamott's *Operating Instructions*. I've combined my academic work with community service, serving on a church vestry and the board of a nonprofit child-care center; and involved my students in service learning as volunteers at local elementary schools. I've written in my specialty of children's literature for a nonacademic audience. And I've mentored students, many of whom have either seen me pregnant or met my children, and who want to know how they, too, can "have it all." While I might have done some of those things without children—and while I might also have been able to add to the list "written an academic book"—I couldn't have, wouldn't have, done the rest. And wouldn't that have been a loss to the profession, to the institution? No one within the profession has ever said so, but I believe it's true. For the university to matter in this day of outcome-based education and ever-heightened expectations for career preparation, we have to be able to speak to those outside our discipline, demonstrate our value to the community at large, and provide a model for our students, both those who will become academics and the far greater number who won't.

So how do we do it? How do we maintain balance, change the world, raise our children, and do our jobs? The changes I listed above, having to do with flexible work, on-site child care, and the like, would be a start. But even more than that, I want us to refuse to "perform childlessness," to make visible the strains and the costs of our striving for balance as we also insist on the centrality of our families to our work.

For me, that's not always terribly hard. As a children's literature specialist (again, not my graduate training) my status as a parent is a plus. I can (and do) bring in "experts"—my own children—to my classes, refer to their reading, demonstrate to my students the ways in which at least two real children respond to the books they are struggling with. (As struggle they do.) But I need to do more, and so do those of us who cannot always make visible the benefits, not just the costs, of their parenthood to their work. What of my medievalist colleague, for example? How has her work shifted since having children? Can she say? Do we know? What of the social scientist whose research may have slowed down, but who is researching the relationship between day-care provider attitudes and success with breast-feeding? What of the scientist whose lab time is limited but who is still active in her research? And in all this, I want fathers, noncustodial parents, adoptive parents, same-sex parents to reattach their heads to their bodies, too, to be acknowledged as whole people. It's far more acceptable for me, a woman who specializes in children's literature—a traditionally female ghetto—to make these kinds of claims than for men in the hard sciences, or gay parents, single mothers, and a whole variety of others. No one would admit to expecting me to "perform childlessness," though they might prefer it if I would; it would make their lives easier. But I refuse to schedule a meeting late in the day, because I need to do the after-school pickup. Not every university, or every department, would accommodate even that.

My children are now seventeen and ten. They can't remember a time when I wasn't "a teacher and a doctor and a mommy," and though they at times resent all three roles, this is the life they know. It's the life I know, too, and while I want to change it almost daily, I don't want to give it up. I want to fight, though, to have it acknowledged for what it is: a whole life, a life of both the mind and the body. So that no one expects them, or anyone else, to be a head on a stick.

Lip Service

JENNIFER COGNARD-BLACK

When I'm at dinner or out for drinks with colleagues, I sometimes joke that my daughter has been orphaned by my profession. It's a line I picked up from one of my students, a young man named Toby—a student who has the odd distinction of having taken me for seven separate courses (he started college-level work when still in high school), who is the youngest son of my department chair, and who, like me, is the product of two academic parents—that rare and aw(e)ful upbringing. Once, when Toby and I met to discuss his senior project, we got distracted and started talking about what it was like to grow up in a houseful of PhDs—about playing "grading" with our siblings (I gave my younger sister As or Fs on her doodles, depending on if I liked them), about learning to drink coffee with lots of sugar and fake cream (all that was available in our parents' offices), and about whooping or skulking through the halls of various college buildings, waiting for Mom or Dad to finish up with a student. At some point, Toby said, "Yeah. I was orphaned by the profession, man. I raised myself." And though he continued, teasing about how he'd carefully learned to avoid using "lay," "lie," "laid," or "lain" in any sentence (another thing we have in common: both sets of parents are English professors), I was too struck with what he'd just said to hear much else. Without meaning to, Toby had just laid (he would say "put") his finger on my own heart's bruising: this tender belief that my own commitment to the profession has forsaken my daughter.

Yet to say that my daughter Katharine has been orphaned by my profession is, frankly, a line out of a pull-on-the-heartstrings Hollywood tragedy— a line that takes the responsibility off my own shoulders and blames, instead, my line of work. If I am honest in the telling, I must write that my daughter has been orphaned by me—by my own choices.

Ask me what the most important thing in my life is, and I'll tell you that it's Katharine. Every night when I kiss her—even if she's already asleep when I get home—I rub my nose in her hair, smell her weedy, warm, little-girl smell and whisper that I love her more than anything. It is my ritual. But take an inventory of my days, my weeks, get inside my head and see how I'm consumed with what needs to happen next—with the papers I need to grade, the novel I need to read, the manuscript I need to edit, the colleague I need to have lunch with—and it's clear that the most important thing in my life is an ongoing mental tally. My work, my work work work. It's clear that putting my family before my work is just lip service—lip service I pay to a version of myself that I project to others. And this version of myself is one I cherish as any reader and writer of fiction cherishes one of her favorite characters. (There's a Web site where a reader can take a quiz and be told which nineteenth-century heroine she most resembles. I'm Anna Karenina: passionate, articulate, taciturn, tragic.)

Lip service—it's an odd phrase. A service is, simultaneously, a ceremony, an examination, a good turn. Funeral service. Escort service. Full-service gas station. To be of service. As a verb, service is synonymous with examine, tune, check, overhaul, and repair, although the Latin suggests a harsher and more candid origin, *servitium* from *servus* or "slave"—the condition of serving, of being a servant. In English, the word has evolved to connote complex and sometimes contradictory meanings. Its tone is devout or reverent (God's service, divine service, a marriage service) but also crass, wanton (to service someone sexually). One can perform a public service, join the Secret Service (or just the Service), polish a tea service, tune in to a broadcasting service, or work in the service sector. A broken ATM is out of service; a landscaping bill is for services rendered; and a plucky or semi-sarcastic restaurant "server" might comment that she is "at your service."

Lip service, then, is the service of lips—the lips wait on, work for, or serve up something for their owner or for others; the lips perform their duties by forming words, by being licked or by smacking loud, or (if lower) by being bit and (if upper) by keeping stiff. And since *lip* is a word that also contains multiple meanings—it is simultaneously an edge and an impudence, an organ of both speech and birth—this saying (perhaps) suggests more than words that cross the mouth but duck the heart. Perhaps lip service might mean something more than false sentiment, a politician's pledge, a mother's wish.

In an English department of thirteen, I am the only female faculty member with a child. In the Arts and Letters Division encompassing five distinct disciplines, I am one of only four women with children. And while my college (small, public, liberal arts) has hired more women in recent years for tenure-track appointments—one might say the college has used the lips of its PR office to insist the school is servicing the gender gap—a significant number don't have children, don't want children, and some wish to remain single. Moreover—and I must admit that I'm about to give a little lip, to be a little lippy—although my college is fastened to a shoreline in southern Maryland (and thus is both beautiful and remote), it offers no campus child care; there is an explicit policy that states faculty are not supposed to hire students to take care of their children on campus grounds ("liability"); faculty and department meetings are routinely held over the dinner hour; and the maternity leave, well, it leaves much to be desired. The assumption here is clear: a faculty member has someone at home to take care of any dependents. Yet, nationally speaking (and sans data for same sex couples), there are still only about a million stay-at-home dads in the United States—which means that my college is also assuming something else: that faculty are men with wives to rear their kids.

But my college is not wholly to blame. Of my closest female friends in graduate school—who have all subsequently had children—only two of us have stuck it out: finished the dissertation, taken the tenure-track job. The others never graduated or are now, themselves, "nonworking mothers." Academia just isn't an appealing place for moms: the hours are too long, the demand to publish too great, the need to professionalize too overwhelming. Our jobs are really three in one, after all: we teach; we are expected to be active in our fields; and we must contribute as invested campus citizens—and in addition to all that, we're also expected to come to our work as a vocation, as a calling (not as a "job"). Last spring, at a Teaching and Learning lunch I attended on living a more committed life, I was told by three senior faculty members to "just say yes." Just say "yes" when asked to chair a committee, organize a reading, write a letter of recommendation, participate in a student-run conference. Just say "yes" to attending music and theater and sports events. Just say "yes" to mentoring yet another one-on-one, year-long senior project, to being yet another club advisor, to writing yet another article for a campus publication. In other words, just say "yes" to forever blurring the boundaries between work and family, work and self.

But saying "yes" in this context smacks of giving mere lip service to living a committed (campus) life—to be a yes-woman is to wear a coat of many-colored caricatures: Cool Teacher; Smart Scholar; All-Around-Good-Gal. A committed life would be, in my definition, a life lived ever aware that we are food for worms—that what we humans have in common is the vacant skull, those eyes starved wide, all that will remain of us after death.

In *Dead Poets Society*, a movie that has been accused of being nothing more than piously uttered platitudes in "service" of a sentimental Hollywood tragedy—and yet a film no English teacher I know of fully accepts as fiction—Robin Williams's character, Mr. Keating, urges his students to seize the day, boys, carpe diem. Mr. Keating's definition of a committed life is to sound one's barbaric yawp over the roofs of the world, to contain multitudes, to suck the marrow out of life (he borrows his best lines from Whitman and Thoreau). In other words, Mr. Keating wants to teach these boys to say "yes" to life—but it's not a "yes" that exchanges selfhood for service (in the most limited sense of service, that condition of slavery). It's a "yes" that considers the magical and precious service one's lips might offer: lips that speak true words, that are vulnerable, that kiss in tenderness, that bear a baby. Saying "yes" to a lived life, a life of full presence and attention, is belied when the "yes" comes after a question to spend more time away from the ones we love, more time away from the tasks we see as joy rather than duty.

Over the past eight years, I have been a yes-woman of the worst kind. In the same month I had a positive pregnancy test, I began the second chapter of my dissertation. Thereafter, as my belly grew and my fingers moved further and further away from the keyboard—as my internal due date forced me to defend my thesis earlier than I had intended—Katharine took a backseat to my work: I didn't sleep as much or exercise or eat as well as I should have. Even on the day I gave birth, I cranked out just under forty job applications before driving to the hospital. And I gave up breastfeeding too early so that I could attend the Modern Language Association conference without having to pump between my job interviews.

From the first, people marveled, called me a supermom. I'd finished a dissertation on Victorian women writers in just nine months; I'd successfully defended that dissertation exactly two weeks before I gave birth; I went on the job market—applying for eighty-eight academic positions—in the first two months of Katharine's life; I did six on-campus interviews before Katharine was six months old; and I landed a tenure-track job in English at an excellent liberal arts college. Since then I've coauthored a textbook; coedited a collection of letters; published my dissertation as a monograph; placed six short stories, two articles, and four encyclopedia entries; taught nine new courses; taken students to England twice; won two teaching awards; received a junior faculty research award; obtained four additional grants to support my work; chaired a collegewide committee; hosted seven visiting writers; presented ten talks and conference papers; and been given the Student-Life Award for committed teaching and supportive mentorship. As this "service record" suggests, I've spent the past few years measuring, measuring—tallying myself up. It's not even mathematics, the elegance of numbers over lines or numbers against lines—a numerical stretch toward eternity. My list is just a tally, hash marks, the work of a stick in the dirt or a pen to a napkin—a slim language of pettiness and doubt. And, of course, my sum has been added up in the expected way: this past spring I got tenure and am now on my first sabbatical, writing my first novel. I am the tally's aggregate: well liked by colleagues, popular with students, and considered productive by members of my discipline. To those who don't know me well, I'm amicable, admired, responsible, and hardworking: almost a nineteenth-century character, a Jane Eyre of the ivory tower—a poster-child for my institution as well as, I worry, other junior faculty members' basic nightmare.

But this service record merely constitutes the qualities of the me on the CV, on the English Department Web site, on ratemyprofessor.com. The actual me is often a wreck—insecure, driven by fears of rejection and disapproval. I don't need Dr. Phil to tell me that I'm a workaholic, that I suffer from a classic case of the Imposter Syndrome—that feeling many academic women have of being not quite/not right, not a true master of their material. The actual me is often a slipshod parent, a partial partner, an inconsistent friend, an absent family member. In the same years that I've made all those lines on my CV, I've also missed being there in the room for Katharine's first word ("book," not a surprise—I'd planted it); being there when she took her first step; being there when she had a temperature of 104 degrees and had to go to the hospital. I've missed taking her to the county fair, to the pumpkin patch field trips, to architectural workshops for kids in Washington, D.C., or to an outdoor Artsfest held each autumn close to the college. I haven't helped Katharine with her homework, haven't picked her up from school; and, most days, I haven't bathed her, brushed her teeth, or put her to bed. Instead, my spouse—initially a stay-at-home, dissertating dad and now an administrator at my college—has borne the brunt of raising our child, of enabling my mania. (Katharine's name for her father is "Madaddy.") And even beyond neglecting Katharine, I've missed flying back home to Nebraska to attend both of my nephews' first birthday parties; I've been in and out of my younger (and only) sibling's life, often making her feel like someone who occupies my heart's margin; I'm currently estranged from the woman who has been my closest friend in my department (I wasn't there for her when she most needed me); and I've slowly disconnected from my spouse—after fourteen years of marriage, we have almost entirely separate lives now, lives driven and dictated by this demanding schedule that I, myself, have created.

At that Teaching and Learning lunch last spring, after we'd all been encouraged to become yes-folk, a young colleague of mine from Education called across the room to me. "Jennifer—I want to hear from Jennifer. She's a mom; she's a great teacher; she's successful; she's published all those books. How do you do it? How? I want to know your secret." It was a terrible moment; without meaning to, this woman (a new mother herself) asked me to strike solace from rock—from my own heart's waste. Tears cornered my eyes. How could I explain the dry ticks that marked my career, marked the time spent away from my daughter? I said, "Oh, Angela. When I'm at work, I feel guilty about not being with Kate. When I'm with Kate, I worry about the work I'm not getting done. I have nothing to offer you. No wisdom. Nothing at all." A few heads nodded; most faces turned away; they'd glimpsed that honest bone, the shape of my skull. The leader of the session said, "Thank you for your honesty, Jennifer," and the conversation moved to a lack of day-care options on or around campus, moved away from this moment when I might have serviced my lips to tell more truths.

For I'd like to put my lips to real service. I'd like to repair some of the damage I've done with my mouth's raw wound: that there is a part of me that doesn't know who she will be if she's not praised for being a super-mom, a super teacher, a super writer, a super colleague, a superwoman. I like those labels. That I don't always know how to be around Katharine—I'm not easy with children; it's not innate. That I take my spouse for granted, have built my career on his patient, broad back. That I won't have another child because I'm too selfish—I want to write this novel I'm working on; I want to travel the world wide; I want to sleep through the night for the rest of my nights. That I fear the frost-thickness of my own heart, how cold I can be to others and their private pain. That I judge others, too, with my absinthe eye. And that I want to make Katharine the most important thing in my life—I want it as I crave sky's color at twilight, as I need to believe in love and in souls—but that I don't know how.

I do not have the slightest idea how to live each day with Katharine at its center.

And yet if I am to tell the full truth, I must also acknowledge that my choices are even more complex—for they are the direct result of trying to live beyond mere lip service to personal politics. I am an English professor, but I am also an active member of my college's Women, Gender, and Sexuality Program. In part, I fell in love with my spouse, Andrew, because he was the one man I'd met who wanted to turn gender on its ear. He and I took each other's last names when we got married (a real headache for him, especially with the Selective Service, an institution that didn't want to select the service of a man who would change his name through marriage). Andrew has never minded that I'm the primary breadwinner, the career woman, the one who brings home more of the bacon and is often too tired to fry it up in the pan. And he cherishes the time he spends at home with our daughter, even though he cringes each time another parent calls him "Mr. Mom" at the playground. Andrew provides me and Katharine a genuine service, a selfless service: he has rescued Katharine from being an orphan, and he repairs me—my spirit—almost daily. Support incarnate.

And so I end with this beginning: I use my lips (via my fingers) to ask a question. Is a child deprived if she is raised primarily by her father, or is it the mother who deprives herself by choosing service over lips? For it is my lips that serve my heart, and when I don't press them to my daughter's head—when I don't make the time to do that enough—I have only the memory of having done so, a mental record of previous miracles. The miracle of my body holding hers becomes a book of faith. And just as the Christian must have faith in miracles through the symbolic record of them, the written memory, I must have faith in my love for Katharine, in her love for me—a love that is both transcendent and everyday beauty. My memory of that love—my record of it—is whether it exists, whether it will continue to exist. And I service myself, my lips, to keep it in existence, to keep it alive. Living. Present. Now.

Body Double

LESLIE LEYLAND FIELDS

8:55 A.M. I stand in the front of the classroom, dressed in a navy skirt, maroon blouse, low navy heels. My hair is freshly washed and styled, my face bright with lipstick. I am waiting for my students to arrive.

"Hi, Mark, hi, Ivan. Come on in. You guys had your coffee yet? There's some over in the corner," I smile, gesturing toward the coffee as if I've been here for hours, serenely doing teacherly things, waiting only for them, my life not beginning until they walk in the door. I pull out the handouts for this morning's class, a week-long intensive seminar titled "Professional Science Writing," with biologists, regional supervisors, and statisticians as my students.

The first class had gone well. I was confident. The students were sharp and funny and appreciative. Now I line up the handouts, twelve to get us through four hours. Everyone is sitting down, in three rows of five or six, each one here in this classroom instead of their cubicle at work because I am going to improve their writing. I am going to lead them through the rationale of science writing, based on its distinct epistemology; I am going to elucidate the obscurities behind science texts, lead them in critiquing reports and studies, and design a rubric with them to edit and critique their own work. That is the plan for the day. My hands shake.

Less than an hour before, I had presided over an entirely different scene.

I am standing in the kitchen throwing sandwiches into lunch bags, looking anxiously at my watch. The babysitter is late. Elisha, seven, comes up beside me and thumps my leg. "You forgot to listen to me read last night, Mom. Can I read to you now?"

"Sure, go ahead. Even if I'm not here, just keep going. I'm still listening."

Isaac, nine, yells, "Anyone seen my shoes?"

Noah, eleven, emerges from his room. "Sign my planner, Mom."

"Fred . . . gets . . . a . . . duck." Are you listening, Mom?"

"Fred buys a dog, yes, go ahead," I call behind me as I retrieve Abraham, fourteen months, stuck between the steps to the living room. His diaper is soaked through.

Naphtali, thirteen, runs down the stairs. "Don't forget I've got piano right after school, Mom. Please don't be late!"

I decide to skip the diaper change, run back for a look in the mirror, frown, pull another layer of red across my lips, head down the stairs, check the window—the babysitter is still not here. I scoop up Abraham on the way out the door.

"I don't have any shoes!" Isaac shouts at me as I speed past.

"Then go barefoot," I shoot back. He loses his shoes every day.

"This is it! I'm leaving," I call. Baby in one arm, briefcase in the other, I stride, head down, out into the rain toward the minivan just as the baby-sitter pulls into the driveway. I about-face, march Abraham over to her as the kids spill out of the house, then sprint back to the van. Isaac is running barefoot, shoes in hand, now diving into the open door of the car.

At the school doors, there are hurried hugs, good wishes exchanged, a kiss from Elisha before he dashes into kindergarten. I spend a few extra seconds watching him as he hangs up his coat and runs to the art box. I don't know how much longer I want to keep teaching. It was a mistake to continue after Abraham was born.

I arrive at the college minutes later. Though I have only twenty minutes to finish prepping for the seminar, I emerge from the van almost calm, hoping that my appearance will mask the chaos of my other life.

I am highly practiced at this magic show. I took my first teaching job at a state university in 1987 while pregnant with my first child: family and career gestating together, like twins wrestling within me. I concealed my insecurity and inexperience with billowing clothes and an inflated vocabulary. No one knew I was pregnant until my sixth month. While working toward a third master's degree, I had two more babies. After giving birth late one afternoon to my third child, I sat up in my hospital bed for most of the evening, pulled out a book and my laptop, and wrote an annotation to turn in the next day. I slept well that night in the hospital bed, happy with my creative output: a son and a paper produced in the same day. And since landing a tenure-track position at a state university, I had perfected the daily trick of alchemizing from one person to another as I drove out of my house, detaching children as I went, to stand authoritatively at the front of the classroom, presiding over essays, research papers, discourse communities, logical fallacies, false dilemmas.

It was a complicated life, far more complex than I ever imagined while in college and graduate school. I had seldom thought about children and family those years, though I had been married through most of them. While living within the walls of the university, ensconced in library carrels, surrounded by stacks of journals and reference books, I could hardly think beyond the literary canon, the accepted discourse of my chosen discipline. When I met with other women in study groups, even in parties outside the university, our girl talk centered on our current research, sharing sources, tips for better organization. We compared theses, lamented the flabby state of our bibliographies, complained about the saturated job market. We were single-minded, whether married or not.

Abetted and tainted by my education, I had developed an extensive list of observations and judgments regarding the state of motherhood, some of which read like this: mothers were boring, clustering in public spaces discussing potty training, swapping chicken potpie recipes, dishing about their children's brilliant scores on their aptitude tests. Mothers were mostly caretakers and janitors, their identities lost in the herding and instructing of beings not yet fully human. Largely absent from public view and influence, mothers were fully absorbed in their private, self-created society, their sphere so diminished that success in public was determined solely by their ability to manage their offspring's bodily fluids and their tantrums in the candy aisles.

Three years after grad school, ten years into marriage, I was ready to become a mother. Nothing I had studied, nothing I had theorized or presented, nothing I had done in the years before, during, and after grad school—extensive travel through dozens of countries, living in the Alaskan wilderness, commercial salmon fishing—had taught me how to temper a predilection to abstraction, an obsession with language, a slavery to self-fulfillment, how to deeply, sacrificially love another human being.

When my first child was born, I knew I had chosen well. With the fourth child, our family was complete. My life was messy and strained, but carefully and manageably parsed between teaching and child rearing. But five years later, when a fifth child appeared unexpectedly, the balanced was tipped, dumping me into an exhaustion that wouldn't sleep away, into guilt, into hunger for another kind of life. And now, this day, the balance was tipped yet further.

I stand before the class, marker in my hand. "What is the basis for the passive voice in science writing?" I ask, resisting the urge to fold my arms over my stomach.

The night before, I had stood in the bathroom over the porcelain sink asking another question. Asking it of a white wand not much longer than my fingers. Am I . . . ? At forty-four, using contraception, teaching full-time, my husband often traveling for his job, with five children at home, one a baby, how was this possible? I knew the science of it, the probabilities, the statistics; I had less than a one-percent chance of becoming pregnant at my age, discounting contraception. Wouldn't intent, schedule, science, degrees, résumé, publications—wouldn't all this, the basis of authority and promotion in the academy and the classroom, count for something in that small private room? Hadn't I already demonstrated my openness to life, my willingness to sacrifice for others? The response was clear.

"Because passive shifts the attention away from the researcher," a biologist named Michael responds.

"Yes, the passive voice de-emphasizes the agent of the action. And why do we do this?" I turn to a woman with glinting eyes, while I stifle a wave of nausea and reach instinctively for my mug on the table, filled with ginger ale now instead of water.

"Because the emphasis is not on the agents of the action," she responds, "but on the results."

Agents of the action. Results. Though I am practiced at keeping my place in the shifting divide between bodies and words, every word in this class reverberates; every phrase is—what else?—pregnant with the intended meaning, and other meanings that creep in unintentionally, unplanned, unexpected. I cannot shut out this second voice, the heavy presence of an other.

"How does the epistemology of science compare, say, with the formation of knowledge in the humanities?" I continue, while my cells, without permission, furiously conjure out of my own body's matter another whole spirit, mind, body.

I nod sagely at the responses, looking intently at each speaker, trying to hear their words through the churning of my stomach, the currents of fatigue washing over me. I pick up a black marker and start a chart to help me stay focused. *How am I doing?* I ask myself as I write animatedly, even excitedly, on the whiteboard. *Trying a little too hard,* comes my critique. *Relax a little.* "So, by contrast, what function does opinion serve in the study of, say, literature?" I ask, poised to write.

As of two years before, my teaching load had been four classes each semester. I had developed a roster of twelve different courses, from literature and composition through every permutation of writing possible: creative, academic, business, technical, science, remedial. But enrollment at our small college was declining. Pressured by the director to increase our flagging numbers, I had created this class, immersing myself in science manuals, blending creative writing techniques with professional science texts. I had labored over this union, joining two utterly different approaches to language and the discovery of truth. And yet each one—science and creative writing—needed the other. It was a logical fusion, but with little precedent, which made it both exciting and exhausting. It had taken weeks to develop the material, weeks to walk it through the university approval process. I first taught the course last year, designing it as a fifteen-hour class squeezed into a week. On top of my other four classes, it had been a huge stretch, but it had been successful. The Alaska Department of Fish and Game had asked that I teach the class again. A dubious reward.

But the creator and designer of this class is now an indifferent parent to a child of her own making. I care nothing about science writing today, and maybe won't ever again. I have a wild urge to breach the wide space between me and my students, to throw away all I have worked toward in a blurted confession that would surely split the earth: "I'M PREGNANT AND I DON'T CARE A FIG ABOUT THIS CLASS!" I could see the blanched faces, the eyebrows frozen, the sidelong glances questioning my mental health. No matter that my students are all biologists who study reproductive cycles (in fish, mostly), who literally milk eggs from a salmon's body, their own hands participants in the bringing forth of life, tending the hatchlings with paternal care and attention. But in the commerce and classrooms of our work lives, we have no language for our loves, and no assigned seats for the admission of either death or a coming life, expected or not.

"Shall we begin the rubric, ladies and gentlemen?" I say, instead, between smiling teeth.

This is the end of my academic life, I know. I am forced to choose sides, to choose between bodies. I feel despair, and, strangely, a twinge of hope.

Two years later, I am standing at a podium. Several hundred conference attendees have listened attentively through my keynote address as I've presented the implications of postmodern approaches to narrative, specifically its application to theology. I've made it all the way through. The applause has ended. I wait for raised hands. A middle-aged man, professorial, asks me a startlingly personal question: "How do you stay grounded? How do you keep yourself in the world of actuality instead of the realm of theory?" I listen, wondering about the question's implied judgment on my address— too theoretical? No, not possible. But more, I am paralyzed with the need to decide: Should I tell the truth? Reveal to this audience of professors, writers, and theologians what I was so good at concealing for so many years? In my writing life, I have already begun to speak down the walls between bodies and selves. At conferences and readings, I quote Robert Briffault, a twentieth-century novelist and surgeon who wrote, "Either a woman writes books or has children." I then cite Alice Walker, who was once asked if women artists should have children. "Yes, they should have children— assuming this is of interest to them—but only one," she replied.

"Why only one?"

"Because with one you can move. With more than one, you're a sitting duck."

After these words, I stand in quiet protest for a moment, then read from my own books and essays, where my multiple children appropriately and unapologetically appear.

But I have not yet done this here, in the realm of the heavily résuméd and erudite. I pause, inhale, reconsider my new resolve to admit, recklessly if need be, to the truths and tensions every one of us lives within every day. I assess the potential damage quickly. Some may walk out. Some will mentally erase all I've just stated. Most will dismiss me from the ranks of the intelligent and worthy. No matter. I'm tired of a divided life, of covering the jagged tear between my public and private self with shaking hands. I lean into the microphone, and speak carefully, so that none can mistake my words: "I have six children." I hear a collective gasp, and I wait, almost defiant, ready for the walkout. The room wavers, titters, then visibly relaxes. It's going to be all right, this time. They ask how old (fifteen down to eleven months.) They ask how I do it (I don't know). They ask, and I speak, in these moments and all such moments hereafter as the person I am, apportioned out to a husband and six others, parceled out to the students I now teach part time, poured out into the essays and books I labor to write, but whole and full, one body, indivisible, speaking openly the truths that bind and free us all.

PART THREE

Recovering Academic

The Long and Winding Road

JEAN KAZEZ

I started off my career as a college professor in a promising way, with four tenure-track job offers. Although the job I accepted wasn't the most prestigious, it offered intellectually congenial colleagues and the advantages of big-city living. That is to say: lots of men. I was thirty-five, and the issues of marriage and family had become, well, pressing. The most prestigious job I was offered seemed perilous; if I found myself on the track to parenthood, I certainly wouldn't want to be derailed by a tenure problem.

My plan succeeded beautifully in the areas of love and children, but not as expected in every other regard. Not badly, but differently. I had been a hard-working and enthusiastic student, thoroughly engaged by my areas of philosophy—primarily language and mind—in a graduate program which was an exciting hub of intellectual activity in exactly my field. But in this new setting, with a small number of colleagues working in other areas of philosophy, doing productive research was more difficult. After publishing two articles based on my dissertation, I ventured into territory that wasn't as safe, and my next set of papers was rejected. Striking out in yet another direction would have been a risky business. I was not going to hold on to my job unless I could quickly produce a tidy stack of publications.

During my second year of teaching I met my husband. The next year, my contract was not-so-smoothly renewed, with strong hints that I was going to perish if I didn't publish. For some, the pressure might have been stimulating. Not for me. The love I felt for my work was gradually giving way to paralysis. Meanwhile, I was enjoying my new relationship and nest building in the home we soon shared. When we got married and commenced "the baby-making project," the never-ending efforts to publish continued, but started to be eclipsed because getting pregnant and staying pregnant at the age of thirty-nine turned out to be a tricky business. After my fourth year of teaching I was granted a medical leave, which—I'm eternally grateful to say—morphed quickly into a pregnancy leave. I spent two months flat on my back in the hospital on labor-stalling drugs, and then finally gave birth to two healthy seven-pound babies.

Although the next three months were excruciatingly difficult (it turns out that after lying on your back for two months, your joints don't work so well; and it also turns out that twin pregnancies put you at risk of gallbladder disease), they were also completely wonderful. I'm not saying I can spend every waking hour giving my undivided attention to tiny children. I remember spending long hours breastfeeding one baby while rocking the other in a car seat with my foot, and simultaneously rereading *Anna Karenina*. But I loved this time. After long years in graduate school (don't ask how long; it's a secret), prone to doubts (was this academic work really worth doing?), caring for my children was an activity completely free of doubt.

The babies were born in the spring and I had a semester's maternity leave in the fall. A year and a half after the birth, I was going to be up for tenure. To have a shot, this was going to have to be a year and a half of round-the-clock work. My children would have to be in the care of a full-time nanny, or placed at my university's on-campus day-care center. Before they were born, I had never for one second contemplated being a full-time mother. I was not secretly plotting an escape from work. But it turned out to be impossible to contemplate the separation required to stay on the tenure track. This was no easy decision. After telling my department head I was interested in adjunct teaching, I felt like a boat cut from its moorings, drifting into the open sea.

I found baby minding a delicious labor of love. Apart from the two objects of my affection, I also loved the new experience of time and friendship. Time flows differently when you're with kids. The camaraderie of women who are brought together mainly by the common ground of motherhood was something new for me. I had spent most of my adult life in the company of intense, combative intellectuals (okay, I *am* an intense, combative intellectual) and it was pleasant to discover I could be other things as well.

I continued to teach one course per semester, sticking with my usual classes in philosophy of mind and language, but it was hard to get adequate enrollments in these "tough" topics at night. After my class was cancelled one semester, I considered what I could teach and be guaranteed at least ten students. With all the new thoughts and feelings I was having about the direction of my life, I decided to teach a course I called "The Meaning of Life." An exploration of "the good life" from Plato to the present, this course turned out to be popular with students and also a stepping stone to the next phase of my career. Gradually, I developed two more new courses in the area of ethics.

Full-time school started for the kids with first grade. Now there would be time to resume Work with a big W. But what to do? It's no secret that adjuncts are not richly compensated. But teaching allowed me to keep one foot in philosophy while being as immersed in my children's growing up as I wanted to be. I'd had all the freedom I could want to offer courses that interested me, and my schedule was ideal. Doing a lot of adjunct teaching, however, would be another matter.

Over the five years of my kids' early childhood, I had become an avid nonfiction reader, discovering plenty of original, engaging, well-written books for nonexperts in geography, religious studies, sociology, history, and other fields. There's not so much readable philosophy out there, even though philosophy can have particular relevance to people's deepest concerns. I decided I would try my hand at writing enjoyable, accessible philosophy, and if that failed, return to full-time teaching.

For the next three years, I worked on a book about philosophy and the good life which (I hoped) would be a genuine pleasure to read. Freed of the pressure to publish in academic journals, I wrote this book on my own terms, in my own style, following my own path through the issues. The success of this project—my book was published in 2007—has given me the feeling of coming into my own. Is this, then, the simple, happy ending to the story of my work and family travails?

It's not quite time yet for a triumphal fade to credits. The fact is that being a freelance philosopher cum adjunct professor is not the same as having a full-time, tenured job. There's far more opportunity for self-expression, which is marvelous, but a lot less money. (Note to Oprah's Book Club: I'd be happy to hear from you.) I am currently working on another book and on other writing projects, so for now I'm staying the course. But I do sometimes wonder whether what I'm doing is really *work* if I'm not compensated for all the hours I put into it. (Or maybe I'm just a puritan: could work be this much fun?)

In an ideal world I'd have a full-time job and my writing would earn me a predictable salary and benefits as well as pie-in-the-sky royalties. I wouldn't have to suffer the indignity of depending so heavily on my husband's income; it wasn't a problem when I was taking care of our children full time, but now, as the mother of two ten-year-olds who are in school all day, it does feel like an indignity. Have I landed in this spot because the academic workplace is ill adapted to mothers? I don't think that's exactly true: I think the academic workplace is ill adapted to everyone.

One culprit is the tenure system. For five years, every new professor must produce reams of publications or be sent into exile. I found the pressure mind-numbing and depressing. Over the years I've been in academia—a lot of years, because I come from a family of academics—I've seen many capable people lose the battle for contract renewal or tenure. The disruption can stop people from starting families or even forming relationships to begin with. It can force people to postpone parenthood until biologically it's too late. It can threaten the livelihood of a primary breadwinner and turn spouses into cargo. Clearly some people do flourish under the system, but the pressure to win tenure can turn people into drones, producing the safest, dullest, most publishable work they can.

Whatever social order we live within, it can have the feeling of being a necessity, no more changeable than the color of the sky. Some academics will tell you the tenure system cannot possibly be abandoned. But in Canada and the United Kingdom, the system is different. A visiting speaker from an elite British university explained this to me, back when I was still on the tenure track: "We hire people and befriend them for five years, and at that point, we can't just send them away." Candidates receive tenure as long as they are productive and competent. The presumption is for it, instead of against. In the United States, friendship isn't part of the equation. If you have to mess up people's lives to make the department shine a little brighter—and that means boast more publications—that's what you do. Academics ought to value excellence (and take care in defining it), but also take responsibility for creating structures within which people can live good lives.

Freed of the tenure burden, would I have continued to work full time after my kids were born? More women would succeed in academia under better conditions, and I think making that possible is important. But me, personally? I don't know. All the particulars of my situation made it irresistible for me to focus on my kids. I adored those first five years. As it turns out, I'm not just grateful for the chance to be an involved mother. Those years also put me on the road to a more authentic kind of work. I don't find myself in a place that's unproblematic, but I have a lot to be grateful for.

The Bags I Carried

CAROLINE GRANT

"Mama," says Ben, as we cuddle in his bed. "Tell me a story. Tell me a story about when I was still in your belly."

"Well," I answer, shifting his weight more comfortably against my chest as we lean together against his pillow, "when you were in my belly I was a teacher. Every day I would drive to a school with long brick pathways and big green lawns. I carried a heavy backpack, bigger than yours, full of papers and books, from my office to my classroom. My students and I would talk about books together, and I would help them write essays about what they read. When the class was over," I continue quietly, listening to his breathing slow, "I would meet the students one by one. We sat in my office together and talked about their essays, and I would help them write out their ideas as clearly as they could."

"Hmmm," says Ben, drifting off to sleep. "And now," he says, finishing the story as I've told it to him dozens of times, "you don't teach those students anymore, you teach me."

It's taken me years to be as easy as he is with the change in my student roster.

I'm twenty-five when I begin graduate school in comparative literature at the University of California, Berkeley. Without a fellowship or teaching assignment for the first year, I work part-time in San Francisco, answering phones at a translation agency; the clients include Dow Corning and Monsanto, the translations are all of patents, but assigning translators and calculating the nickel-a-word fees is the closest I can come to working with languages. I cart my books back and forth across the bay so that I can attend seminars in the morning, go to work in the afternoon, then head back to Berkeley at night to attend film screenings or use the library.

I wish I could immerse myself more fully in graduate school life. I wonder if I am missing out on something. I remind myself that it's not meant to be like college, an all-absorbing, self-sufficient world of friends and books and parties.

No, I think, school is a job like my office work. My professors remind me all the time that I need to "professionalize": present my work at conferences, publish papers, package myself to future academic employers as an expert in a specific field.

Yes, this is a job. I log the hours in the classroom, at the library, reading in the wavering fluorescent light of BART trains and Muni buses, in order (theoretically) to put the work aside when I get home. This could be good, I naively hope, when I have the family I desire; I'll be able to pursue my career and be available to my children.

Except I can't ever put it aside; it's never a nine-to-five proposition. The research, the preparation for seminars, always spill into my time as surely as my books keep spilling out of my too-small, college-era backpack. I can sacrifice the time for myself, for now, but what if I had a family?

I dive more deeply into my studies, and finally land a position as a teaching assistant, so I quit my real world job and move to Berkeley. Now I can take my seminars in the afternoon and hold mornings free for teaching, totally immersing myself in graduate student life. The teaching stipend is so small, I take out a student loan to help cover the rent on my tiny cottage apartment, grateful I'm not trying to support anyone but myself.

I hunker down and do my work, reading widely in American, French, and Latin American literatures, feminist and film theories. Once my literature requirements are satisfied, I'll be able to dig into one field, and I plan to focus on American literature and film. For now, fulfilling the disparate requirements keeps pulling me in different directions.

My first teaching assignment is as an assistant to a more senior graduate student, the mother of one, who teaches a literature course titled "Female Grotesques and Demons." The figures turn out all to be mothers. She is the only graduate student–mother I know, yet she never alludes to her family life in class. Teaching this course, she tells me, is her subtle way of bridging her academic and personal lives. I wish instead she could bring in a picture of her son and teach our students about less monstrous moms.

Soon I start developing my own courses—"Language and Landscape," "Nationalism and the Family"—broad themes which allow me to teach writing I love, writing my students respond well to.

❧ ☙

I follow my professors' advice about professionalizing: I buy a sleek black leather bag and start teaching in the university's College Writing Program. In the hierarchy of what graduate students do, teaching composition sits at the very bottom, below teaching literature, far below doing research. But I know I'll always have work.

We teach out of a ramshackle wooden house, a far cry from the beautiful stone buildings around the rest of the campus. The stairs up to my office are creaky and slanted, and six of us share the cramped space. My beautiful new bag is too small to hold much more than my teaching notes and my students' drafts, so I lug books in my arms from office to classroom and back again. The teaching load is twice that in my home department, but the sense of community is strong; both graduate student instructors and adjunct faculty receive abundant training and support in teaching basic composition to first-year students. We gather for monthly faculty meetings, sharing our frustrations and our small successes.

Meanwhile, I'm still single, still feeling light-years away from combining academic and family life. Since I am a good student, I use this time to research that project. I collect anecdotal evidence.

Item: My older sister, now a tenured English professor at a small private university. She married a fellow graduate student midway through course work and had a daughter midway through dissertation writing. She hates to give me advice, but when I began considering graduate school she couldn't stop herself from warning me about the bleak prospects for job seekers with PhDs, the difficulty of balancing school and family. I forged ahead anyway.

Attending my sister's graduation after my first year at Berkeley, I sit in the auditorium with my blonde niece on my lap, clapping for each graduate until our hands sting. So then we clap just for the women, then just for the women in science, then just for the women in science holding babies; we cheer and whistle for the two of them, but my heart sinks at seeing the statistics about women in higher education walking across the stage. At the end of the ceremony, my sister walks up the aisle past us and scoops her daughter up out of my arms into her own, so that's the image I cling to as I continue my studies: my sister's new doctoral hood resting across my niece's shoulders, too. Later, after two years of looking, my sister finds a good job and moves her small family cross-country. I never question her too closely about how she handles school and family. I see that she does, but also see that she waits seven years to have a second child. I look on and applaud her successes, not wanting to know what toll it takes.

Item: A senior professor, the mother of two grown children. She tells me a story of the Dark Ages, as she puts it, when she boarded an elevator, eight months pregnant, only to have her department chair recoil at the sight of her and stammer an excuse to take the stairs. I never witness behavior like this, but mostly because I don't see many women, professors or students, trying to bring any aspect of their personal life to school.

Item: My advisor, the mother of two young children. She earned the job at Berkeley without the obligatory campus interview because she had been too pregnant to fly—a huge concession in a competitive market. She seems like a success story. Now she rushes from seminar saying that her kids will be put out on the curb if she's late for preschool pickup again. Prioritize, she reminds me; original research gets a person hired, not teaching. Put teaching on the back burner, she insists. But when I wonder about how to apply this thinking to a family, I'm stymied by images of small kids and hot stoves.

I don't know any other faculty who will discuss their family life, and so give up this research.

I complete my doctoral exams and write my dissertation prospectus on family relationships in 1940s American films. I use it to apply for a departmental fellowship—a year's relief from teaching, with enough income that, for a change, I won't even need a loan to help cover my steep Bay Area living expenses. With the prospectus finished and the fellowship application submitted, I agree to a blind date with a guy named Tony Grant. We go hiking—my backpack holding homemade banana bread, his carrying a couple of perfectly ripe peaches—and quickly realize we go together as well as our snacks. Within a few weeks, Tony and I are a solid couple and I've earned the fellowship. My friends joke about the two grants I've received this spring.

Graduation day. My parents fly out from Connecticut to witness me receiving my PhD. On the way out to Berkeley, we all stop at City Hall, where my mom snaps a picture of Tony and me applying for our marriage license.

I give myself the summer off—we marry, take a two-week honeymoon—secure in the knowledge that I have cobbled together plenty of work for the following year: one job teaching in the film department at UC Berkeley, plus a position teaching writing at the San Francisco Art Institute. It's an adjunct's life: holding student conferences in cafés instead of a proper office, spending more time in my car than a classroom, paying out too much of my small salary for parking and bridge tolls. I've given up that smart leather bag in favor of a smarter backpack. I don't see much of a future in this life; it wouldn't work if I had children, and we want to have children.

But for now, I'm employed in the fields I trained in, living in the same city as my husband; I know many who have it worse. Much worse. I don't dare complain.

Fireworks explode into a fog bank over San Francisco Bay, making the sky glow in soft shades of pink and blue. I'm used to the baby pastels of fog-muted fireworks here, but this year they have a special resonance for me. Pale pink or baby blue, I wonder? I lean back into Tony's arms, surrounded by friends at this rooftop party, happy to share one of my two bits of news. Yesterday, I announce, Stanford called me in to interview for a teaching position. And this morning my pregnancy test read positive.

I spend August lying on the couch, queasy and enervated, relieved that I am no longer on Berkeley's earlier schedule. I tell my department chair about my pregnancy after I am hired and she, a childless woman in her late fifties, is delighted. I wonder briefly if she ever wanted children. At the first faculty meeting, she asks us all to introduce ourselves by revealing something personal that has nothing to do with teaching. I ponder the question as others mention their hobbies: romance novelist, marathon runner, gourmet cook. When it's my turn, my new boss blurts out, "Caroline's pregnant!" before I can say a word. And so my identity here is fixed: Caroline Grant, mother to be. During the break in the meeting, I field questions about morning sickness and gender preferences. No one asks me anything about my teaching or research interests.

As my first quarter winds down, I reflect on my experience teaching here as a pregnant woman.

Item: At a faculty symposium, a colleague taps my growing belly and urges me to read Naomi Wolf's *Misconceptions*. As I try to back slowly out of her reach, she continues to touch my stomach and question me about my obstetrician's C-section rate. "Do you have children?" I ask, trying to redirect the conversation. "Oh, no!" she laughs, "I have a horror of pregnancy!" Later, in the privacy of my office, I rub my belly, crooning to the baby, apologizing for the assault.

Item: The winter quarter schedule is published, and my chair notices that my three-hour seminars will be held in one of the trailers. They're unheated, and don't have bathrooms. "Is that going to be an issue for you?" she asks kindly. It's a hassle to petition for a classroom change, but she initiates the paperwork and sees it through for me.

Item: I'm standing at the front of the classroom when I realize that my students are distracted, staring not at the chalkboard but my belly. I look down to see that my baby is putting on a quite visible gymnastics routine. Now I try to teach sitting down, a minor concession in an altogether uneventful pregnancy. My students are occasionally interested—taking bets on the baby's gender, lobbying me to name the baby after them—but for the most part they do their work, and I do mine.

Item: A colleague engages me in conversation about accommodating the needs of the job to the needs of the family. The first year or so is intense, she warns; the little ones need you so much, but as they grow you'll develop a good routine with them, and find ways to get your work done even while they're around. Finally! I think, a role model! I start to pepper her with questions about flexible teaching schedules, sleep deprivation, day-care options. "Well," she says, "I didn't need day care for my dogs, of course; when I attended conferences, I just put them in a kennel."

A kennel? So much for my role model.

I schedule thirty-minute conferences with students, knowing that they run out of steam after twenty minutes' close attention to their essays. I spend the time remaining between students making calls to different people in the university's human resources department, trying to get a clear answer about maternity leave benefits. I finally learn that I can take six weeks' paid leave after six months' employment.

Six months. I began work September 1. I just need to make it until March 1. My baby is due March 14. I cross my fingers for an easy third trimester and make my contingency plans.

And then? Then I have six weeks to decide if I'm coming back.

A six-week leave would bring me back in the middle of the following semester, so my chair offers me a position in the tutoring center. I can work a flexible schedule, even bring the baby with me, she urges, and then return to classroom teaching after summer vacation. Her proposal makes so much sense, and yet I doubt my ability to pull it off.

I want some model of how it can be done, but I don't see anybody holding student conferences while bouncing a baby. I don't notice women shouldering breast pumps along with their briefcases. I haven't even had the baby, and yet already I feel isolated by it.

I'm eight months pregnant and trying to remember exactly where on campus I parked the car this morning. Shuttles run to the outlying lots, and often a passing van slows and the driver opens the door for me, gesturing me inside. Hefting my new rolling suitcase on to the shuttle turns out to be more difficult than just walking. I continue along, pulling my books behind me, belly and bag nicely balanced.

I find the car and drive the few miles to Tony's office. While I wait for him, I walk laps around the parking lot, wondering again what it is about the weight of this baby that makes sitting still so uncomfortable. I've given up trying to keep the baby's kicking hidden from my students; they're now used to me circling our conference table during class, and lately I have to stand during office hours, too. I'll squirm and shift in my seat the whole hour it takes us to drive home, though it's not all physical. Our conversation unsettles me.

I'm thrilled that my job comes with maternity benefits (it didn't even come with a parking permit), but I'm not sure, I tell Tony, whether I want to take just maternity leave. "What if I don't want to go back? What if I'm so happy, or so distracted, or so busy being a mother that I can't go back? Will we be okay?" "Yes," assures Tony, "we'll be okay." And I sit quietly a minute, thinking. "All right," I say finally, "but I reserve the right to open up this discussion again at any time, okay?" "Okay."

I continue teaching, but also arrange for back-up teachers and film screenings in case the baby comes before the end of the semester.

At my thirty-eight-week checkup, my obstetrician asks me how long I plan to continue my two-hour daily commute. "Well," I answer, trying to look professional in my paper gown, "I've got two more weeks of classes, but I'm showing a film the last week, so I—" She cuts me off and repeats her question. "I could probably just go in a couple—" I try to answer. She cuts me off again, this time rephrasing her question: "How comfortable would you be with going into labor in the middle of your class?"

Six months to the day when I started teaching, I turn my classes over
to my colleagues, remind my students that I am available for conferences
via e-mail, and give them their final essay assignment. The next day I go to
an afternoon movie and buy a baby journal. Tony and I spend the weekend
relaxing; we install the car seat, visit friends, secure in the knowledge that
we have two, maybe three, weeks before becoming parents. Sunday night
my water breaks, and Monday morning, just as I would have been walking
into my morning class, Benjamin arrives.

The next six weeks, my maternity leave, are a blur. Ben eats, sleeps, and
cries. I nurse him, and when I'm not nursing, hold him, marveling. "He's
as engrossing, as addictive as a new boyfriend," I tell a friend. "Except I
made him." I learn how to make and eat meals one-handed. I e-mail my
students about their final essays, typing over Ben's head while he nurses,
and submit their final course grades on time. I believe they all did very
well. My leave is ticking down and I have barely left the house. Commuting to school seems as simple as flying to the moon.

Part of me wants to go back to work, just to prove that I can. But the
plan that had sounded so manageable, so reasonable before Ben's arrival
now seems laughable. He's not a potted plant, sitting quietly in the corner
while I meet with my students. He's a demanding, noisy, perfectly typical
baby. But it's not just that his presence would be distracting; his very existence is distracting to me. He is too new, *I* am too new, to keep my head
at work no matter where he is. And I hadn't even thought, before his birth,
beyond the one semester. After those weeks in the tutoring center, I'd be
teaching again. The university doesn't offer on-site child care, so I'd need
to find something nearby, or closer to home? Day care or nanny share? Just
thinking about the various options wearies me.

Meanwhile, I realize that while I love teaching, love working closely with
my small groups of students, I don't actually love the job. All the baggage of
professionalizing (presenting at conferences; faculty meetings spent debating curriculum requirements; advancing through the academic hierarchy)
preoccupies my colleagues and threatens to draw me in.

So I quit. My colleagues are supportive and understanding. They tell
me to be in touch when I'm ready to come back to work. I am lucky, I keep
reminding myself, so lucky, that I don't have to work.

But I miss work. I miss discussing books and movies. (I miss books
and movies!) I miss the community that develops in the classroom each

semester, the welcome ebb and flow of intense interaction with students and colleagues and then solitary work at my desk. I miss the exchanges with my students about their tricky paragraphs, miss seeing the light in their eyes when they catch a big idea with their words.

With Ben, now I'm never alone but I'm lonelier than ever. I'm not above playground conversations about sippy cups and sleep deprivation—I initiate my share of them—but the playground community develops briefly and then dissipates like the fog as the strollers retreat, each to their own homes, and Ben and I are left on our own, again. I study him every day, but he is not my student. He is gorgeous and interesting, amazing evidence of what my body can do. But I want a UC Berkeley T-shirt that says "PhD" in big, bold letters to remind myself—and, yes, prove to others— what my brain has done.

One day, my sister tells me about a writing group for mothers she's heard about in Berkeley, just a block from my old cottage apartment. I've started writing about my new life, trying, as I always did as a student, to figure out what I think by reading what I write. But after all this time, Berkeley still means "school" to me, and I can't imagine choosing that commute again, and walking down that sidewalk with my new baby.

A year or so later, that writing group has started a Web site, *Literary Mama*, and my sister one of the many editors trying to manage some combination of motherhood, writing, and other work. She invites me to share her editor's position, and urges me again to meet the writing group in Berkeley. I finally get up the nerve to drive out one morning with Ben and a messy first draft of an essay stuffed next to the board books and plastic snack tubs in our diaper bag. The group meets in a kindergarten classroom (the irony doesn't escape me) and I enter nervous as a kid on the first day of school. The women circle metal folding chairs and discuss each piece of writing in turn as the kids weave in and out around our legs, playing in the piles of crayons and Lincoln Logs set out for their distraction, offering us cups of imaginary tea, climbing onto our laps for a snack or a cuddle.

Despite the interruptions, my writing gets closer attention here than it ever did in graduate school. I'm energized by the feedback, eager to race home and incorporate the suggestions I receive. Working with the mother-writers in the group and those who send essays to *Literary Mama* returns me to my favorite part of teaching: helping writers bridge the gap between the ideas in their heads and the words on the page. We work together, alternately paring away and polishing, until the essays shine.

⇛ ⇚

Today, I'm pulled in different directions like in those early days of graduate school, but now I feel grateful for it: my family, my writers, my writing all demand my attention and I struggle to give them all what they need. I drive to writing group now with a sleek orange bag carrying my laptop; Ben's now graduated from writing group so his little brother, Eli, accompanies me, carrying his own small bag, packed with a diaper, snacks, and a sippy cup. At home, I prop my computer on the kitchen counter or on the floor next to the boys' wooden train tracks, taking advantage of quiet moments to e-mail a writer or jot down an essay idea. And at night, when Ben and I cuddle up, I can finally tell him his bedtime story without any twinges of the ambivalence I once felt about leaving academia.

One of the Boys

MARTHA ELLIS CRONE

When I was young, my mother told me that I could be anything I wanted to be. I see now that she, mother of two, employed in a series of part-time jobs, may have meant this as encouragement in the face of certain obstacles, or simply as a message of hope. But I took her literally. By the time I decided I wanted to enter academia, every mentor and support person in my life had echoed my mother's sentiment. Of course I, a woman, could become a professor of political science. All I had to do was to work hard and follow the prescribed career path.

In the fall of 1988, when I began graduate school at The Ohio State University, my husband, David, and I developed a plan for our lives that seemed both sensible and doable. He would take a stopgap engineering job for a few years to pay our bills, while I attended OSU on a fellowship. My career would be primary in our family, we agreed. Not only was an academic career extremely demanding, but it would also require me to move around the country. David's engineering degree was more marketable, so he could get a job wherever my career took us, or so we assumed. Or maybe, once a baby came along, he'd start his own business so he could work from home and watch the baby at the same time. It never occurred to us that having children would interfere with either of our careers. We simply plunged ahead and put our plan into action.

During my first week of graduate school, I was shocked to find only a few women students among my new colleagues. At first I thought I was simply unlucky to get stuck in an incoming class that was mostly male, but gradually it dawned on me that this was the norm in political science: men far outnumbered women at all levels of this discipline, not just at Ohio State, but everywhere. It was my first inkling that maybe the work of the women's movement wasn't done, as my college friends and I had blithely assumed when we planned our careers. It turned out I was going to be in a minority.

My response to minority status, which worked well for me as long as I remained childless, was to adapt until I fit in. Beginning that first quarter, I taught myself to be one of the Poli Sci Boys. I did whatever the boys did: I read voluminous amounts of literature, took sides in academic arguments (restrainedly in class and then more contentiously in the hallways), competed for computer time in the student lounge, and complained about statistics class. When they partied, I did too. I learned how to keep up with the boys beer for beer in bars and at department social functions. I became proud of my ability to drink at least some of them under the table. Around midnight we'd drunkenly plan each other's brilliant academic careers, scribbling promises on bar napkins to coauthor papers when we became assistant professors.

As far as the other women students went, I developed great relationships with those who chose the same path as I did: fitting in with the men in the department. For the most part, my female friends and I were satisfied with our treatment by the faculty and by our male peers. Other women, those who expressed an interest in feminist theory or who spoke up about perceived gender inequalities, didn't fare as well. The male graduate students mocked them, and more importantly, the faculty ignored them. One doctoral student, a few years ahead of me, was virtually shunned because her dissertation focused on political gender bias in the third world. She didn't get offers from faculty members to present papers with them at conferences, nor did she receive the expected dissertation-year solo teaching placement. The reasons were never discussed overtly, but it wasn't hard to speculate that the department didn't want students or parents complaining about her strident tone and touchy political views.

I didn't want my reputation tarnished by association with women like these. I wanted a normal career studying topics that would get me faculty support and eventual publication. If that meant fitting in with male expectations, I didn't have a problem with that. In exchange for my acting like one of the boys, my professors treated me like one.

A woman with a better-developed feminist consciousness might have viewed our department as gender biased. Perhaps a woman who had lived through, or at least embraced the philosophy of, the women's movement of the 1970s would have grasped its patriarchal nature. But I, who came of age in the can-do 1980s, chose instead to appreciate the gender-related affirmative action practiced in my department. At least partly due to those policies, I received fair access to funding and research opportunities, and at the time, that was enough to win my respect and gratitude.

For example, I was awarded a prestigious five-year University Fellowship with no apparent discrimination against me as a female. This fellowship provided me with a substantial cash grant, equivalent to a research assistant's pay, for my first and fifth years, and guaranteed assistantships for the years in between. In my second year, I was assigned to work in the department's survey research lab, an important placement for those in my chosen subfield of electoral behavior and public opinion. The lab director explicitly balanced gender in appointing students to these positions. In my third year, I was chosen as intern to the editor of the *American Political Science Review*, where I got to see inside the remarkable world of publish or perish. Again, the *APSR* editor consistently selected both a man and a woman for the two intern slots. Further, the male chair of my general exam committee chose me to coauthor a paper for the American Political Science Association's annual conference. It's difficult to know what combination of gender and achievement helped me land these kinds of opportunities, but clearly I wasn't experiencing any overt discrimination in access to the sort of assignments that provided strong career preparation. And once I had them, I worked hard, and I loved them.

I started to hear whispers from professors like "We're expecting big things from you." One professor confided that the faculty bet I could get an Ivy League placement, since Ivy League political science departments were eager to hire women to fulfill affirmative action goals. Being a woman seemed like a bonus, an added feature that would make me more desirable on the job market. Around the time of that conversation, the fall after my triumphant copresentation at the APSA, only a semester away from general exams, I decided it was the perfect time to get pregnant.

David and I dearly wanted a baby, and I thought it made sense to have one before I got hired for my first academic job. In fact, I thought we'd timed things very well. The baby was due in July, two months after I would take my general exams. I planned to take the summer off to give birth and rest, starting my dissertation in the fall. I gave myself a year to finish the dissertation, and I even thought that having a baby would help me be more focused than my colleagues on my research. I'd be more "settled," which seemed like it would be an advantage. I was certain that by fall of 1992, I would have the dissertation completed and be ready for the job market.

The physical facts of pregnancy were my first hints that I really wasn't one of the boys. I was often tired, and had to push myself to keep up with my course work. I began to feel out of place physically, because I was the only pregnant person in the department and (it often seemed) on the entire OSU campus. I felt the baby move for the first time during an extremely tedious comparative politics seminar, and at seven months pregnant, as I was sitting for general exams, the baby kicked and squirmed while I wrote my essays. I was definitely the only one in the room experiencing *that* side of generals.

Even with all those reminders of my femaleness, I still felt like one of the boys, like one of the department's stars. So it came as a shock when, after I passed the oral portion of my general exam, my committee chair expressed doubt about my ability to combine work and motherhood. I brought it up to him, jokingly, when he gave me the good news that I had passed. I patted my belly and said, "Well, I guess you guys aren't worried about whether I'll finish the program and get a good job, right?" Instead of responding with the good-humored denial I expected, he avoided my eyes and said, out of the corner of his mouth, "We're all just waiting and seeing."

Pregnancy may have begun the process, but the birth of baby Laura separated me from the boys permanently. Everyone always says that nothing can prepare you for motherhood, but I think my special combination of naiveté and cockiness made me doubly or triply unprepared. Having lived completely in my mind for years, I was blindsided by the sheer physicality of life with a newborn. Before Laura, I was accustomed to controlling everything; now I only reacted, biologically and instinctually, to this tiny person who shared my DNA and needed me around the clock. I was forced to just *be,* moving through my days and nights without accomplishing anything except the repetitive tasks of mothering an infant. I was reduced to a bundle of sheer love and terror—completely bewildered.

Many PhD students experience a difficult phase of isolation when they pass exams and begin their dissertations. The loss of structure and community throws many people off balance. For me, that occurred at the same time that I had a baby, an event also recognized for causing isolation and depression. Going from prolonged daily contact with friends and colleagues in the department to being by myself with a baby most of the day made me crazy. Most of my graduate school friends, it seemed, suddenly lost interest in me. Occasionally a woman friend would stop by my home, or I'd arrange to meet someone for lunch, but even my closest friends seemed puzzled by my new role as a mother, and unsure of how to react to a baby.

For my part, I was too sleep deprived and hormonal to have much to talk about on the political science front.

I valiantly tried to shake it off, as if giving birth and becoming a mother was a bad virus I'd get over soon. I reminded myself that I would be starting my dissertation at the end of September, that I was going to stick to the plan despite the life-changing event of having a baby. But I started to harbor doubts about my master plan. Just a few intense weeks of motherhood forced me to realize that my fantasy of writing my dissertation from home while Laura slept blissfully in a bassinette next to me was hopelessly delusional. Having it all would be a lot harder than I had expected, and I could already see that success would hinge on child care.

Child care was rarely discussed in the department, either as public policy or personal necessity, but it became the key issue of my academic life from the moment Laura was born. When I had reliable babysitting, I could do my work; when I didn't, I couldn't. In discussing my child-care needs with my advisor, he made me understand (without actually saying so) that I'd be expected to solve the babysitting issue on my own. This conversation brought to mind a different discussion I'd had with another professor long before I became pregnant. He was mystified by a student who dropped out of her program to stay home with her children. "Why doesn't she just hire a nanny?" he asked. At the time I shared his bafflement, but once I had Laura, I could have given him an entire list of reasons: The money. The scarcity of Mary Poppins clones. The problems of hiring, supervising, and firing, when necessary, said nanny. The money. The guilt. The genuine desire to connect with one's child for more than a rushed, crazy moment at the end of the day. The delight of motherhood. The money. Why not hire a nanny, indeed.

Insensitivity to the needs of parents seemed rampant among my colleagues once I became a mother. One afternoon, months after Laura came along, I was walking across campus with a few other students and a favorite professor of mine, a departmental representative to the University Senate. The senate was scheduled to vote on a proposed policy (subsequently defeated) that would grant time off the tenure clock to assistant professors who became new parents. Professor P. opposed this policy. "Why should people be given preferential treatment for choosing to reproduce?" he pontificated, possibly without giving a thought to his own grown children, who had been raised by his stay-at-home wife. "Yes," a male colleague piped up in toady fashion. "If they get to stop the clock to have a baby, why can't non-parents get time off to go mountain climbing in Nepal?" Chuckles rang out all around. I'm ashamed to say that I silently burned with indignation, but felt too concerned about my need for dissertation support from Professor P. to reply.

In a stroke of good fortune, I did locate a terrific undergraduate baby-sitter, a woman named Kristen. For a year and a half, I accommodated my teaching, research, and writing work to her class schedule in order to keep her as Laura's caregiver. We could only afford to pay Kristen for fifteen hours a week, so I had to squeeze in most of my work during those hours and on weekends when David was home. And squeeze I did, becoming efficient and hyperfocused. No more "study breaks" chatting with friends or walking to High Street for an ice cream. Every second that I had babysitting, I worked like a dog. And every moment that I wasn't working, I mothered just as ferociously, because I really missed Laura when I was gone.

Missing Laura was something I couldn't discuss with anyone at the university. Having a baby exhausted me, yes, and it interfered with my academic work. But it was also marvelous. I loved being with her, especially once we left the madness of the newborn phase. I loved playing with her, making her laugh, and watching her learn to crawl and stand. I loved dressing her up, brushing her wispy hair, reading her board books and singing her Beatles songs. I loved the single tooth she finally produced at eleven months, and the way she used it to scrape mashed sweet potatoes from a spoon. My academic colleagues expected to hear about the negative aspects of babies, so sleeplessness, diapers, and colic were acceptable conversation topics, if they were brief. But being smitten with one's child was intellectually nonrigorous, and if I shared even a bit of my pleasure with motherhood, people tended to look at me warily and escape rapidly, as if I was exhibiting a bizarre and possibly contagious mental deficiency.

With Kristen's help, I started to make real progress on my dissertation while teaching my own introductory American politics classes. For a while, things fell into a routine, and once again I began to believe that I could do it all, that I could balance motherhood and career. Having a child made it much harder than I'd expected, but I was doing it. I even made tentative plans to go on the job market in the fall of 1993, a year later than originally expected, but not bad, I reasoned, considering my situation. But then, in June of 1992, I found out I was pregnant again.

This pregnancy was unplanned and initially unwanted. I felt humiliated by my body, by the birth-control failure, by my rampant fecundity. One baby might have been smilingly tolerated by my advisors; two babies in nineteen months would be seen as completely insane. Furthermore, I had lost my innocence about motherhood and work, and could no longer entertain fantasies of pleasantly puttering along with the dissertation, teaching, and job search while caring for a newborn and toddler. Interviewing for jobs in particular seemed forbidding, since it would entail week-long trips out of town, and would require that we locate (not to mention pay for) temporary full-time care for the children. Even if we could do all that, I had no desire to leave a young nursing baby for that amount of time. Another option was to bring the kids along, but that would require finding a nanny to travel with us, and even if I could find one, how would we afford it? This job-market dilemma sparked my first genuine doubts about my ability to manage an academic career and mothering.

Daughter number two, Madeline, was born via emergency C-section in March of 1993. It took me six weeks to recover from that difficult birth, during which time I experienced unfathomable fatigue and needed my mother to live with us just to keep the household running. A year or so afterward, the OSU department hired a young assistant professor who was pregnant. She also gave birth by emergency C-section, on a Monday. By Friday, she was back at school teaching her graduate seminar. I felt a sick combination of envy and dismay for her willingness to make the birth of a child look like nothing more traumatic or life changing than having a tooth pulled. To me, her actions were an example of what was necessary to combine motherhood with a job at a high-powered research university, and I was both unable and unwilling to do anything like that.

Once life with two babies began in earnest, my academic life fell apart. Madeline was a different baby than her older sister. She was more needy, less prone to sleeping on a regular schedule, and less accommodating to babysitters. I learned, in hindsight, how much of my prior ability to balance work and mothering I owed to *Laura's* flexibility. Kristen, our gifted and trusted sitter, had graduated, and I never found anyone that flexible or reliable again. Most importantly, Madeline's birth ignited such fierce love and attachment in me that higher education by comparison seemed pale and pointless. My attachment to Laura grew, too, as a result of my new attitude toward mothering, and family acquired for me a gravitational pull beyond my resistance.

My journey out of political science was slow and meandering. It took me years of waffling and agonizing before I made a real decision to quit. I'd get enthused over my research and teaching experiences, then get overwhelmed by the pull of my family. I'd get blissed out on motherhood, then panic about losing my career identity. I felt enormous guilt about leaving. I felt guilty that I was letting down the sisterhood, those who had fought so hard for a woman's right to an equal career. I also felt like I was letting down the university faculty, especially those who had awarded me a fellowship and supported my academic work.

So I continued to work on the dissertation. I taught classes at both Ohio State and Otterbein College, a private liberal arts college in a suburb of Columbus. I presented research at professional conventions. I cobbled together child care, even relying for ten agonizing weeks on an appalling day-care center because I'd gotten a last-minute teaching contract. But my attention was permanently fractured. When I was working, I thought about my kids. When I was with the kids, I thought about work. Of the two sides of the fracture, work and home, home was winning as my interest in political science withered.

My husband David's life was changing, too. During the long years it took me to finish my PhD, his "stopgap" job that he'd once planned to leave whenever I said "go" turned into a successful career with tremendous responsibility and a substantial salary. We both knew it would be difficult for him to contentedly leave that job. Furthermore, his increased commitment at work left me with more of the burden of child care and household work. Without our consciously planning it, the babies had brought about a more traditional gender division of labor in our home.

As my graduate school friends either got jobs or moved on, I shifted my social connections outside of the academy. Several years into mothering, I had developed a close group of women friends: intelligent, fun-loving, dedicated mothers who were staying at home with their children. More and more, that was what I was doing, too: staying at home with my children. My academic work began to seem like a distraction from what I truly wanted, which was to fully immerse myself in mothering. I wanted to be one of the girls. I wanted to dump the guilt and stress and just relax into my family's life.

Four years behind my original schedule, in June of 1996, I defended my dissertation. Laura was five, Madeline was three, and I was thirty-four weeks pregnant with Julia, our third daughter. In a strange reversal of roles, the four men on my PhD committee seemed afraid of (or at least highly intimidated by) my enormously pregnant self, while I felt nothing but calm and confident. In part this was because I knew I had written a good dissertation, and I was fairly certain I'd earn the doctorate. But it was also because this group of men, and the academy they represented, held no power over me anymore.

Three of those uncomfortable men were fathers who'd left the child rearing to their wives. The other man had no family. None of them knew what it was like to feel a baby move inside a womb, or to push a baby out into the world. None of them had completed a dissertation (albeit in five long years, racing the qualification deadline) while also giving birth to two children, gestating a third, and pouring their souls into parenthood.

So when they asked puzzled questions about my plans for the future, I felt comfortable with my responses. No, I said, I don't want to go on the job market. No, I don't want to try to get the dissertation published as a book. No, I don't even want to teach as an adjunct. If I change my mind, I finally said, I know where to find you. I walked away from political science the day I defended my dissertation, having made a quirky but ultimately right decision for myself.

I won't say I never wonder what would have happened if I'd made a different decision, nor will I say that the path I chose is right for everyone. There's a certain degree of guilt and regret in my story, as I think there must be in everyone's, because every choice we make entails a universe of unlived possibilities. My life is different than the one planned by the idealistic and driven young woman I was two decades ago. But I set out to become anything I wanted to be, and that is what I have become: a mother and a writer with a doctorate in political science. Yes, I tell my own daughters that, of course, they can be anything they want to be when they grow up. And I smile to myself, because I can only imagine the sweet and painful choices that wait for them on the journey there.

Free to Be . . . Mom and Me

Finding My Complicated Truth as an Academic Daughter

MEGAN PINCUS KAJITANI

As a former teacher of feminist studies, I can easily tear down the whole have-it-all myth with a few choice words about our flawed patriarchal system and media spin. Yet this pesky cultural ideal has nagged at me, personally, for many years. That happens when your own mother is its living embodiment.

A PhD in accounting, my mother has gone from popular professor at one major business school to highly respected department chair in another, was thoroughly present for me and my brother growing up, *and* has a happy, thirty-seven-year marriage to my father, who is also an academic. She defies the studies I have cited in my *Chronicle of Higher Education* columns on the challenges of career/family balance in academia—studies that show women on the tenure track are less likely to have as many children as they want, and to make their marriages work, than tenured men or nontenured women. Several of my academic mentors fit the studies' disheartening description. But my mom pretty much has it all.

This knowledge, while on some levels inspiring, was not easy to live with when I found myself at twenty-nine, two years into a PhD program, realizing I didn't think I could swing the career/family balance I wanted. The total commitment required in my humanities discipline—including complete geographic flexibility and willingness to live for a decade on subsistence wages—became less and less appealing the deeper I went. And I was a West Coast soul (broken up with a West Coast boyfriend) holed up in a Midwest library, alone and cold on Saturday nights.

As Barbara Lovitts explains in her book *Leaving the Ivory Tower*, most of the 50 percent of all doctoral students who don't complete their programs were actually doing quite well when they decided to leave.[1] I was no exception. I'd earned a prestigious fellowship, won a graduate student award, presented at international conferences, and even published an academic article before the end of my eventual four years of course work. It wasn't that I couldn't do it. It was that I wasn't really happy doing it. I wasn't living where I wanted to live (and even when I transferred to a California PhD program, I knew I'd have to leave again to get a job); I wasn't married and having children, which, hard as it was to admit as an up-and-coming feminist scholar, I intensely wanted to be. I wasn't in the right place for me, literally and figuratively, at that time.

My mother never pressured me to have an academic career like hers, and she never pressured me to get married or have babies. In fact, her pressure actually came in the form of subtly urging me *not* to marry young (even though she did and got "lucky," as she calls it). The only outright requests she ever made of me were that I not become a cheerleader and I not pursue a career in acting, my adolescent fantasy. The cheerleader request was for obvious reasons from a 1970s feminist mother (and is a request I plan to pass down to my own daughter), and the acting because, living south of Hollywood, we knew many talented but starving actors, and CPA Mom didn't like the odds. Other than that, she just told me to do what made me happy.

To my surprise, it turns out I did all my mother told me. I was never a cheerleader. (Being thrown in the air and watching football were both wholly unappealing, so that was an easy one.) And I left acting behind at my performing arts high school after losing a big part and realizing I didn't have thick skin or overwhelming theatrical talent after all. I went to college back East and became a journalist instead, until deciding, after several years, to follow my roots to graduate school. I even got married at age thirty (to the aforementioned West Coast boyfriend), as my mom always recommended.

That I did not eventually become a doctor wasn't in any way breaking the mother-daughter bargain. It was never really even discussed. When I asked for her opinion, in the throes of my decision to forfeit my future in the professorate, she still said she just wanted me to be happy. Deep down, I knew she meant it. After all, this was the woman who bought me *Free to Be . . . You and Me* and read to me nightly from that weathered 1974 volume.[2] I absorbed the enlightened writings of Marlo Thomas, Gloria Steinem, Judy

1. Barbara Lovitts, *Leaving the Ivory Tower: The Causes and Consequences of Departure from Doctoral Study* (New York: Rowman & Littlefield, 2001).
2. Marlo Thomas, *Free to Be . . . You and Me* (New York: McGraw-Hill, 1974).

Blume, and Shel Silverstein about fighting gender stereotypes, embracing our feelings, and being whatever we wanted to be.

But it still bothered me immensely, as I stepped off the PhD path, that I wasn't going to be a superstar professor-mother like my own mother—that she had made it all work and I could not. As much as I knew it was the right choice for me, I still had an unsettling sense of failure—not helped by comments from family friends, friends of friends, or random people telling me "not to give up," that I "just had to finish or I'd never forgive myself." (Whose issues were those anyway?) It was a heart-wrenching, self-questioning time, and it took all my strength to walk away, with lip trembling, but head held high.

In an ironic turn, upon leaving my doctoral program I accepted a job as a career counselor for PhD students. I landed the offer through what career counselors call "planned happenstance." As a graduate student, I went to the career counselor's office and became interested in her work while she helped me decide to ditch the doctorate. When she happened to retire, I just happened to be ready to leave my program. So I used my well-honed research and presentation skills, and my by-then inside track, to land and nail the job interview. Fate with intention, let's say.

For nearly two years, I channeled my mother's wisdom each day as I helped troubled graduate students feel better about themselves. Yes, I edited résumés to the last detail and taught interviewing skills with the aplomb of a former actress, but my real contribution was the subtler support I offered to the many angst-ridden students who slinked into my office each week. I gave them validation that it's normal to have doubts about the long haul to the PhD, it's no small feat to earn a master's degree, and it's not wrong to do something else that might make them happier. While I of course supported those who were well suited for careers in academia, most of the notes in the collage of thank-yous tacked to my office bulletin board were from the questioners, those whom I steered through the heartache of self-doubt, away from the "shoulds" and useless comparisons, and toward a peace within themselves.

Partnering with a campus psychologist, I launched a support group for PhD students called "Questioning Career Transition"; it instantly had a waiting list every quarter. I wrote advice columns for the graduate student newsletter, which eventually evolved into *Chronicle of Higher Education* columns, offering a broader audience these confirming messages. "It's okay to change your mind," I called out to the unsure, overachiever doctoral students of the world. "You are not a failure. Academe is right for some people but not all. There are other places to use your education. And that's fine." Many wrote back, telling me no one else had said this to them before, and they had needed to hear it. In a way, these were my mother's lifelong lessons to me, but for the first time I was actually beginning to believe them, deep down inside myself.

Every week, men and women (but more women, who are also more likely to leave PhD programs) came into my office torn between the tenure track and the parent track, not knowing how to balance it all and stay sane. "Do we need to do it all, to drive ourselves into the ground?" they asked. "Isn't there another way?" I told them they did not need to have it all, at least not all at once, as the media taunts us to try for; few women are able to accomplish that as my mother did. "All," I explained, "is relative." In this counselor role, I blossomed, becoming like Marlo Thomas and Friends singing about being free to be who we are, about not comparing ourselves to others or trying to fit in to narrow stereotypes. (And by the way, let's fight the system, not beat ourselves up.) Finally, I was embodying all of this in my own life; the wisdom was becoming my own. As I spoke to these students, I also spoke to myself, and I was setting myself free.

It was during this time that I began to accept that my mom and I are just different. She is a math brain, in the male-dominated business-school world where a good woman is a gem, and there are jobs in desirable cities and money to go around. She had already started her family when she went for her doctorate, and graduated in the early 1980s when the market was in her favor. In personality, she is unflappable and even keeled—sensitive but not often outwardly emotional—and lets pressure, pettiness, and downright rudeness slide quietly off her back. I am a creative type, who attempted an academic career in a female-saturated humanities field that offered very few jobs and little money. I was still single, but deeply desiring a family, when I embarked on my doctoral program, at the top of this millennium with its glut of PhDs. As unflinching as my mother is, I get stressed out easily. Harsh comments, so common in academe, can crush me; I have actually been known to cry when someone flipped me the bird on the freeway.

My mother's personality is ideally suited for academic administration, and she loves it. My personality, I have come to embrace, is better suited for an eclectic mix of freelance work, activism, creative pastimes, and family life. We are both feminists, and in that way we are more similar than dissimilar. We both married men who are equal partners in marriage, and sensitive, involved fathers, which in her generation was atypical but thankfully in mine is growing more common. We both fight the patriarchal system, in our own ways—she, from within, in a position of power to influence department and university policies; I, from out here, through writing and speaking. We have both gravitated to what we do best and need most.

I left the university for good after my baby was born seven months ago. It was another turning point. The old system did not work for me. My department shunned part-time and job-share arrangements and the campus offered no child care for children under age one. Commute and day-care costs would nearly equal my staff salary. A full-time workload plus travel time, I decided, would not leave me even close to enough time with my child. I spoke out about the archaic injustice of policies on my campus; whether anyone really heard me, I'm not sure. I continue to write in various forums about ways academia can be more family friendly for faculty and staff (part-time and flexible work options, campus child care, manager training, teaching tenure, to name a few).

But, for me personally, the complicated truth is that I wanted the time at home with my daughter. The impossibility of keeping my job on campus, while infuriating on one hand, on the other hand forced me to figure out another path, which, in hindsight, suits me better. I had waited a long time to be a mom, and I wanted to savor and be fully present in it. The injustice is in the fact that I was not allowed a real choice. That I may have chosen to be home anyway is beside the point. This is where my feminist training serves me well—I can articulate this critical message and I know it is true. It took me a long time to get there, but I now understand that I can still be a feminist, and still fight the system that offers only a façade of choice, but also still be at home for now and feel happy about it.

And I am happy, happier than I've ever been. Full-time parenting is a grueling, 24–7 job, but I love it. Waking up with my curly haired cherub cooing at me, watching her discover how to scoot across the room or taste bananas for the first time—there is no job I'd rather have. This doesn't mean I don't have my moments of frustration and exhaustion, when she wakes up screaming at 2:00 A.M. and doesn't go back to sleep until five, or when those bananas end up in my hair and stay there for two days until I get a four-minute shower. It just means that, even in those undignified moments, I actually feel fortunate.

I still write professionally, as a freelancer, mostly pieces that challenge my mind and allow me to express myself, some that simply help pay the bills. Most days, I have intelligent conversations with my husband and friends. And I can usually laugh when I'm so sleep deprived I can't form a coherent sentence. My career is not on the fast track, but I'm keeping my engine running and will seek on-ramps to shift back into high gear in years to come. Living on my husband's schoolteacher salary and my sporadic freelance income is a stretch in Southern California, but every day we recommit to it and know it is right for us. For now, each day I have at home with my daughter is a gift, I truly believe, to both of us.

In the end, I'm doing things differently than my mother did, but I have created a career and a family nonetheless. Different women, different times, different circumstances. Both loving mothers, both women fighting inequities, both finding happiness in some combination of fulfilling work and loving family lives. A generation before her, my grandmother had no choice but to stay home, then my mother's generation fought hard to give women a place in the professional world. Now my generation takes on the fight for more balance, and more diversity of career/family options.

I still think my mom's ability to create an exemplary professional life and a functional family in these times, in this country, is rare. And to achieve this, she has worked harder and smarter than anyone I know. She still works through many a weekend, can often be found in her office at 10:00 P.M., and travels weeks out of each month. But she never fails to stop and pay full attention when her children or grandchildren call. I can now take lessons from my mother, but know I can never be her. And, once and for all, that's okay.

So, my journey carried me down the road to professorhood, swerved onto the avenue of counseling others, then jackknifed me back into my own driveway. Here, at last, I can sleep peacefully (in three-hour fragments) and embrace the lessons of my mother (although still make my choices by the heart, not the odds) and my 1970s childhood. I am now, in my thirties, free to be me, and to appreciate my mother for being her.

Nontraditional Academics

At Home with Children and a PhD

SUSAN BASSOW, DANA CAMPBELL, and LIZ STOCKWELL

Every year, PhDs leave academia to raise their children; many, perhaps even most, find fulfilling, nontraditional ways to remain intellectually productive. It is difficult to track those who leave for family reasons, since most lose any formal institutional affiliation. Social scientists who study women in academia may be able to follow the career paths of PhDs right to the point at which they leave academia, but even where reasons for departure are documented, there is little understanding of what happens to these smart, dedicated women (and men) once they have left traditional academic positions. In this essay, we reject the common notion that a PhD who has left academia to raise her children has lost her drive or somehow failed. Instead, we suggest that often the opposite is true: our own experience proves that leaving the traditional ranks of academia can bring intellectual freedom.

We are three biology PhDs from well-respected universities who left academic careers after our children were born. Today, we call ourselves Nontraditional Academics, or NTAs. We are dedicated to parenting as our primary career for the long term, and also to fostering independent writing, education, and consulting projects steeped in our academic backgrounds. We know that we are not alone (each of us is aware of a handful of peers who took the same track), but we are few and far between. We have no support group, as we would in traditional career tracks, so we each learned to tackle the balance of family and our academic interests individually. Upon meeting one other, however, we discovered that we share strikingly similar experiences and values that we had not realized were so integral to our identities. Finding these similarities gave us a heartening sense of normalcy and dispelled our fears of going it alone; it validated our commitment to be with our families, to integrate our love of learning into our children's lives, and we determined to support each other, and others in our position, as NTAs.

While a common notion claims that a woman can "have it all"—that is, the job and the family—this view is unconsciously skewed toward the mother who balances these by finding others to care for her children and working a forty-plus-hour week in a traditional career field. We represent a different, less publicized and recognized section of the have-it-all spectrum, those who intertwine our academic interests and caring for our children while our spouses are at work, and pull out our intellectual pursuits in off-work hours and nontraditional work environments.

Many reasons led us to emphasize raising children while giving up the next logical steps of our academic careers. We were motivated by the desire to experience and nurture our children as much as possible. We value the benefits of simplifying life during the child-rearing years and of turning our focus to family and community; we relish the joy of teaching and learning with our children while reducing the effects of the hectic pace of professional ladder climbing upon family life. Here Liz tells her story of making the decision to parent full time:

> The deeper I moved into my graduate research, the more disillusioned I became with pursuing a traditional tenure-track academic path. By the time I finished a postdoctoral position, I found my research had taken me farther away from the natural history and love of the tropics that truly excited me. Just before my first child, Henry, was born, I thought that part-time university teaching would be a satisfying way to stay intellectually active. I naively assumed that I could write new lectures, grade assignments, and prepare for class with a cobbled-together combination of child care from my husband in his off hours, eight hours a week from a paid babysitter, and long stretches of baby naps. However, not only did I grossly underestimate the time it would take to prepare a new class and grade assignments, but baby Henry preferred to sleep in twenty-minute catnaps during the day, and needed frequent feedings at night. I found myself staying up all night, overusing Baby Mozart, and feeling oddly resentful of my son. Subsequent years teaching the same course went more smoothly, and were very enjoyable, but still required more time than specified by my job description and salary. Furthermore, to feel fully satisfied as a teacher, my attention was always focused on my students and course responsibilities at some level, even when I was with my family. On a family trip to a local beach one glorious fall afternoon, I spent more time alone identifying seaside plants in preparation for a class field trip I was to lead the following week than I did playing in the sand and looking for sea creatures with Henry. The difficulties I had switching gears between my roles

as biology instructor and mother were all the more wrenching when I could see the happy moments I was missing with my son, and it became clear that I needed to rethink my priorities.

When my husband accepted a position at another university, I opted not to negotiate a position for myself, but rather decided to spend time with my son. I justified it to anyone who asked as "the maternity leave I never had with Henry." My daughter, Rachel, was born shortly after the move, and both the cost of child care for two children and the desire to be with my daughter during the developmental stages I missed with Henry confirmed for me that part-time teaching was not a viable option. I now realize that stepping away from the hectic juggling of child care and teaching was an empowering choice. I have actually found more thoughtful, satisfying time to develop my interest in tropical ecology and teaching by writing a book and developing a college-level curriculum on the natural history of tropical fruits and the animals with which they have evolved. I look forward to teaching a course one day in which I use my book, but for now I can fulfill my intellectual needs within my familial obligations by immersing myself in book research when I get time off from mothering.

When the three of us sat down together and figured out our similarities, we found that for all of us our parenting reflects our interest in our field, and we constantly share our love of science with our children. Whether it is taking our kids on outings into natural areas, going to the local science museum, or volunteering within our children's classrooms, we instill in our children the importance of education. We talk about science at the dinner table and in the car, and we instill a far different threshold for squeamishness about biological critters than is common in our suburban neighborhoods. Our children's pets might include pill bugs, darkling beetles, snails, or cockroaches, and we've even been known to bring ethanol home from the lab to preserve dead pet fish for later dissection. We motivate with biology: "Let's see how many different kinds of birds we can see on our walk to school this morning!" Science-related games, toys, and books spill off our children's shelves. We parent this way partly because we love going to the science museum or the zoo, so we spend our time with our kids there. It feels natural to help out in our children's schools, and wonderful to be heroes in our children's eyes. Finally, we simply want our children to have the opportunities to love what we love. For all these reasons and more, we share our love of science and education with our children, and they adopt this love without prodding.

We focus intently on our families, and have taken on our new jobs of parenting with as much drive and enthusiasm as we had when we began our dissertation research. Just as our academic careers have been altered by having children, our children have caused a shift in our academic interests. We are no longer constrained by the specific niche we had cut out for ourselves in the course of graduate and postdoctoral research. Our children have helped us to follow our interests and passions toward the intersection between science and important aspects of our family lives: education, child development, sharing our love of natural history with our children and our responsibility for Earth's stewardship, for example. Along these lines, Susan tells how her background provides a valuable and rare resource for her children's school:

I have loved ecology since I was a little girl. I marched through college and then graduate school focused on biology, ecology, and climate change, and even held a science-policy postdoctoral position at the White House Office of Science and Technology Policy. Once our children were born, however, my priorities shifted. My desire to study ecology transformed into my desire to teach my children about the world in which we live.

Ever since our daughters were born, my husband and I (both ecologists) have brought them outside to explore and enjoy nature. We are known in the neighborhood as the parents who take kids on nature walks—we explore the open fields nearby, finding interesting insects, plants, lizards, snakes, and other ecological wonders. When my older daughter was six, she went to a natural science camp and had such a great experience that I, in turn, became involved with this environmental education organization, as a board member. For the first time since my children were born, I had a title that I felt was worthy of my PhD.

My other "job" is to advocate for the promotion of math and science in my daughters' elementary school. In my experience, teachers welcome educated scientists to help enrich the science curriculum. Last year I helped out with my daughters' school's Science Fair. This year I wanted to do more, so I organized the first series of PTA-funded after-school science sessions, with the theme "science is fun." My enthusiasm for science proved contagious: nearly half of the school's five hundred children attended our sessions. I selected activities and designed simple experiments aimed to show kindergarten through sixth-grade students how fun science can be. For example, the children learned about polymers by making slime; simulated how an eardrum works with plastic wrap and salt; and learned about food webs by dissecting sterilized, regurgitated owl pellets full of the indigestible remains of the owl's prey. By the end of their afternoons, they were all smiles, and had even learned a bit of science. I do not get paid for this work but I have the satisfaction of knowing that our neighborhood school has excellent opportunities for science education, and equally important, my kids are filled with pride that their mother is known throughout their school as the "science lady."

Despite our dedication to raising our families, the interest and drive to continue academic pursuits does not dissolve with the choice to raise a family; in fact, it bubbles up in every possible venue. However, because the structure of academia does not currently fit or support the NTA's lifestyle, staying intellectually engaged becomes a fight for many reasons. This fight, ironically, produces many of the frustrations that squelch drive and wear down self-esteem in women like ourselves.

As full-time parents, we still thrive on the intellectual stimulation of working on the kinds of activities that gripped us in our academic work, and all three of us have thrown ourselves into projects—writing books and articles, teaching events, consulting—during any free time we can get. Here we share several challenging issues common to our experiences in pursuing intellectual activities.

A major issue for NTAs is keeping up with research or work relevant to the fields in which we completed our degrees so that we can continue to connect with and relate to our former colleagues, advisors, and peers. After several years out of academia, on a path that is so different from our expected career trajectory, we are often dismissed as "not working" and therefore no longer useful contacts. It becomes hard to ask for letters of recommendation from the very people who know our work the best.

After terminating formal academic affiliations, our projects are no longer externally endorsed, and aspects of academia that we took for granted are no longer at our disposal. We have no advisor, no department, no borrowing privileges at academic libraries, no institutional address or e-mail, no letterhead (even to write recommendations for former students), and no access to granting agencies to approve or fund our work. These are great liabilities. As NTAs we need to assure ourselves that our projects are both feasible and worthwhile, with little external feedback and without academic facilities. We then need to justify to ourselves (and to our partners) our spending from the family budget to carry out our unendorsed projects. We need to fund computers, hardware and software purchases, photocopying, Internet access, and anything else that used to be funded through grants or an institution, and with no tech support service in our home offices. Sometimes it is possible to obtain library and equipment privileges and endorsement through an unsalaried academic affiliation, such as research associate. However, departments vary in their requirements of affiliates, and this type of position may bring with it expectations of productivity and department involvement that are difficult for a full-time parent to live up to.

Of course, there is also the issue of engaging one's brain in an academic project after spending a day engaged with children. Staying intellectually active is a second job that demands creativity and mental energy, and often there is not much of either left when the day is done. Many times we try to set our children up with an activity that will completely engage them, such as running through the sprinkler. We carefully put out snacks, towels, and plenty of toys in anticipation of any possible issue that could come up, so that we can sit on the sidelines with our computer, but inevitably, as soon as we get that first thought going, someone needs a Band-Aid, or the drinks have spilled all over the towels. Often, even in the intervals between interruptions, we spend more time watching the fun than typing on the keys anyway. So we wait for the evening, another potential time for attacking writing or research projects. After homework, good-night books, brushing teeth, and the long task of getting everyone into bed, we make lunches for the next day, call the soccer coach to find out why our child is no longer on the team, tend to our sunburns (what parent remembers to put sunscreen on themselves?), check our e-mail, and then sit staring with glazed eyes at that computer file again before realizing that in less that seven hours we'll be starting a new day with energized kids—and we know it's bedtime.

Another challenge for the NTA is dealing with judgment from the rest of the world. Caught in between traditional paths, our self-esteem deflates as we watch the blossoming careers of our graduate school peers (where we could have been right now), while at the same time often keeping a low profile on our own extensive educational background and our "advanced" (relative to other parents) age as we try to fit in to our current set of (less academic) parent-peers. Even our own family members sometimes comment, "It must be frustrating to have wasted all those years in school and then not use your degree."

The tenure process is so rigorous and time consuming that many opt out of this path to pursue career alternatives that are more amenable to spending time with family, such as lectureships or research positions. This choice in itself is often wrenching, but is considered acceptable by traditional academics, and may even allow for a tenure-track option down the road. Taking time away from the scholarly schedule to raise children full time, however, so obviously derails one from the academic track that it is hard to explain this as a career choice rather than as not making it in academia.

The three of us have all heard supposedly sympathetic, falsely self-deprecating comments like "I could never stay home full-time with my kids, I would just go crazy." We are not necessarily more *able* to stay home with our children, (or better able to withstand the reduced intellectual environment of raising children), but perhaps we are more *committed* or *willing*. Parenting is our choice; we didn't opt out of academia because we were looking for a reduced intellectual input, but because we see full-time parenting as an advantage to our children and as a way for us to use our extensive education and enthusiasm to make valuable contributions to the next generation. Being a parent is, of course, excruciating work, in part because the choice to parent at the expense of one's traditional career is often underappreciated. Here are Dana's tangles with self-esteem:

I have more than a vague feeling that I let my PhD advisor down by not going on to the postdoc that awaited me. I have lost touch with people I love from my graduate school days who are now professors; they are busy, I am busy, and phone calls can get a bit awkward: after they describe their latest research paper I am often stumped by the question "So, what have you done that is interesting?" From my early elementary school years I have been a hard worker, studiously searching out any opportunities for extra credit or more advanced work. So when I recently overheard a colleague say, "Dana is not very motivated," I felt terrible and unappreciated.

But I enjoy and value what I do. I love working on my book, in which I have adapted a series of experiments from science literature that helps parents actively explore their children's cognitive development—this aspect of child development fascinates me, especially now that I am experiencing it firsthand with my children. I love that my children's lives are not frenzied by my career, and yet my children (occasionally) see me research and write on my own project. I also love that I have the time and energy to explore the outdoors with my kids. I want my kids to appreciate the simplicities of owning one car and not depending on long commutes, and to avoid the rampant pressures of consumerism and excessive conveniences to save time. Even as the world gets smaller and tighter I realize how little access children have to enthusiastic role models who demonstrate how to enjoy and protect, rather than consume, their world.

Seeing my daughter choose to put on her boots for a walk down the stream behind our house instead of watching her favorite TV show, or grab her friend to show her the bug she found on the sidewalk and watch her friend be a little more receptive than the last time she did this, seeing my three-year-old recognize a woodpecker and enjoy the analysis of what it eats and where it finds its food, all this makes me more secure that I am doing the right thing in sharing my values with my children. I do not need academics to understand or appreciate what I do, but I would love it if they did, and maybe one day they will.

NTAs enjoy few academic benefits, but it would not take much to empower NTAs to use their skills fully and productively. In the long run, assisting the NTA will benefit not only the individual, but also the institution that has already put considerable energy into training and forming the individual as a scholar.

The Whiteley Center at the University of Washington Friday Harbor Laboratories stands out as an institution that exemplifies the rich realm of possibilities for supporting NTAs. We highlight this facility because all of us have worked there extremely productively, and because it offers a clear, concrete example of how an academic institution can successfully support the intellectual activities of an NTA and simultaneously enrich the experience of other scholars. The Whiteley Center encourages established scholars of all types to study and write on specified, approved projects for periods of a few days to a month. Most important to the NTA, the Whitely Center accepts applications from those not currently affiliated with an academic institution, and motivates the NTA by endorsing and validating her project. The Center provides convenient office space, computer equipment and Internet access, extensive library facilities, space for collaborations, a forum for intellectual interactions, and housing for families in a wonderful setting.

While having all these benefits in one location such as the Whitely Center is ideal, any university could, at little additional cost, open its facilities to NTAs and provide one or a subset of amenities to support our intellectual activities. Free or reduced-cost access to library facilities may be the simplest way for institutions to encourage NTAs, especially now that so many resources are available online. Providing space, affiliation, computer equipment, and software is also of great help, as is creating opportunities for intellectual interactions. Perhaps just as important as any of these services individually, however, is recognition by the academic community (and perhaps society as a whole) that NTAs make valuable intellectual contributions through nontraditional venues and can connect traditional academics with broader sections of society, such as school-age children.

Universities are working to make academia more family friendly. For example, the Berkley Parents' Network, in connection with the University of California's Family Friendly Edge initiative, puts out an online support and informational newsletter for people who are "balancing academic goals or careers with family life." Bristol University in England offers regular quarterly meetings for academics to discuss issues of academic family life. There is no equivalent support for NTAs. Since NTAs' choices are uncommon among our academic peers, since we tend to disperse away from our home institutions (as do most academics), and since we're usually academically unaffiliated, the three of us feel there is a great need for better networking to increase interaction and discussion and decrease isolation among NTAs. Networks would help NTAs maintain a larger presence and greater recognition in academic horizons, reduce anxiety about being the only one out there forging an unconventional path through unappreciated terrain, and create a community in which we belong—all of which would make NTAs better, more secure parents and scholars.

We believe full-time parents with doctorates and other graduate degrees share many issues and experiences without realizing it, and we have found that strength comes in identifying others with similar goals, values, and frustrations, and banding together. We envision creating a forum for full-time parents with graduate degrees to share experiences and ideas with like-minded others and to get productive feedback and support. Our current vision is a Web site in which members can contribute to current discussions, read archived discussions, post to and read from a bulletin board of time-sensitive topics, and explore links of general interest, such as grant opportunities and calls for papers. We expect ongoing discussions to include an array of topics: ideas for projects, suggestions for balancing family and intellectual life, connections to potential collaborators or contractors, parenting and school concerns, and successes and frustrations. We hope that meeting and comparing perspectives with other PhDs from all different stages in their careers will build a supportive community of full-time PhD parents, which will reduce feelings of isolation and provide encouragement for intellectual creativity, parenting, and academic connections.

Making the decision to leave accepted career paths and care for our children full time has empowered us to explore new intellectual directions while enriching our own lives tremendously. However, it is a difficult road.

The three of us feel extremely lucky to have found each other and to be able to analyze critically what we do and how we feel about what we do, and identify ways to make it easier and more satisfying to remain active in intellectual pursuits. We call on other NTAs to join us in building a community for support and activism. There is tremendous societal value in affirming the lifestyle choices made by NTAs, and supporting their continued contributions to intellectual discovery and educational improvements, but we need to draw together as a group in order to get this done.

A Great Place to Have a Baby

REBECCA STEINITZ

I had my first child in 1996. I received my PhD in 1997. I had my second
child in 2000. Now it is 2007, but I am not the tenured professor my
timetable suggests I should be.

Ah, you think, you've heard this story, in all its variations. She and her
husband met in graduate school; she followed him to his first job and started
adjuncting; the first baby came and she didn't publish; the second baby came
and her husband was busy in the lab; before she knew it, she was a stay-at-
home mom. Or maybe they both got jobs, four hundred miles apart, and
when push came to shove, she gave hers up so the family could be together.
Perhaps before she even finished the dissertation she decided that professor
and mom were mutually incompatible, so she got the degree, got a real job,
and got on with the business of a family. Or it could be—though you hope
not—that she's one of those sad cases who went on the job market half a
dozen times without success and decided to compensate with another child.

Nope. We've all heard these stories, even watched them unfold, but none
of them are mine. For me, academia and motherhood went together like
Gilbert and Gubar, Deleuze and Guattari, Big Bird and Snuffleupagus, diapers and wipes.

Graduate school seemed like a great place to have a baby. Having worked
for several years before returning to school, I turned thirty as I started my
dissertation. I had no intention of following in the footsteps of the junior
faculty I knew who, postponing children for tenure, found themselves childless at forty and, if they were lucky, parenting toddlers at forty-five. I had
excellent health insurance and a dissertation fellowship. There seemed no
reason to wait.

Indeed, graduate school turned out to be a great place to have a baby. I
was five months pregnant when I went on the job market for the first time,

with one chapter of my dissertation completed. It was a relief when my interviews went nowhere, leaving me free to devote myself to preparenting and dissertating. The baby was born in May, I took the summer off, and by August, I was back at my computer, with the help of a part-time babysitter and my husband's days off.

There were certainly some hairy moments, like scrambling to finish my writing sample with the baby lying on the floor next to my desk, which sounds charming, but wasn't. Overall, though, it worked. I nursed in the Hilton hotel ladies' room between Modern Language Association interviews and managed to find time to pump on campus visits, which department chairs were kind enough to schedule so that I was away from home as briefly as possible. (I had enough frozen breast milk to get the baby through the first, but by the second, a week later, we succumbed to the ease of formula.)

I got a tenure-track position, we moved two-thirds of the way across the country, and before I knew it, I had transformed from grad-student-mom into professor-mom, which I did not find much harder. (Okay, I am slightly exaggerating the ease, though not the outcome: we arrived in Ohio on the first of August and, having finished my dissertation just three days before we left California, I spent the next two weeks in a panicky search for child care while I was supposed to be preparing classes. I had finally talked myself into a home day care that I could tolerate, when—I am not joking—a trained British nanny called me up, said she'd heard I was looking for child care, and announced that she was coming to work for me. Because we lived in a small town in Ohio, and her salary was her family's second income, I could even afford her. It seemed like a sign that everything was meant to be.)

Though it was disconcerting to be the only person in town who occupied the overlapping sets of mother and assistant professor—at parties, I never knew whether to talk shop with my colleagues or talk kids with their wives—I found my job ideal for motherhood. My schedule was flexible, I had summers off, and there was an endless supply of student babysitters. I could bring my daughter to work if she had a day off from school, and if I had to cancel class because she was sick, nobody raised an eyebrow. I stayed up way too late preparing for class, spent every Sunday in my office grading essays, and nearly lost my mind every time I had to give a conference paper, but I could go to Halloween parties, take Friday afternoons off, and be at the sitter's or school in five minutes if someone threw up.

My good fortune was due partly to my institution, a liberal arts college that genuinely placed teaching first and hired with the expectation of tenure, unless someone really screwed up. Writing mainly in the summer, I was able to publish at a reasonable clip, and good teaching evaluations and prodigious amounts of service helped me feel reasonably secure, even as a junior faculty member.

I was also lucky to have a supportive chair and provost, both active fathers who appreciated the logistical challenges of combining professing and parenting. One thing the college did not have was a viable maternity leave policy: on paper, faculty got six weeks off, which made no sense at all, especially for a baby due at the end of December, as my second was. But when I proposed to my chair that I substitute the six weeks for one of my courses, and committee work for another, he suggested that I teach a once-a-week honors tutorial in place of the third, and, voilà, I essentially had a semester off, coming in just one afternoon a week for office hours and my tutorial, and showing up at department meetings with the baby asleep in her car seat.

The following year, when I heard that a woman in another department had received no maternity leave after the birth of her daughter, I proposed to the Faculty Personnel Committee that every new mother (I couldn't get as far as fathers, though we did include adoptive mothers) receive the equivalent of a semester off, to be taken as she and her department determined, either in one full semester, as I had, or in several semesters of reduced load. The new policy was rapidly approved by the faculty, demonstrating both an institutional will to support mothers and the power of individual mothers within the institution.

The spring I spent on maternity leave, I received early promotion. The next year I got tenure. The year after that, I was awarded a special scholarly leave which I was able to combine with a semester-long sabbatical for a full year off, during which my family spent ten weeks in London, funded by a generous faculty development grant. My children were thriving at the on-campus preschool and the local public school.

What a triumphal narrative, you're probably thinking. Let's get to the happily ever after already.

Except wait. Something is not right.

It's okay. You can flip back to the first paragraph.

Yes, you're remembering correctly.

After all that, I left. Walked away from tenure, at a good school, where they liked me (most of them) and I liked them (most of them). What was I thinking?

I was thinking that academia really wasn't for me. Though I liked the classroom and my students, the idea of teaching first-year writing and *Jane*

Eyre over and over for the rest of my career made me want to cry. Research was fine when I was doing it, but I didn't miss it when I wasn't. And after publishing several articles and finishing my first book, I realized I had nothing else to say—at least nothing else scholarly to say. When I went to conferences, I had little interest in what anyone else had to say either. Academic politics? Don't get me started.

I suppose I could have become one of those alienated academics who shows up only to teach, but alienation has never been one of my career goals. And beyond academia, my husband's career had stalled and we were hundreds of miles away from our families, living in a place we had no desire to live.

We kept at it for several years, though. I mean, I had tenure! We could afford our mortgage, we had lovely friends, and life wasn't terrible, most of the time. As significantly, I couldn't imagine how I would manage motherhood if I wasn't a professor. Would I send my kids to camp for the entire summer, while I shivered in an air-conditioned office, counting the days till the single week of vacation I could spend with them? Would they have to go to afterschool five days a week? What if I had a finite number of sick days, and it wasn't enough? What if I wasn't allowed to bring my kids to work? How would I find babysitters if I didn't have students? And who would I be if I wasn't a professor and a mother?

I'd be a mother and something else, I realized, when we finally acknowledged that the reasons to leave were stronger than the reasons to stay. I quickly discovered that the rigidity of a nine-to-five office life was not for me, but I was able to craft an alternative career path that grafted the flexibility I had as a professor on to work that I love: I now divide my time between freelance editing, writing, and a half-time job running a program for high school teachers. I still stay up late at night to finish editing projects and write essays like this one, but I also can still stay home with a sick kid and make it to the Halloween party. My children are minutes away from their grandparents, my husband's career has taken off, and we can get to the beach in less than an hour.

But my point here is not simply the eventual happily ever after (so far) of my own narrative. Rather, I want to argue that the academy has the potential to be a radically family-friendly work environment. Professors have the flexibility and autonomy only dreamt of by most working mothers—whether they work at Wal-Mart or on Wall Street. The university is, at least theoretically, an environment which places a prime value upon the individual mind, whether that mind is teaching or learning. It would be wholly logical to extend that value to the individual's body, life, and family, which enable that mind to function. And I'd argue, too, that it wouldn't be that difficult. Indeed, my experience could serve as a model.

It is not insignificant, though, that I taught at a mid-level liberal arts college rather than a top-tier research university where the demands to publish or perish could give pause to any but the most avid procreators. Still, even those institutions have started to realize the possibilities: Harvard University recently set aside additional funds for faculty and staff child care, while Princeton University and the Massachusetts Institute of Technology now automatically extend the tenure clock for junior faculty who have babies.

Academia is not just a place where students learn and faculty teach and research. It is also, again theoretically, but often practically as well, one of the primary incubators for the ideas and practices that shape our society. Why not use today's universities, then, to birth a new vision of academia and mothering, indeed, of work and parenting? A vision in which these dyads are neither mutually exclusive nor oxymoronic, but rather symbiotic and productive?

What it would take? Oh, the usual (or maybe I should say the obvious): a commitment to partner hires, reasonable maternity leaves and no punishment for taking them, affordable and available on-campus child care, flexible scheduling for courses and meetings, an equitable distribution of teaching and service across departments (not to mention across genders), transparent tenure expectations that emphasize quality over quantity, supportive senior faculty. That is to say: a bunch of things that would be eminently feasible if academia, which supposedly consists of the smartest people around, would just decide that they mattered.

I know, I'm talking like a cockeyed optimist, but, hey, isn't cockeyed optimism fundamental to the very act of having a child? So why not take it bigger?

Today motherhood, tomorrow the university, next week the world!

Recovering Academic

JENNIFER MARGULIS

Jenny flounced into my office and threw herself in a chair. She was crying before I had even managed to say hello. She gripped a cloth handkerchief in her hand as tightly as my daughter held Blue-Blue Blankie at home, drawing it rather brutally across her eyes to wipe away the tears. She seemed to be willing herself to stop sobbing.

"What can I do for you?" I asked, unsure how to respond to this display of emotion from a student. When my two-year-old cried I usually knew how to comfort her. I'd take her in my arms, or nurse her, maybe distract her with a silly joke, or tell her a story about Chica Persona, a made-up misbehaver whose antics often mirrored my daughter's. But what was I supposed to do with Jenny, a grown woman and my student? Should I hug her? Offer her Kleenex though she already had a handkerchief? Crack stupid jokes?

I sat listening to the faulty radiator backfiring in my dingy gray basement office and waited for Jenny to pull herself together. After a few minutes she stopped crying and started hiccupping.

"I. Just. Don't," she began. "Understand. Why. I. Got. An A-. And not an A. (Hiccup.) On. This. Paper." She thrust the essay under my nose.

Her paper, about diabolic images in Nathaniel Hawthorne's *The Scarlet Letter,* had a grammatical error in the first sentence. And the second. And the third. After three years in one of the top colleges in the United States, Jenny, an English major, could barely write a sentence without making a mistake.

I've. Never," she continued, still sniffling, "gotten anything but a . . . a . . . an A on a paper before."

I rubbed my belly. I was almost seven months pregnant with my second child. What was I doing in this dim office with this spoiled student? Why wasn't I home playing with my toddler? I had originally wanted to become a professor because I loved to teach; more specifically I wanted to teach people who wanted to learn. Teaching at anything but the college level didn't appeal to me because I did not want to be a disciplinarian. I wanted to help open young minds, learn as much from my students as I taught them, engage in debates that would move the world forward. But Jenny wasn't interested in talking about the cogency of her argument, the misplacement of her apostrophes, or even the larger issues of good and evil, conformity and socialization that were raised in Hawthorne's text. She couldn't care less about either logic or grammar. She was only interested in her grade. And the grade, an A-, was not something she earned or merited; it was something *I* had done to *her*. If I learned anything from the students at the all-female, elite college where I was a visiting assistant professor, it was that I didn't want my daughter to grow up to be anything like them.

I received three job offers my first year out of graduate school: a tenure-track offer from an upstate school in the State University of New York system, a lectureship at Michigan State University, and a visiting professorship at a top women's college. I felt an instant intellectual affinity with the chair at the SUNY school who was courting me, and the idea of working at a university that catered to regular kids, most of whom were first generation college-goers, appealed to me. But when I went to visit the school the faculty seemed so unhappy. They didn't understand the dean's system for merit raises, they felt overwhelmed by the number of students enrolled in the courses they taught. The people who would become my colleagues seemed stuck. The dean talked enthusiastically about moving my tenure clock forward since I had already published a book in graduate school, but when I asked him for a higher starting salary and money for moving expenses, he turned cold.

"One doesn't refuse a tenure-track offer," the chair of Graduate Studies at Emory University, where I had earned my PhD, said when I went to talk to him about the campus visit. He was restless, rearranging books on his desk. He placed a hardcover edition of *The Scarlet Letter* on top of a paperback *Gulliver's Travels*.

"But I've got another one, at a school that's on the map. It's not tenure track but they're offering me over five thousand dollars a year more."

"One doesn't refuse a tenure-track offer," the chair intoned.

I thought of a brilliant colleague who had moved to Nevada for a tenure-track position, and was miserable. And another who worked at a big research university in the middle of Ohio who was also struggling to find her way. I thought of a professor at Emory who never wanted to be in Atlanta, who hadn't bought a house or an apartment because she felt like her time there was just temporary. Ten years later, tenured, she was still in Atlanta. Instead of living her life, she was waiting to leave. She hadn't married or had children. My husband, James, and I talked about our options for hours: we decided that we weren't willing to move somewhere we didn't want to live just for a job. We made the decision that we would make over and over again: our family, our children, and our quality of life all came ahead of academic success. It was a decision that would soon catapult me out of academia and into a more flexible, child-friendly, and risky career.

"What university are you affiliated with in America?" a professor from the English Department at L'Université Abdou Moumouni, Niger's only university, asked me, years later, as I handed him a business card.

"I'm not," I said.

"You don't work for a university in the States?"

"No," I explained. "I'm a recovering academic."

I had turned down the tenure-track offer and taken the job at the women's college, happy to be back in the Northeast and thrilled with the prospect of teaching motivated students. It was there, in faculty housing, that our second daughter, Athena, was born at home. She emerged from my womb whooping her war cry, gray eyes flashing. James and I wanted to have our children close in age, so we planned for Athena and her older sister, Hesperus, to be only nineteen months apart. For us, going from no children to one (an easily comforted, smiley baby) was much easier than going from one to two (Athena was a lusty baby who was very vocal about her needs just as Hesperus morphed into a terribly trying toddler). I found myself completely overwhelmed by the needs of my children and the needs of my students. To my surprise, the school where I chose to work was far from idyllic. Instead of having lively discussions about literature over tea (isn't that how professors at elite New England colleges nestled in the mountains spend at least some of their time?), I found myself in a competitive, unsupportive department where the professors were more interested in their evaluations than in academic standards and where the students, like Jenny, seemed to care stridently about their grades but feel nonchalant about the quality of their education. Worse, when I told the chair I was pregnant and due in the spring, he cringed visibly. "You can take a week off," he said, sounding like he thought he was being generous. "We'll get someone to cover your classes." Something had to give.

"What would your ideal job be?" I asked James one day while we were visiting my mom. Hesperus had found a pair of scissors and was cutting the fibers of my mother's dining room carpeting. Newborn Athena was nursing.

"To be paid to write," he said without hesitating.

"Paid to write?" The idea was so novel I had to ponder it. Most young academics are so desperate to get published in scholarly journals that they rarely even consider remuneration. The first royalty check I received for the academic book I published in grad school—a classroom edition of a little-known eighteenth-century play that I coedited with a colleague because I didn't have the confidence to do it myself—was for $31.22. I was so delighted I skipped all the way to the bank to deposit the check. But it's not like those royalties would pay the rent.

"Paid to write, like how?"

"Like, you know, long articles for the *Atlantic Monthly*."

"They pay you for that?"

It was such a good idea! Why hadn't I thought of it before? Writing for a living. What could be more perfect?!

The idea seemed even better when I found out just how much some magazines and newspapers would pay. I wrote to *FamilyFun Magazine* for their writer's guidelines. They came back on a page that had been Xeroxed so many times they were barely legible. But the information contained in that fading type was hard to believe.

"A dollar a word!" I told James. "A dollar a word?! They pay you a dollar for one word. 'The,'" I said, holding out my hand. "Give me a dollar!" I ran around the house, changing Athena's diaper and picking up Hesperus's toys, humming to myself. I need only write the word *the* and I would make a dollar.

"So you're not teaching in America?" my Nigerian colleague asked again.

"Not anymore," I explained. "In the States I make a living as a writer."

The problem with becoming a writer when you have an academic background is that you have to undo a lot of what you're taught in academia. Academics write obscurely, intentionally limiting their readership by masking their ideas behind abstruse prose. In fact, unless you're Henry Louis Gates, Jr., if your work is too popular your colleagues become suspicious.

At tenure reviews they don't necessarily want to see that you've published in *Ms. Magazine* and the *New York Times* but in journals with names like the *Journal of Andrology* and the *Ontology of Semiology*.

Though establishing a career as a writer wasn't as easy as I'd thought it'd be when I went dancing around the house, it was a relief to make my own schedule and escape the classroom. I missed the summers off and the overseas conferences, but I didn't miss teaching or the cold shoulders I got from my colleagues. After all, being a parent was as much of a performance as teaching, it involved as much energy, as much social interaction, and as much hand-holding. By the time our third child was born, on a clear October night in our little red farmhouse in Greenfield, Massachusetts, I had found my voice as a parenting writer and journalist and had established a consulting business to help other writers (many also trying to undo their academic training) polish their prose and publish.

A year later a writer friend (a mother of four boys who had become a successful writer even though she never finished college) forwarded a call from the Fulbright Program folks saying they were looking for applicants. I'd lived in West Africa in the 1990s and always planned to go back. But life and work and baby making had gotten in the way.

I didn't know that as a professional writer I was eligible for a Fulbright, but I was. A year after I learned I could apply (it's a long process), I found myself in front of a classroom again for the first time in six years. I was awarded the Fulbright to return to Niger, the landlocked Sahelian country where I had worked thirteen years before. I would teach my specialty—nineteenth-century American literature—in a country where only 15 percent of the population is literate. I knew a little about the university, as I had taught English as a Second Language there before. The University of Abdou Moumouni, named after a famous Nigerien physicist, was once the jewel of West Africa. Students from Mali to the West and Chad to the East, as well as those from neighboring Benin, Togo, and other Francophone countries, would come to study there. But I also knew that the current government was openly opposed to education, and that over the past ten years the university had steadily declined. The president of Niger, Mamadou Tandja, had actually said in a televised address that people in Niger don't need education, they need to grow millet and sorghum. Army men, in full riot gear, are dropped off by the truckload on campus every morning to "keep the peace." But even though I was prepared, theoretically, for difficult teaching conditions, I really had no idea what I was getting myself into.

I had eighty-four second-year English students packed into one small room, with three squeaky ceiling fans and a very dusty chalkboard. The students in the back were so far from the blackboard they had to stand up to see what was written at the bottom.

This was a far cry from Emory's tree-lined campus, where marigolds, tulips, and daffodils bloomed on every walkway, where most of the classrooms were equipped with PowerPoint projectors, podiums, pull-down screens, and world maps, not to mention clean chalkboards, working outlets, doors that close, and brand-new desks. For the past three years Niger has been classified as the poorest country in the world by the United Nations. Instead of teaching some of the most privileged people in the world, I would now be teaching some of the most disenfranchised.

But after my family and I arrived in Niamey and settled in (a process which took months longer than I expected) it became unclear whether I would actually get to teach. During the first months of the semester we endured what the American Embassy called "seasonal striking," students protesting government policies and commemorating the deaths of their comrades in past protests. The two months of sometimes violent striking included large protests blocking traffic for hours, angry students burning tires and torching cars with foreign plates, and gendarmes dispersing crowds with tear gas, which (I found out one day while I was trying to hold a class, despite the political difficulties, about slave narratives) sounds like a bomb explosion when it's fired outside one's classroom. Just when I was despairing of ever getting to teach, the political situation finally settled down, and my students and I dove gratefully into the nineteenth-century American literary tradition.

The peace lasted for exactly three weeks. Then, at eight o'clock one morning, I heard someone call "Madame!" A large man filled the doorframe of my classroom. "You are in my room!"

"I beg your pardon?" I had been writing the day's lesson plan and homework on the board. I walked to the door where the man was waiting, bringing my chalk with me. It was the only piece I had, the only piece I had access to. If I left it in the chalkboard well, it would disappear.

"This," he said grandiosely, "is my room. Tell your students to leave at once!"

I looked at him in disbelief, sure there was some mistake. Nigeriens are known for their graciousness and hospitality and I was flabbergasted that the professor was talking to me this way. "I've been using this room since the beginning of the semester," I protested, moving away from the door so my students wouldn't hear me arguing in French. "I was assigned this room by the English Dep—"

"The English Department has no jurisdiction over rooms!" he interrupted. "Assigning rooms is the responsibility of the Registrar's Office. And if you follow me, you will see that YOU ARE IN MY ROOM."

The professor swept away, his white robes hovering about him like a ghost in one of the Edgar Allan Poe stories we were reading. I followed him past a bathroom where one sink was ripped out and the other was leaking, making a *drip drip* sound as the water spilled to the floor. The air in the hallway was thick with the stench of backed-up sewage.

The clerk in the office simpered as we came in. He swayed when he greeted us, slurring his words. I had been in this office verifying classroom assignments with the English Department chair just two days before. But now the professor pointed triumphantly to the room assignments, handwritten on a huge piece of white paper tacked onto the wall. My name had been crudely blotted out and his name written over mine in ink.

"Get your students out of my classroom," the professor said.

"Where should we go?" I asked.

"*Je m'en fous* [I don't give a f—]," he answered. "You're wasting my time, Madame. I just came back from Mecca and I have no time to waste."

The clerk suggested the conference room, so my eighty-four students and I piled into a classroom with enough space to accommodate thirty. Squeezed elbow to elbow, knee to knee, we started class. There was no blackboard, so I wrote on the door. Half the class couldn't see the door so I broke my coveted piece of chalk in half and asked a student to copy what I wrote on a metal window shutter in the other corner.

"Oh, Mommy," my three-year-old son said the next morning when he saw me putting on work clothes. "You going to work *again*?" My daughters were attending an international school and left the house a few minutes before I did but my son was at home most mornings, either with my husband or our housekeeper. He sounded disappointed. "I miss you when you is gone," he said, encircling my legs in his arms and hugging me for a long time.

"I have to teach my class, honey," I told him.

"Why?" he asked, looking sad. "You is not a teacher. You is a mommy."

I pulled my son into my arms and kissed his cheek. "You're right," I told him. "I miss you when I'm gone, too. I'm a mommy first. And I love being your mommy. But I'm a teacher sometimes, so I can help people learn."

I hugged my son for a long time, feeling his heart beat against my breast. James, finishing a book we were cowriting, would be home with him this morning, but I still felt bad about leaving. Unlike at the elite New England college where I had last taught, my Nigerien students were anything but spoiled. They were engaged with their studies, fascinated by the window I was opening for them onto American culture and history, and grateful for the presence of a native English speaker with an interactive teaching style among their Nigerien professors. I was eager to teach but my heart was still heavy. I gave my son one last kiss and went to class.

That day I brought a slide projector and slides to class to show my African students scenes from a 1799 book, sold by subscription, of early Philadelphia. The book, which Thomas Jefferson owned, showcased the triumphs of the new nation's capital, with its tree-lined streets and mansions under construction. Alongside those images I projected slides of an artist's rendition of Poe's stories: gruesome black-and-white images of the ancient house of Usher falling into the tarn and of a man's back being eaten by a seagull, his head nodding in death. I was using the slides to illustrate Toni Morrison's argument in her book about nineteenth-century American literature, *Playing in the Dark*, that much of our nation's early literature is antithetical to the American Dream. This was a theme that we explored all semester as my students and I saw how the rhetoric of America often contrasted with the imagination of early America in the literature of some of our most talented writers: Poe's grotesque rendition of the human psyche, Hawthorne's exposure of hidden sin and human depravity, Frederick Douglass's exploration of how slavery dehumanizes the slaveholder.

But the woodwork around the only outlet in the classroom had been so eaten by termites that it no longer conducted electricity. Several students assisted me, and the janitor helped us run a long extension cord down the hall and into another room, so we managed, finally, to turn the projector on. Sun streamed in through the curtainless, west-facing windows. The images were projected onto a yellow wall and my students, sweating as profusely as I while we all baked in the packed room, could barely see the slides.

I thought of Jenny. I thought of another of my American students, who complained all the way up to the dean because, after missing 80 percent of the semester, he got an F for class participation (he overslept, he told me unself-consciously, even though class started at 10:00 A.M.). And I thought of the parents who called the chair to defend their daughter's actions after she was found guilty of plagiarism (she purchased a term paper off the Internet).

"Good morning, sir," one of my students greeted me a week later as I walked through thick sand, blown all the way from the Sahara by a fierce wind called the Harmattan, to our newly assigned room. On the day's schedule was a discussion of how Frederick Douglass surreptitiously taught himself to read when teaching literacy to slaves was illegal in many Southern states.

"Sir?!" I cried, turning around in an elaborate pantomime to see whom she was greeting. She apologized profusely and we laughed, walking the rest of the way to class together. I realized then that I was always doing what I had longed to do: teaching people who wanted to learn, exchanging ideas with students who had as much to give to me as I to them, exposing expanding minds to new ideas and new ways of thinking.

Despite the unbearable heat, the gendarmes on campus, the tear gas that interrupted our class time, the inedible food served in the cafeteria, and the fact that four to six students were sharing dorm rooms that accommodate two, my students were doing everything they could to learn. I was still glad that this wasn't my full-time job, but at the same time I realized that what I was doing in Niger complemented my parenting instead of replicating it. Maybe, I decided as I took some chalk out of my backpack and wrote the day's agenda on the dusty blackboard, I wasn't really a recovering academic. Maybe I had recovered so fully that I could fall off the wagon and come back into the classroom from time to time.

PART FOUR

Momifesto

The Orange Kangaroo

NICOLE COOLEY and JULIA SPICHER KASDORF

Utopia 1a. An ideally perfect place, especially in its social,
political, and moral aspects.[1]

NICOLE

I had driven by the building several times, intrigued. At home, I looked it
up online: "The Orange Kangaroo, Children's Art Studio and Café, Opening Soon!" And I was one of the first customers, with my young daughters,
the week it opened. The place was beautiful, spacious, and bright, run by
artists who were also parents. There were two rooms painted orange and
blue, separated by open French doors: one where children painted, glued,
crayoned, built with pipe cleaners and molded clay, and one where parents
sat at wooden tables, talking, drinking coffee, reading, and writing. From
the moment I entered this light-filled, happy place, I felt something deep
within myself lifting. I felt at home.

My daughters were two and five, and I believed I'd already flunked
motherhood. The academic metaphor is telling, an exam my only frame
of reference for talking about early motherhood. My daughters and I were
kiddie-class dropouts; we'd quit music, swimming, several kinds of dance.
When we moved to northern New Jersey from Queens, I found myself
astonished by the world of mothering held up as the ideal in our town.
Toddlers taking French lessons, elaborate birthday parties that rivaled my
own college graduation, a constant pressure on mothers to be perfect in
every respect, induced by a fast-paced, money- and achievement-obsessed
dominant culture. Yet my husband, also an academic who was sharing
the care of our daughters with me, felt none of this pressure. It was very

---

1. Definitions of *utopia* are from the *American Heritage Dictionary of the English Language*, 3rd ed. (New York: Houghton Mifflin, 1992).

specific to mothering. Over and over, as I tried to fit in to the world of our new town, I recalled my graduate school qualifying exam that required me to survey all centuries of British and American literature plus literary theory. I felt like a grad student who could not keep up.

Yet, ironically, my own position in the academy's family romance has always been "the good daughter." For years I'd been the exemplary student, moving without a break from BA, MFA, and PhD to my first tenure-track teaching job, following the perfect academic narrative. I had always obeyed the academic code of conduct that demands that you focus on nothing but your work. I'd gotten married in graduate school, but I made up for that, I reasoned, by publishing my first book the year I turned thirty, and another two years later. All through my twenties and early thirties, I was striving to be the perfect academic.

Perfection is seductive, but as Sylvia Plath astutely pointed out, "it cannot have children." As a grad student, I kept a list of when certain women poets, Plath and Adrienne Rich among them, had published their first books, won their first poetry prizes; I set my own deadlines to match. Oddly, I never considered Plath and Rich as mothers, never thought about how motherhood affected their lives and work.

Essentially, although I knew I wanted to have children, I didn't consider motherhood at all while I was in graduate school. There was, literally, no space for such a thought. Never in all of my undergraduate or graduate work, from the time I was seventeen until I was thirty, did I have a pregnant professor. Rarely did I encounter a female professor who had children, though I knew many male professors with children. Several women I knew had children as graduate students, but I am ashamed to admit I never imagined what this must have been like. I had no idea how difficult it must have been to balance academic work and childbearing and rearing, or how challenging it would be to do this on a grad student stipend with no mentors or models.

And, then, at thirty-four, when my first daughter was born, I experienced motherhood as a seismic shock, far and away the greatest upheaval of my life. As hard as it is to admit now, I was one of those people who believed that having a baby would have no impact on my life. I thought I could balance everything—I had written a novel while getting my PhD; I had always written poetry and fiction at the same time. Having a child would just be like writing in a third genre. Never mind the fact that I would be the only full-time member of my department with a young child. Never mind that my public, urban university—where many of my students had children, in fact—offered no child care for faculty or staff. Continually sick throughout my pregnancy, I taught until three days before my due date, and never even inquired about maternity leave. Through incredible good luck and hard work, I won a research leave from the college president's office, a semester of release from teaching that would begin shortly after the birth.

I was still caught in the trap of wanting to be the perfect academic, but as my daughter's birth approached, this was becoming harder and harder. When I crossed the stage to accept my research award and make the required brief speech, I was seven and a half months pregnant, and, instead of pleasure in my accomplishment, I was gripped with an intense anxiety, as I imagined the audience of fellow professors disparaging me, thinking I must only be using my fellowship to have a baby. Two weeks after my emergency C-section, I graded all the projects and papers for my classes and turned them in on time, then started to write an academic essay. The model of mind/body separation was so internalized that I could not rest or relax or enjoy my daughter's early weeks of life.

Then, in the fall of 2001, when my daughter was ten months old, that strict binary of mind and body underwent a shift. After months trying to take care of an infant and finish writing a book, I was happy to be teaching again. On September 11, one week into the semester, I was at home in Queens with my daughter on my lap, preparing my classes, when the first plane struck the World Trade Center. For the next few weeks, like most New Yorkers, my husband and I walked around in shock, trying not to breathe the terrible burning smell that floated through the streets, hung in the air, and seeped into our apartment. In front of the TV coverage of "America's New War," I held my daughter as tightly as I could. Suddenly, being the perfect academic seemed irrelevant.

And my students were devastated. They had lost relatives and friends. Many had family members who worked for the Port Authority of New York and New Jersey as firefighters. All at once, it was impossible not to talk about what had happened to our city and our country in class, to invoke the personal, the bodily, the part of life that was supposed to be extraneous to academic life. It was impossible, too, not to write about it.

Nevertheless, the poems I wrote after the birth of my daughter, after 9/11, made me uncomfortable because they violated the borders I'd set for myself in writing. I was anxious that mothering was becoming significant material for my work. I still fought the impulse to unify my two selves. Uncharacteristically, I never sent out my poems about mothering, didn't show them to colleagues, nor read them at poetry readings.

I didn't show anyone my work about mothering because I was afraid of being judged. I realize now, reflecting on how difficult I have found it to be an academic and a mother, that both roles are performed under the gaze of others. For years, I had enjoyed the approval of my professors and colleagues for my singular focus on my work, and I had thrived in the competitive sphere of the academy. Once I had a child, and still more after my second was born, I no longer felt such approval. And then, as a mother, I became conscious of the watchful eyes of other mothers, all of whom seemed to be doing a much better job at mothering than I was. Again, I felt as if I were taking my exams over and over again, stumbling through questions about aesthetics and poetry that I felt ill-equipped to answer.

And yet I knew I was lucky, even privileged: I had a good full-time teaching job and two healthy children. I had a husband who shared the work of parenting. Why did I feel so on edge and troubled as a mother-academic? Why did I feel both roles demanded a kind of perfection from me that I could not offer? Why did I care so much about the approval of others?

When my friend and fellow poet Julia and I sat down together to think through these issues, we asked ourselves: what is it about academia, the life of teaching and writing, that feels so totalizing? For one thing, university life is still predicated on a medieval model of the transcendent, priestly professor, draped in academic regalia in accordance with the clerical tradition; he has no body—let alone children. A recent study in *Academe* found that of tenured female faculty members, 62 percent in the humanities and 50 percent in the sciences have no children at home. The priestly professor, male or female, is devoted to the higher calling of the life of the mind, while someone else is cooking or upholstering or tending to the garden back at the convent or monastery. For much of our academic careers, we lived simply in cramped quarters and held ourselves to this model.

Until our children were born. Then the question became: what is it about twenty-first century middle-class motherhood that feels so totalizing? Motherhood today suffers because it is grounded in two competing yet simultaneous models, which conspire to produce exhausting and impossible expectations. First is the post–World War II model of the fifties housewife that retains cultural power today. The good woman took care of everything at home, everything "domestic" (read: trivial), everything, too, related to the body. As Betty Friedan wrote in 1963, the nurturing housewife-mother provided a secure base for the entire family in a country plagued by cold-war anxieties: Korea, Senator Joseph McCarthy, and the atomic bomb.

Now at the start of the twenty-first century, women following such paths are sometimes called the New Traditionalists; they are described in Lisa Belkin's infamous article as "opting out" of careers to be full-time moms. In her terms, middle- and upper-middle-class, educated women who "delayed" childbearing until after age thirty, have become a new kind of stay-at-home mom, one who channels all her considerable energy—formerly focused on her career—into her child and the construction of a home. And, yet, at our current historical moment, in which war, terror, and a radically destabilized world feature prominently, these women perhaps also echo those post–World War II housewives who sought to provide comfort and stability for their veteran husbands and young children, by creating a beautiful and secure domestic space.

As mothers in academia, as women teaching, writing, mothering young children, we find ourselves caught between these two models. To be a professor, you need to give up the other aspects of your life, to devote yourself completely to the life of the mind. And, unfortunately, you simply can't put an academic career on hold for several years, returning to it when your children are older. To be a mother, you need to forget or at least subdue your previous intellectual life and devote yourself completely to your children and to building a stable environment for the family. You need to become "the angel in the house"—that paragon of maternal nurture and self-sacrifice who was first named in the Victorian verse of Coventry Patmore. To perform either role incompletely is to be inadequate.

What still amazes us, again, is how we have internalized these models. Despite the fact that our daughters have fathers who parent equally with us and despite having tenure at our teaching jobs—in other words, despite the privileged positions we occupy in both mothering and work—we remain caught in this opposition. We have felt, over and over—since we can't stop using the academy's language—as if we were failing at both roles.

So when I sat for the first time at the little café table in the Orange Kangaroo with my coffee and the book of poetry I was teaching, when I was able to watch my daughters making collages, pictures, and paintings as I did my own work, when all three of us were happy and relaxed and having fun, I experienced a revelation: for the first time out in public with my children I could be my mother-self and my academic writing/teaching-self *at the same time*. The boundaries between selves began to dissolve, and rather than the painful struggle I'd experienced several years before when I tried to navigate both selves, what I felt now was joy.

Utopia 1b. A work of fiction describing a utopia.

JULIA

When it first appeared in an e-mail message from Nicole, the Orange Kangaroo intrigued me with its impossibility: a creature that cannot be found in nature. Indeed, that place seemed to be the only space outside her home where she felt she could be fully herself in her community of SUVs, Ray-Bans, and slender, stay-at-home moms. She promised a visit as we planned to get our children together over spring break. Recently separated from the father of my four-year-old, I was determined to pursue whatever pleasures I could afford, determined to prove my autonomy, and a four-hour drive into the congested suburbs posed an inviting challenge. We'd planned obsessively in the early morning and nap-time e-mail exchanges that sustain our friendship and provide essential ranting vents and reality checks. I would arrive late at night so my child would sleep for most of the trip; Nicole would leave the door unlocked so I could carry the sleeping bundle to bed. She had already stocked up on kiddie and grown-up snacks and beverages. Perhaps most significant of all, we arranged for this visit to occur during the annual conference of our national professional organization, the Association of Writers and Writing Programs (AWP). To stay home from the conference with our children felt transgressive the way that playing hooky thrills dutiful students, or that getting a good massage moves mothers of small children to tears.

By the spring of 2006, we had attended so many academic conferences with our kids that the memory of each event seemed more marked by milestones in their early development than by our own intellectual or artistic exhibits—they were strapped to our chests in Baby Bjorns, wheeled in strollers, sitting on our laps with sticker books while we listened, and participated in, readings and panel presentations. In one particularly vivid moment, Nicole stood outside a panel on the confessional poets with her fifteen-month-old fussing and crying. Another woman, a writer with children of her own, walked by and said, "Are you trying to remind people of why Sylvia Plath killed herself?" At another conference, someone discussed my book, *Eve's Striptease,* in terms of Simone de Beauvoir's idea that "imminence," determined by the female's reproductive potential, traps and prevents women from reaching the "transcendence" men attain—hence, *The Second Sex.* No joke, I thought as I listened to the paper, crouched on the floor in a back corner of that crowded room, my ten-month-old sprawled across my knees, nursing like mad.

At the AWP national conference in 2003, where that child learned to walk by pushing her stroller down a Baltimore hotel's long, empty hallways before dawn, Nicole and I co-moderated a panel hopefully titled "Women Poets and Motherhood in the New Century." Having arranged child care for the session, we joined Diana Hume George, Gale Walden, and an overflowing crowd. The audience, mainly women, was eager to share heroic stories, confessions, complaints, and laughter; we exceeded the time slot set for the session. On a conference program alongside literary readings and pedagogy forums, that panel felt brave and important to us, even transgressive (that word again!). But not new. Thinking of it now, I get a sick feeling of déjà vu when I consider that passionate conversations such as ours must have occurred for least thirty years—although perhaps not on the official schedule.

Our panel asked how the questions raised by Adrienne Rich (*Of Woman Born*) and Tillie Olsen (*Silences*) are reflected and refracted today. Ultimately, thirty years later, not only have some university human resources offices not caught up to the reality of the times by granting maternity and paternity leaves but, more fundamentally, the mind/body split remains a governing principle of the academy, and academic culture—with its expectations of late afternoon and night meetings, out-of-town conferences and research abroad—is still predicated on a family structure in which professors with stay-at-home spouses are scholars and writers, free to focus on their work because family, if it exists at all, remains sequestered in a safely distant realm.

I think of my friend Danny, who teaches visual art at one of the State University of New York colleges, telling his chair that he would have to arrive a bit late for an early morning meeting because he needed to drop his daughter at day care.

The chair, a tenured woman, replied, "We hired you, not your wife and child."

She expected Danny, who had not yet achieved tenure, to act like a man, perhaps as she had. I mean a man like my father, who left our suburban home at seven or eight o'clock in the morning and returned for dinner at six, his life neatly divided between apparently separate spheres. Because he worked in the research laboratories of a large corporation sustained by defense contracts, the division was especially stark: wives and children weren't allowed on the grounds without a pass from the guard at the security booth; we never met his colleagues or saw where Dad spent his days. Before e-mail or home computers, work stayed at the office. His black briefcase, which mostly served as a lunch box, fell by the front door with his shoes each evening, and usually remained unopened. Rarely during my childhood did his professional and domestic lives overlap.

"Accidental overlap" is the term I learned from a doctoral student who shadowed me several years ago for a research project designed to see how faculty with families use their time, and whether we take advantage of the so-called family-friendly policies available at large research universities. For three full days—at home, in my office, in the classroom—she trailed me while scribbling notes and filling bubbles on Scantron sheets. "Accidental overlap" means *unintentionally* attending to family or personal matters while you think you're doing research or teaching or administrative work. When I asked what she'd learned from watching assistant and associate professors at two Big Ten universities, the researcher cautiously said it looks like women are more subject to accidental overlap than men.

The study was headed by Carol Colbeck, a Pennsylvania State University professor who investigates the ways social and organizational contexts shape academic work. Her team of researchers found that faculty members try hard to keep work and family as separate as possible, but work appears to intrude into home life more than home intrudes upon work. We prepare for classes, read and write at home, but rarely do our children's concerns come to school. The researchers identified two coping strategies of faculty parents that will come as no surprise: multitasking and integration, such as making a family vacation out of a research trip. Another finding was that universities' work-family policies have had little influence on the daily lives of young faculty members—and we may even be unaware of them—because departmental culture, including norms and interpersonal interactions, set the agenda for most of our choices. So, while there may be a paternity leave in place, an untenured father doesn't take it because to do so would run counter to departmental customs.

I also discovered that the so-called family-friendly policies may be more symbolic than substantial. At my university, for instance, a thousand children were waiting for on-campus day care when I put my child's name on the list (then luckily found a less costly and immediately available spot elsewhere).

Participating in the study was surprisingly wearisome because it made me mindful of my everyday life, one more layer of consciousness added to days already full of simultaneous thoughts: I was suddenly aware of the fact that I nursed the baby while reading a student's MFA thesis while wondering what I'd find to cook for dinner, or whether I had time to run out for a few groceries.

But, the project got me thinking. Children are a lot of work, but haven't I always been a worker and done many things at once? Don't I fundamentally believe that all things are connected—including the work we do for money and the work we do for love? How can I—a poet who has always worked quite literally from life experience—divide the public from the private now? Why, after earning a PhD *while* working forty hours a week as a writer of grant proposals, should I now separate mind work from body work? Come to think of it, even my father's lives overlapped: Marie, the secretary I never met, sent my mother recipes for my father's favorite cookies and typed my high school research papers, the separation of those spheres merely an illusion enabled by two women's unbounded labor and cold-war prosperity. Maybe the term "overlap" is improper, assuming as it does a neat division of the professional and domestic spheres in the first place. Perhaps the split between domestic and professional is a utopian fiction, a dream of purity as false and ultimately impossible to sustain as the split between body and mind, and becoming a mother has driven that fact home.

When I became pregnant, I learned that maternity policies for faculty in my college, beyond the standard six-week paid leave, were negotiated case by case with wildly different results (a policy which has since changed for the better.) In my department, among tenured professors, there were more than twice as many fathers with babies under three years old as mothers, mirroring the national gap in tenure achievement between men and women who are parents. My department has few tenured or tenure-track women, and of the faculty women who had children when I became pregnant, all but one were at least ten years my senior, according to my informal observation.

This is why turning up for class visibly pregnant felt good, once I got used to the sense that I was doing something I wasn't supposed to. Due to deliver at thirty-nine, a decade after my first book won an award, I was what the nurses sadly termed "of advanced maternal age." Nonetheless, I felt like the willful teenager I never was, the knocked-up chick who insists on attending high school anyway. Like Nicole, I'd never had—never even recalled seeing—a pregnant professor in my fifteen years of post-secondary education. At New York University, there were rumors of a slim comparative literature professor who had two children, a live-in nanny, husband, and a tailor so skilled no one ever noticed when she was pregnant. As graduate students, we thought we knew better than to show up pregnant for a job interview. In our early thirties, Nicole and I spent a lot of time in anxious conversation wondering whether it was even possible for poets negotiating the academic job market to land a decent teaching position before becoming infertile.

Recalling those moments, I think there may be anecdotal evidence for some kind of change. Lately I've noticed some pregnant graduate students in my department. Apart from financial worries, they seem to be doing fine, in contrast to the stories I heard a few years ago when I started "to show." At a holiday party in my small town, the local dermatologist cornered me and described what it was like to get pregnant, drop out of medical school in the 1970s, then be denied readmission because her professors didn't believe she would ever practice. A fifty-something art professor told me that when her pregnancy became evident during her last semester of art school, she was forced out of her studio space and had to finish and mount her thesis exhibit without institutional support. The acting head of my department—hugely sympathetic to my circumstances—related her own: she had had to quit, then reapply for, her job, because in the 1960s no one knew what to do with a pregnant professor. I respect the tales these women carry around, like smoldering coals waiting to flare, and it's hard to question the implication that their experiences have made way for younger women like me. But I find that their stories typically invite gratitude and praise rather than real conversation about current conditions.

In fact, I hear very little about these matters in academic circles. Maybe the same old problems—human rights—have just become tedious relics of the 1970s? Maybe the gaps in creative production that Tillie Olsen traced in mothers' lives are just too hard for us to accept in a culture of competition and inflated professional stakes. Perhaps fear of failing to get a job, to achieve tenure, or to maintain post-tenure security silences us now. Following the ethos of these assessment-obsessed times, corporate universities such as mine have adopted absurd measures to quantify faculty performance in the humanities. In addition to asking our students, now figured as consumers, to evaluate every course we teach, the university measures our writing and publications against a system of weights and balances. We must report the *number* of pages of our publications in annual "activity reports" and rank journals or presses in order of their status—an essentially impossible task in my field—to set up a hierarchy whereby our output can be judged. Those professors deemed insufficiently productive are called up for post-tenure review. Of course, many professionals face job performance evaluation, and work has grown increasingly stressful and demanding for nearly all Americans. Yet I worry that the nation's academic culture of creativity and critical thought—once a global model—may devolve into a culture of superficial productivity. Even tenured faculty can internalize an attitude of surveillance toward their intellectual and creative activity, an attitude that is hardly supportive of the most daring and original work. Tenure—once designed to protect intellectual freedom in the belief that our democratic system depends upon serious and engaged thought—isn't what it used to be.

Those few days standing around in thin March sunshine while our daughters rode tricycles on the sidewalk were a great affirmation of life beyond academia. In New Jersey daffodils bloomed, though snow banks still clogged the curbs in my tiny post-agricultural, post-industrial town in the mountains of Pennsylvania. In New Jersey we shopped at an upscale children's clothing consignment shop, one of the many advantages of that advantaged community. And we visited the Orange Kangaroo, where the children painted paper kites shaped like fish while Nicole and I sat in that light-filled room, talking about our writing and lives. Granted, the price of admission was eighteen dollars per child, plus a few more bucks for hot beverages; utopia comes with a price in the suburbs, but afterward we all ran down the street, laughter and Japanese fish trailing in the wind.

> *Utopia* 2. An impractical, idealistic scheme for
> social and political reform.

And then it closed. One day Nicole went to the building with her daughters and the Orange Kangaroo was dark, shut down forever. The children were distressed, but she became obsessed. She asked everyone she knew, searched the Web, inquired of nearby shopkeepers what could have happened.

Eventually, a notice arrived in the mail: the business had gone bankrupt. Maybe the artist-parent-entrepreneur couple found the Orange Kangaroo to be financially unsustainable in that town of good schools and nice homes and traditional, nuclear families. Perhaps a space like the Orange Kangaroo cannot survive in a culture that pays lip service to family values but, at bottom, does not support the lives of parents and children. Such a precarious utopia must be funded privately—and therefore be accessible to only the middle class. Could we even imagine the existence of a public, not-for-profit space like the Orange Kangaroo? That miracle—that place where mothers and children could both experience creativity and joy—was, sadly, unworkable, the financial reality of utopia suddenly clear.

Forgetting money for a moment, let us take the Orange Kangaroo as a metaphor for the space where a woman can be both a mother and scholar or writer, all identities integrated and satisfied. That space where we could find solitude for reading or writing, or time for an intellectual conversation, and also be with our children—is it an impossibility? Or is that at the heart of the very definition of utopia: unworkable perfection?

We've experienced the rare conjunctions of our mothering and academic lives as transgressions, thrilling departures from the all-or-nothing commitment both jobs demand. Maybe those moments of integration are utopian spaces, too, rare and fleeting delights not usually found in nature, given the fact that most of the time, we find ourselves "just switching channels," as one professor friend describes her life of work and children.

Perhaps the challenge lies less in seeking those spaces where our separate spheres of operation overlap, but in valuing all the kinds of work we do when others may not. We can see ourselves not as failures unable to succeed at the totalizing roles we were born to play, but as accomplished actors refusing to give up any of our big parts. That's one way to revise the metaphor of performance. As mothers and as academics, we need to consciously shrug off the feelings of failure, the sense of ourselves being under intense scrutiny and always found lacking. Life's energy is finally found in the improvisation, in negotiating the demands of mothering and teaching and writing when they conflict, and in keeping our own bodies and spirits healthy enough that we have the strength to refuse to comply with impossible requirements—internal or external.

At some point the good girl grows up and refuses the scripts that will ultimately be her undoing. *So what* if we are all supposed to be as autonomous, efficient, and productive as that man from the suburbs whose labor was invisibly buttressed by a wife and secretary? Lessons in resistance and change don't come from good students or the lovely, good mothers hovering on the edge of the playground. It's as important to identify and critique those totalizing paradigms, and to work for institutional and social change, as it is to personally refuse to comply with their demands—that is, we can deliberately find ways to live otherwise. To start, we can refuse to hide the facts of our lives in defiance of the culture of an academy that would rather we all just publish excellent texts (about "the body" even) and give excellent lectures, but keep our children to ourselves. Refusing to hide the facts of our work lives also defies the image of "the angel in the house," who from the last two centuries and into our own time still haunts the dream of domestic perfection.

Ideal Mama, Ideal Worker

Negotiating Guilt and Shame in Academe

JEAN-ANNE SUTHERLAND

A few years back I presented at a sociology conference, discussing my dissertation on mothering, guilt, and shame. I spoke of the social construction of the good mother ideology, the impact this ideal has on the lives of women, and specifically the manifestation of guilt and shame. Afterward, I was meandering through a reception, making my way down the hors d'oeuvres table, when I struck up a conversation with a female colleague who had attended my session. The tone was, "Ah yes, what we women go through," as we considered the egg rolls and the little quiches. She then said to me timidly, laughing a bit, "Yes, but, aren't good mothers supposed to feel guilty?" I had spoken for twenty minutes on the social construction of good mothering, how it sets mothers up to feel badly about ourselves, and to feel guilty, which makes us doubt ourselves and we then pay the psychological costs. And yet, what she revealed to me was the prevailing orientation to mothering: if you are a mom, you feel guilty, and if you don't, well, you must not care very much, ergo you're a bad mom. And all I could say to her in that moment was, "Um . . ."

Working my way through graduate school, soon after the birth of my daughter, I was all too familiar with the phenomenon known as "mother guilt." It can start as early as pregnancy and creep up behind us, even when we are anticipating it. But, in the midst of graduate school, I found that I experienced another variety of guilt simultaneously—worker guilt. A good worker produces quality work. A good graduate student is competitive and devoted to her studies above all else. If she fails, even for an instant, she feels guilty. And if she doesn't, well, she must not be very serious about her work.

Guilt is one of those words tossed about so frequently that it has no shock value. We even jokingly compete over inflicting the worst kind of guilt. (Catholic and Jewish friends of mine claim to know it best, though coming from a southern, Protestant background, I can attest to its presence there as well.) We are not entirely sure of the meaning of *shame*; we tend to call it all guilt. Yet scholars of social psychology and emotion draw a distinction between guilt and shame. Guilt is typically thought of as a negative self-evaluation focusing on specific acts or behaviors. Shame tends to strike at one's guts, igniting negative self-evaluations about the entirety of one's self. I think mothers feel both. There were times when I felt I should be doing more. That's guilt. There were times when I questioned how I could call myself good, or scholarly when my very method of *being* in graduate school felt less valued. That's shame.

Work, Family, and Guilt

Academic studies and the popular press make clear it's difficult for mothers to combine work and family. In her book *Unbending Gender: Why Family and Work Conflict and What to Do about It,* Joan Williams describes our culture's glorification of the "ideal worker." The ideal worker, designed, of course, around norms of masculinity, puts in more than the requisite forty work hours per week, experiences advantageous mentoring and social contacts, and earns promotions at rates exceeding those working in part- or flex-time positions. As Williams points out, the ideal worker has a family life only if a "marginalized worker" performs the family work. More often than not, that marginalized worker is the mother. This is to say, being an ideal worker and mothering necessarily conflict. As Williams notes, "[W]hen women find that they perform as ideal workers, they are condemned as bad mothers; if they observe the norm of parental care, they are condemned as bad workers."[1] Williams's analysis is applicable to all manner of work, whether blue- or white-collared.

Working mothers have a difficult time negotiating the labor force within the boundaries of what our culture deems the good mother. Good mothering, or "new momism" as Susan Douglas and Meredith Michaels describe it in *The Mommy Myth,* has three key features: motherhood completes a woman; mothers are a child's best caretakers; and mothers must devote themselves fully to their children: physically, intellectually, emotionally, and psychologically.[2] When we fall short, we often blame ourselves, second-guess

1. Joan Williams, *Unbending Gender: Why Work and Family Conflict and What to Do about It* (New York: Oxford University Press, 2000).

2. Susan J Douglas and Meredith W. Michaels, *The Mommy Myth: The Idealization of Motherhood and How It Has Undermined Women* (New York: Free Press, 2004).

ourselves, and feel guilty. I am not suggesting that all mothers, across racial, ethnic, sexual-orientation, and social-class lines, perform work and mothering in the same manner and experience them the same way. However, within the context of these differences, mothers in our culture still share common experiences. The macro-level good mother ideology is simply too dominant and pervasive for most to escape. While different groups of women work in varied contexts, mother in different ways, and have different fears and concerns for their children, the ideology of the good mother still affects us all.

But isn't the academy so much more sensitive than corporate America, finding ways to value the mother *and* the worker? Well, yes and no. Some academic programs do accommodate motherhood. But, like corporate America, the halls of the academy also revere the ideal worker, rewarding those who work the longest, produce the most and, in terms of graduate school, finish first. Subsequently, mama-guilt can go both ways. As mothers we often feel guilty when we do not perform according to the ideal for good mothers, such as when we are away from our children, allowing others to provide care. The guilt also kicks in when we feel we are not living up to some ideal of scholar-in-training.

My daughter, Savannah, was born the year I transitioned from the MA to the PhD program. I was a nontraditional graduate student (a delicate descriptor for the older ones), and an "off-time" mother (the medical field was less delicate, slapping "advanced maternal age" on my medical chart the day I turned thirty-six). I wanted to finish my PhD in a reasonable amount of time. I also wanted, as the expression goes, to be present for my daughter. Thus, I found that I felt guilty a lot of the time, both as a worker and as a mom. And so, I went out and talked to some mothers; not surprisingly, they felt much the same way.

My experiences juggling motherhood, graduate school, guilt and shame prompted me to write a dissertation titled, "'What Can I Do Different, What Could Be Better, What Could You Do More?': Guilt, Shame and Mothering." I was amazed at how little systematic research existed on this topic, not only in my field of sociology but across disciplines. When I told others, male or female, about my dissertation, responses included comments like "Well, you should talk to my friend/sister/wife. SHE could tell you about guilt!" Another response was often nervous laughter, which suggested, "Well, of course mothers feel guilty. Do you really have to *study* that?"

My discussion below focuses on mothering in the context of graduate school, though I suspect it is applicable to those in faculty positions.

Mothers in the academic world, as in the broader work force, feel pulled between the ideals of the good mother and the good worker. We want and need to be both, but the struggle is tiresome and frustrating. We forego sleep to the detriment of our health. We bounce between worlds, merging the two when and if we can. While we experience the pull in myriad ways, there are three specific areas in which it is acute: pace, focus, and frenzy.

Pace

As most of us know, there is an acceptable window of time, varying from program to program, in which one is expected to complete her PhD program. There is also a less formal window of time to which many of us hold ourselves accountable. In this case, there are two important *Don'ts:* 1) Don't finish an awkward number of years behind those who began with you, and 2) Don't wait around your department until colleagues begin to joke, "Are you *still* here?" In the race to avoid these don'ts, one must establish a steady pace of course work, comprehensive exams, dissertation research, and writing. Clearly it is much neater, faster, and more efficient to fit through this window when one is performing as the ideal worker.

Unfortunately, graduate school is all but neat, fast, and efficient. Most graduate students are not only taking a full course load, but are also working as teaching or research assistants and trying to publish their work. All of these activities add up to fifty or sixty work hours per week. While we would like to think that enlightened scholars grasp the complexities of work/family balance and the ideal worker, we know that, in most cases, the graduate student who plows through at breakneck speed, puts in those long hours, and produces the most is the most valued and revered. The grad student–mother then has a series of choices to make. First, we will assume that she does not have a marginalized worker at home, performing the family work. (I am not gendering parenthood here, just acknowledging the ample research which indicates that while fathers are performing more child care and housework, the majority still falls to the mother.) She can slow her pace, take fewer classes, or postpone comprehensive exams. Or, she can work at the ideal pace, spend less time with the children, and also work what Arlie Hochschild terms the "second shift." If she chooses the former she runs the risk of feeling less than her colleagues. If she chooses the latter, she runs the risk of feeling very, very tired and possibly quite guilty. Her choices strike her at the level of her identity: bad worker or bad mama?

During my pursuit of the PhD, I knew I was not keeping pace with traditional students, though in the end, I finished roughly one year after other members of my cohort. I thereby avoided Don't number 1—I finished before hitting the awkward mark. But I did not escape the second, encountering "Are you *still* here?" countless times until one day it morphed into, "So you *finally* finished?" When Savannah was a baby, I took her to class with me, to department gatherings, even to brown bag lectures. In those days she fit snuggly on my body and I could slip into my office to nurse her, or she slept. But as she grew, it became increasingly difficult to bring her along and increasingly difficult for me to not spend time with her. Instead of three classes, I often took one. Like so many other mothers, when I was at work, I often felt guilty, as if I was missing out on such a sweet and fleeting time in her life. But, when I was with her, I often felt guilty that I was letting my work slip by.

I've heard others talk about pace, about finishing on time. My department once held a graduate student brown bag discussion on this topic, but I was not invited. I suspect I wasn't asked because I wasn't yet finished, though I initially feared it was because I embodied the model my department wanted to shield from new graduate students. From what I heard, they discussed how to finish quickly, with praises given to a graduate student who had just finished the program in a jaw-dropping three years. I realized that my department, which provided such a safe and comfortable zone for me as a mother, still at its core valued the ideal worker and I simply could not play that role as long as I also played the role of mother. Enter the feelings of guilt and shame.

Focus

How many times has a new mother complained that she is having a difficult time focusing? As every new mom knows all too well, we are tired a lot of the time. Of course, we don't have to be *new* moms to be tired. Braun Research's survey of some five hundred mothers found that 54 percent say they don't get enough sleep.[3] And when many of them finally get into bed, they lie awake worrying. (Mothers reading this may now collectively emit a resounding and sarcastic "Really?") Sociological research has also shown that mothers experience parenting differently than fathers do. Mothers, for the most part, feel responsible for the minutia of parenting; the hair, the teeth, the clean sheets, the doctor's appointments, and the scout meetings. I am not suggesting that fathers are not involved, are not tired, and

3. Reuters, "Yawn! Most Mothers Don't Get Enough Sleep," MSNBC, October 20, 2006, http://www.msnbc.msn.com/id/15347691.

do not feel pulled between worker and parent identities. However, gender differences arise in terms of how the work/family pulls are experienced. Of course, when a mother feels hyperresponsible and pulled in numerous directions, her ability to focus on the academic work before her can be affected. Is her focus forever impaired? Of course not. But, for us to not acknowledge it allows the guilt to fester.

While pregnant with Savannah I was enrolled in one class. I thought this approach ideal. By taking one class, I could maintain a good pace, show everyone that motherhood needn't interfere with my progress and have something to focus on besides the impending duties of a new mom. Sure, I thought, I will birth this baby one day, and return to class a few days later. My body was in good shape, and my energy for academic work was thriving. And then labor came. All of my plans went awry. Instead of the healthy, natural birth I envisioned, I experienced every medical procedure the hospital's menu had to offer: epidural, forceps, suction, episiotomy, and a cesarean. Toss in a fractured tailbone to make the story more dramatic. Instead of bounding from the hospital with my newborn cub and rushing back to my social inequalities class, I was wheeled to the car, crouched over and groaning from aches and cuts in every conceivable body part.

My first few weeks at home with Savannah involved not only physical recovery, but emotional and psychological recovery as well. I could not walk very well. I looked something like Tim Conway's old man character on *The Carol Burnett Show*, who shuffled along, face to the ground. I was instructed to avoid stairs and since we lived on the second floor, I spent the first two weeks largely indoors. I had to find interesting ways to nurse considering the two locations of stitches and the sore tailbone. As if any of this needed an additional cloud, one existed in the form of postpartum depression. I sat there in my rocker, on my pillow, wearing my big skirt (the only one that fit), in that strange land where the ecstatic meets the melancholy, holding my guts in, and trying to read something about socialist societies and stratification theory. Two weeks earlier I had found this material engaging. In that moment, however, it felt like something I could grow very old without. The harder I tried to read it, the guiltier I felt that I was somehow failing as a serious graduate student and potential scholar. I didn't plan for the blues that made me want to hide away with my daughter. I certainly didn't plan for the multiple injuries that made sitting in one spot without an odd pillow excruciating. I didn't plan on feeling so tired, physically, emotionally, and psychologically, that focusing on work would become an issue.

As time passed, so did the postpartum depression. The ability to focus on more than a favorite sitting position returned. Of course, other aspects of mothering affected my focus and always will. When Savannah didn't feel well, I felt more present to her fever than to advanced data analysis. When she started preschool, I cried when I left her, and didn't get a lot done that day (okay, so I *thought* the postpartum depression was handled). The truth is, we learn to work within the context of mothering. Our children always distract us, breaking our flow and focus at times. This does not make us bad workers or less-valued scholars. It is important to acknowledge it so that the conflict itself does not breed the guilt and shame.

Frenzy

I cannot recall how many different ways and times I was told that graduate school would be a frenzy of work and overload. That is what training often is—a frenzy. We can live with that. But what if we have children too? Now, there is a frenzy of sit-com proportions. In the pursuit of our degrees, we are trying to keep pace and trying to remain focused. We are teaching, grading, attending classes, reading, writing papers, and researching. It can feel frenetic. But in the midst of it all are these creatures, or in my case, just the one creature, who create and sustain a unique frenzy of their own. On any given day a mother has to decide which frenzy gets her full attention. And, rather like the popular children's book *If You Give a Pig a Pancake*, if you give a mother this kind of choice, well, she's just going to feel guilty.

One way I sought to resolve the dilemma of mama-and-worker guilt was to study it. While researching mothering, guilt, and shame I came face to face with some of my own issues of guilt, and with good mother ideologies. I also found that many mothers struggle with similar issues and place similarly high expectations on themselves. Yet, even with a topic as engaging and personal as mine, life was often frenetic, and writing was often difficult. I taught two to three classes a semester, which meant writing lectures and grading, grading, grading. I picked up Savannah from school two to three days a week and spent those afternoons and evenings with her. I had a number of life events colliding, and some days it felt like I lost my scripts, and played all of my roles badly.

A wise friend suggested that, for the sake of sanity amid the frenzy, I get myself a mantra. Something I could repeat and live by. Something that would help me to focus and—look at that coincidence—keep the pace! My mantra became: "Savannah, Self-Care, Dissertation." Nothing more, nothing less. My job was to take care of myself, which provided the energy to take care of my daughter, which gave me the space to write the dissertation. Another wise friend made an addendum to my mantra, which she wanted posted on my office door: "Not Even a Casserole." She knew all too well my tendency to say yes—to this committee, or that organization. Draw the line, she reminded me. Just say no. If the task at hand did not involve Savannah, self-care, or my dissertation, I was to rethink it entirely.

The frenzy of graduate school only adds to the mama-and-worker-guilt dance we so perfect. I was told by many that the dissertation would "consume my thoughts." Some told stories of waking in the night with fresh ideas that had to be written down. Others told of working to the detriment of their health in order to meet deadlines. What of the mothers in this scenario? In the frenzy we are again confronted with questions of competency. Are we performing as good enough mothers? And, are we producing good enough work?

Savannah, by now in first grade, took a picture of me during the final weeks of my dissertation writing. My office was a complete horror. My mantra did not include words synonymous with *organized* or *clean*. Articles and books lay spread across the floor. My wall of Post-it notes was almost artistic in its seemingly random display. Dirty coffee cups sat perched on the edge of the desk. Mounds of drafts spilled off a table. Savannah and I reveled in it. She had been counting down the weeks with me. I had kept her informed of the process and she was living amid the frenzy. As I wrote to Savannah in my acknowledgments page, "I won't soon forget the day I felt the weight of deadlines and asked, once again, for your patience. Temporarily forgetting all of my understanding of the trappings of maternal guilt, I said to you, 'Give me two more weeks and I'll go back to being a good mama.' You smiled at me and so lovingly said, 'Okay, but, you're already being a good mama.'"

Conclusion

As it turned out, I did finish my PhD. While it was at times a struggle, I found that I could be both a good mother (however *I* defined that) and a good worker. Sometimes one upstages the other, but both are key components of who I am. When Savannah was born, I wasn't prepared to negotiate guilt and shame as I bounced between worker and mother identities—trying to be good at both. As mothers and workers, we need to give ourselves permission to slow down when our bodies tell us to. We need to remember that it is okay to be with our children when we feel pulled to them. We need to remember that doing so does not make us bad workers. We need to also give ourselves permission to truly love the time we spend in our work. Working well does not make us bad mothers. Recognizing the ways in which we are set up to experience guilt and shame is progress. It's not easy to negotiate this paradox, but naming it is the first step.

In Theory/In Practice

On Choosing Children and *the Academy*

LISA HARPER

In my earliest years of graduate school, it seemed the perfect plan: I could finish my course work, pass my preliminary exams, and get pregnant while writing my dissertation. No matter that a father existed neither in theory nor in practice; my thinking was captive to the kinds of abstractions endemic to students pursuing advanced literature degrees, and I thought life would hold up very well to the model I had envisioned. It helped that two women in my program had done just this. They were bright and accomplished, and both had managed to have their second children during the final years of their doctoral degrees. When one remarked to me, with only a little sarcasm, that she was lucky if she had time to wash her hair, I laughed with her, but really, I was too dumb to take her comment at face value. Instead, I admired her ability to balance career and family, and I imagined that birthing a child and birthing a dissertation were compatible—if not complementary—processes. Naively, I imagined that gestating involved a long, silent stretch of time during which I could sit and think and write and be responsible only for myself: I would have no course work, no classes to teach, just a grant and a blank page, an idea and an embryo. A book and a baby made sense.

But truly, I knew nothing of the consuming process of dissertation writing and even less about the potentially consuming distractions of pregnancy. I knew nothing about complications or bed rest, nothing of morning sickness, or restless, insomniac nights, nothing of bone-numbing fatigue. I had never heard of sciatic pain so extreme that it made sitting intolerable. I knew nothing about hormonally induced stupidity or stupidly insane mood swings. And I certainly never considered the aftermath: the daunting job search, the career to be faced, the even more daunting child to be raised.

Mine was a bad plan, as abstracted from reality as only the most abstract theorizing can be. My career certainly would not have survived my first pregnancy, so it was lucky that the opportunity didn't present itself. Instead, in extreme solitude, I finished my dissertation in record time (probably because of the extreme solitude), served a pleasant year as a postdoctoral fellow, and took up a visiting professorship at a local university. I considered myself lucky: my job was in a good liberal arts college, in a beautiful and vibrant city, and while my teaching load was a heavy four courses per semester, I taught literature—not composition—at introductory and advanced levels. I designed senior seminars, taught frequently to my interests and specialties, and had a number of welcoming and supportive colleagues. I had a private office, a phone, ample administrative and technical support. My students were bright and interesting. I thoroughly enjoyed teaching my courses. After years of poverty-level wages and mounting debt, I had a good salary; after the infantilizing apprenticeship that is the life of a graduate student, I began to feel like an adult with a career of consequence and momentum. I enjoyed the prestige of my institution and my title, and I took great satisfaction in belonging to the academic community. As my career began to take root, my engagement to my husband established certainty in my personal life. And so, at the same time that I began to dig into an academic career, I began to think—this time seriously—about having a family.

But as it happened, the paradise I thought I had found in academia was soon lost. Among my department colleagues, only one had a young child, and I saw daily just how tired she was. I knew how much of her salary went toward day care (though the financial cost was not her primary challenge as a mother), and I saw clearly her struggle to balance the demands of motherhood, the pressures placed on any marriage by parenthood, and the crushing life of a junior faculty member who, in order to achieve tenure, must attend to course work, research, and, at our institution, a substantial demand for community service. Being a junior faculty member is always rigorous and consuming, but to combine it with mothering a young child is challenging in the extreme. In time, I would learn that this potentially crushing intersection of issues is endemic to anyone who attempts motherhood during her time as a junior faculty member, but I think it added to my colleague's burden that she was the only woman in our department who faced this challenge, and, at that point, we were not an especially supportive department.

Family life was discussed furtively, usually behind closed doors or at a secluded lunch table, as if it were a guilty secret apart from one's life in the academy, as if it had no place there, as if to be an academic one had to pretend to be complete within the bounds of the institution. What happened at home was something to be left behind and disavowed; motherhood was not to influence in any way one's teaching and scholarship. In theory, at least, I knew that this was an absurd proposition. One of my closest advisors was a feminist scholar who'd built her academic career on the kinds of theorizing that acknowledged the influence of childbearing and child rearing and domestic labor on women's writing. But I had not yet practically confronted these challenges, nor were they visible among my colleagues. It's not that my colleagues didn't care about family life—in theory and in practice they most certainly did. It was simply that, within the boundaries of the department, we were not allowed to be complete; we could not acknowledge fully the complex relationship between our lives in and out of the academy.

By the time my two-year appointment was finished, I had also learned something about the politics of motherhood in other departments. From some, I learned there were strongly suggested months in which to get pregnant and bear children, so as to ensure that the pregnancy would have minimal impact on career advancement and teaching schedules, and I knew several junior faculty members who were attempting to plan their families around these "suggestions." In all honesty, I don't know where these timelines came from, nor what the consequences were for deviating from them. For all I know they were nothing more than rumor and innuendo passed from one nervous junior faculty member to another. But what was clear to me was that academic culture demanded that motherhood be secondary, and that to put it ahead would be unwise. And although I believed I saw clearly the challenges of balancing family with academic career, I also began to see that the problem was not simply in the challenges that motherhood posed to the individual in the academy. It was a problem rooted much more deeply in academic life. What I saw was a division between motherhood and the academy that seemed germane to the culture. This fault line meant that women who became mothers were in it alone, and it meant that they would face particular hardship on the already difficult path to tenure. It meant mothers would work harder, endure greater emotional and psychological strain, and be expected to deny—or at least to downplay—to great extent, a significant aspect of their lives. They would live in a world clearly divided, moving between private home and public academy, private parenting and public pedagogy. Even more, pursuing motherhood and tenure simultaneously meant living and working

at least half of the time in a community which did not especially value
pregnancy, or parenting.

   To this day, I am not sure exactly why this is the case. Is it because academics tend to deny the life of the body for the life of the mind? Or because
we often seek a rarified community, one unsullied by the practical concerns that can muddy daily life? Or because parenting is not considered
a rigorous (enough) intellectual activity? Whatever the case, it seemed as
if the last thirty years of feminist theory had made no impact; they certainly had not raised much understanding of the challenges faced by real
women who balanced life with career, practice with theory. Nor had the
academy understood in a practical sense what mothers—as mothers—
might *add* to the culture. If motherhood was seen not to nurture the academy, neither was the academy nurturing the mother. I didn't understand
why the two things I wanted most in life, mothering and writing, had to be
so conflicted.

As it happened, the funding for my position was renewed once, but not
twice, and I faced the dismal prospect of entering the academic job market. By then the veil had been lifted and I had no more illusions about academic life. As I considered what I would do next, my overriding thought
was that I would leave the academy. The thought disturbed me, for I had
worked so long to get where I was, and to forfeit it all—the stable teaching
post, along with the respect and security it offered—seemed like such great
failure. But I was deeply unhappy with the politics of the community, and
I suspected that motherhood would be largely incompatible with this career.
In the end, there was a third, deciding factor: I had lost interest in pursuing the writing necessary to achieve a successful tenured career. There was
much I wanted to write, but none of it involved criticism and theory. I had
begun my writing life as a fiction writer, and I wanted to pursue that, along
with the kind of creative nonfiction that would be supported by my research skills, but accessible to more general readers. In short, I wanted to
leave the world of theory, and attach myself to a life lived more practically.
Call it a sensibility, if you will, but I knew, ultimately, that my path lay outside the academy. And so, with the emotional and financial support of my
husband, I left the community that I had always assumed would be my
professional home.

Then, two things came to pass: I rather quickly became pregnant and I rather quickly was offered an adjunct position in the MFA in Writing Program at the university I had just left. As it was part time, and a creative writing position, I leapt at the opportunity. Ironically, in just a few short months, I found myself pregnant and back in the academy.

But the department I joined could not have been more different from the one that I had left. It was not simply the fact that the program was self-sustaining and independent of the undergraduate English program. Beyond sharing a very few faculty members, we existed solely for the benefit of our graduate students, many of whom were older, with professional careers and families. We had our own staff, our own relationship with the university administration, our own control over course development and content, and we were housed in an altogether different part of campus. Our classes met two evenings a week, during which time faculty and students would convene in their separate seminars, but we often came together in the hours before and after class meetings. For all intents and purposes, I found myself working in a new institution.

Conventional wisdom has it—and my earlier experience had certainly confirmed—that adjunct faculty serve as second-class citizens on most university campuses. Lower pay, the absence of benefits, the lack of job security, poor course assignments, and overwork are only the most pragmatic problems. Compounding these difficulties, in many institutions, part-timers are largely excluded from the life of the department, from administrative responsibilities (and, therefore, from administrative power), from the intellectual and collegial respect afforded their full-time colleagues, and from the possibilities for career advancement in their own and other institutions.

But in my new program, I worked with a group of writers, almost all of whom served as adjunct faculty, who seemed genuinely to like one another, and who were happy to be teaching together. Although the practical, financial challenges of adjunct work remained, we also were largely freed from the administrative burdens that took time from the primary pleasures of writing and teaching. As part-timers, we were all equals. As part-timers, it was a given that we had families, occupations—in short, full lives—outside the academy. This fact was respected by all, including the students who had their own demanding lives outside of our program. Contrary to prevailing academic wisdom, here was a program that thrived *because of*—not in spite of—part-time labor. My colleagues and I talked about pedagogy, supported each others' book releases, and traded manuscripts. We attended programwide readings and read each semester from our own works in progress. There was a clear, communal sense of purpose and a devotion to the art of teaching that equaled our primary calling to write. It was a rare find and a great freedom to be part of such a community.

The success of this community was due in large part to the leadership of its two directors, who had made a commitment to creating a rigorous MFA program that also fostered a rich sense of community, a sense of being a writer in conversation with others, across disciplines and genres. This ethos affected how faculty treated students, how students treated other students, and how faculty treated each other. It was a program that valued diversity, too, especially of age, and this brought many unconventional, deeply experienced, and interesting students into the classroom. And because it was a program designed for working adults, all classes met on Tuesday and Wednesday evenings, which meant that everyone in the program—students, faculty, and directors alike—met on campus at these times. Such critical mass led to impromptu meetings in the cafeteria, in the hallways during breaks, and at the entryway after class, when many students, sometimes joined by faculty, would head off to a local pub. Ironically, because the program was understaffed and underfunded, some faculty assumed administrative responsibilities (and earned additional compensation), including course advising, final thesis reading, and participating in the admissions process. We attended faculty meetings, where our voices were sought and respected. Perhaps most important, after teaching a certain number of units, we were eligible to apply for entry into the university's Preferred Hiring Pool, which offered job security and priority in hiring, health-care and retirement benefits, and a one-time pay raise of around 20 percent. In short, although I was a part-time faculty member, I gained a certain security, and I participated in many aspects of my program—from admissions to course development to thesis approval. In fact, I felt more involved in shaping the direction of the program than when I had voting rights in my undergraduate department.

The fact of job security and ownership, in tandem with fulfilling, part-time teaching, and the visionary leadership of my cochairs, created an academic position that was fully compatible with motherhood. For beyond its intellectual, writerly, and professional pleasures, this community allowed me to be mother *and* writer *and* teacher. Practically speaking, the schedule was ideal for a mother of young children. I could teach my course one night a week, hold office hours earlier that evening, and do my prep at home: during my daughter's naps, in the evenings, during my scheduled babysitting time. I could spend the lion's share of my time with my daughter, and still have time to write.

But even more important were the not-so-subtle psychological benefits of this new position. In my program, which rigorously pursues an ethic of compassionate critique and actively seeks to create a community between and among students and faculty, I found that being a mother and being a writer-teacher were finally coterminous. My colleagues and students were single and married, gay and straight, parents of young and grown children, and childless by choice. Yet in my pregnancy, I felt supported by them all. In fact, I felt supported by the program itself, as if the institutional life of the program gave its blessing to my choice to be a parent. My cochairs didn't blink when I rather bashfully announced (as a very new hire) that I was pregnant; I continued to teach and advise students—even, rather famously that first summer, during the early hours of my labor: "Was that a contraction?" a student asked, after an especially long silence that I hoped sounded thoughtful. "Yes," I answered. "But it wasn't too bad." (Which was certainly true given what they would become.) We laughed and moved on. This same student, a terrific writer and also a highly skilled technician in the research hospital where my daughter was delivered two long days later, brought flowers to my recovery room, which neither of us found strange or embarrassing. Other students sent notes of congratulation and small tokens for the baby. But what astonished me most was the matter-of-factness with which the community at large accepted my maternity: it was neither sentimental nor sequestered. It simply was. Being in the midst of such a community even helped me to adjust to my strange new status. A few of my colleagues are parents of older children, and their advice and support has often been invaluable. Not only do they understand my life in these early years of motherhood, they have real advice about how they have managed teaching and writing and parenting. We talk about our writing, but also simply about parenting, and, of course, about the many ways that parenting has influenced our writing.

Now, even after the birth of my son, my colleagues continue to ask about my children, a fact for which I am eternally grateful simply because the question (never mind the genuine interest in my response) allows me to be a whole person. And if—so late in my career—I am still abashed that I am allowed to be all of these things in one place, it just goes to show how hard that path can be for women. Finally, my work has become a place reconciled with parenting.

⇒ ⇐

Of course, my return to and reinvention in the academy has not been without strain. When I moved to part-time/adjunct employment, I gave up quite a lot of money, a nice retirement plan, and a certain amount of stability in my professional career. I've partially recovered some of these things, but I don't pretend, as the program expands and more full-time faculty are hired, that the ideal relationships and politics I've enjoyed to date might not change or even jeopardize my employment. And I would be remiss if I did not acknowledge that a part-time model, even one as appealing as I have outlined here, is still insufficient for some. I have part-time colleagues who would absolutely prefer full-time, even tenured academic employment. But the structure I have benefited from these past years has given me a clear vision of what *is* possible in academia, and so it has helped to shape clearly my priorities and commitments both within and outside of this privileged world.

What I gave up by committing myself to mothering my children full time and not pursuing a more rigorous academic job was precious time to write. It is hard (some days or weeks or months, it is *very* hard) to carve out what should be that sacred space of writing. But if motherhood has diminished the time that I can devote to writing, it has also made that time more valuable, and thus more productive. I have found it to be true, as more than one of my colleagues has said, that I will never again have the luxury of writer's block, that I will always have something to write about, not because I will write about my children (though I have) but because my writing time is so much more precious. Sometimes, my diminished productivity makes me anxious. I would like to have my first book sold; I would like to be further along in my second book; I would like to finish the pieces that exist only in notes by my bed and in fragments on my computer or simply as recurring chants in my head. But my life is full and rewarding, and I know that as my children grow, they will need me less and I will write more. I know, too, that my first pregnancy helped me to forge a voice and a relationship to writing that would not have been possible before my maternity, when some mysterious alchemy taught me to integrate my critical training with my literary sensibility. And as for the teaching, which places great demands on my time, it has kept me in a community of writers, given me an intellectual home, and helped to maintain my sanity and my stability. In fact, I believe that this part of my career has helped to make writing possible during these difficult early years of motherhood, and I think it has made me a better mother, too.

As my teaching and department responsibilities have grown over the past five years, the birth of my second child has made the struggle to balance teaching and writing and mothering even more difficult. I need more day care. I need a cleaning service. I'd like a quieter office, with sentries at the door equipped to hand out snacks or braid doll hair. I constantly need more sleep. I would prefer more often to read for pleasure instead of for workshop, or to spend a weekend in the mountains instead of grading papers.

But what mother doesn't have these needs?

I have no illusions but that this struggle will continue at least until my children are school age, simply because I am unwilling to work full time, for that would mean giving up these years when my children are allowed to be so close to me. It would mean not bearing witness to them, and missing all of the small pleasures, even the trials, which have, quite literally, changed my life. They have, quite literally, made my life.

For me, the benefits of part-time work in the academy have been so satisfying that I don't know that I will ever again seek out a full-time tenure-track position. I don't know if I will ever be willing to commit such a large portion of my life to the academy. I know, now, that there are other options for me, and I know with certainty that the professional sacrifices that I have made in recent years pale in comparison to the personal ones that I would have made in order to continue on the tenure track. Now I know that there is part-time work that challenges and bestows ownership, where a full professional life can be balanced with a vibrant personal one. Now, I hope that I can raise my children to value the practice of life as much as their ambition, and that I will be able to teach them how to balance career and family in a way that will fulfill both callings, the theory and practice alike.

Motherhood Is Easy; Graduate School Is Hard

TEDRA OSELL

My baby helped me write my dissertation. Or rather, my baby plus my husband's job. After his birth (the baby's, not the husband's), we were able to afford three hours a day of child care. From nine to noon, Monday to Friday, Lena came over to take Linus out in the stroller, put him down for a nap, and do a little straightening up. Because I knew that that was the only time I'd get to write, because I was paying for it, and to be honest because Lena was around the house and I'd have been embarrassed not to be seen working, I wrote.

I was more productive in those three-hour blocks than I had been the entire year before—during which I had told myself I had all day to get some writing done, then gotten distracted by various smaller tasks, and then been frustrated and angry at myself for not working harder. Now, when I wasn't writing, I was able to do other things, guilt free. I could nap, then take the baby shopping, or pop him in a carrier and go over to campus to return old library books and get new ones. (Let me add here that toting a twenty-pound baby and a bag of library books to campus on a bus is an excellent weight-loss program.) When there were campus meetings to attend, I took him along; if he fussed, I breastfed him (deal with it) or, if that didn't help, we stepped out of the room until he calmed down.

I was lucky. I had a husband with an income that allowed me to take a leave from teaching, I had friends who were willing to lend me their office keys and library cards (since being on leave meant I lost my library privileges), I lived in a city with good public transportation, I'd had an easy birth and Linus was an easy baby. I even had a brother- and sister-in-law in town (both single, both fond of babies) who were willing to help out, plus an extended network of graduate student friends who were always willing to do us a favor or pick up thirty or forty extra bucks by babysitting for an afternoon or evening.

I look back on those days now with a kind of nostalgia: how happy I was, despite being stressed out with dissertating and job-market worries and new motherhood. And how little I realized at the time that, in fact, I had it pretty good. My daily schedule, once I got back to teaching, was demanding but enjoyable. A generous (and underpaid) mama friend of mine, Krista, would show up with her twins at 8:00 A.M. to watch Linus for the day while I took the bus to campus, taught, applied for jobs, prepared for my dissertation defense, held office hours, bolted out of my office to walk a mile to my friend's house in order to pick Linus up at four, strapped him into the stroller with the snack I always packed in my book bag, rolled him to the bus stop, packed up the stroller, boarded the bus, brought out the children's book that always accompanied my grading, and read to him before reaching our stop right next to the grocery store—where I'd shop and then tote groceries, baby, stroller, and papers up the hill to cook dinner and spend a few hours being a mama before my husband came home and I started my grading. It wasn't easy, but in and of himself, my baby wasn't bad for this graduate student.

What is bad for graduate students, though, is insecurity. And although, in retrospect, my situation was an excellent one, at the time I felt all too keenly how contingent it all was: my work depended on my husband's job, friends' willingness to lend me their library cards, babysitters showing up. When Krista called to say that her boys had chickenpox and she couldn't take care of Linus, I had to beg my brother-in-law to come babysit for the day and was late for class because I couldn't leave until he showed up. If my husband was late from work, my grading didn't get done. And all the while I wondered if I'd get a job when I was finished. And if I did, how in the world I'd reproduce the support system I had in an entirely new city.

Graduate school, with the job market being what it is these days, is a time of enormous stress. Grad institutions can't wave a magic wand and fix the job market, or prevent graduate student neurosis. But they can, and should, support their students. Given the ages of most graduate students, pregnancy will happen—what, we're supposed to wait until we're on the tenure clock?—and while most students probably have friends who'll share library cards and office keys, few have partners who make enough to support a family. Students without high-earning nonacademic partners and conveniently local in-laws often find themselves having to choose: is it better to keep the stipend by teaching or working in the lab, knowing that between work and the baby you'll end up choosing between sleep and research, or to take leave and be unable to afford child care, maybe even rent, but hope you can write your dissertation during nap time?

Thankfully, graduate institutions have begun to realize the nature of the problem. As I am writing this, major changes are taking place in graduate education: Princeton, Stanford, and the University of Pennsylvania have all instituted broad new policies supporting women graduate students during pregnancy and early motherhood. Importantly, these policies are focused on childbirth, and therefore apply specifically to women: they supplement, rather than replace, existing family-leave policies available to both women and men.[1]

These policies will likely establish a baseline that other graduate programs will follow. They provide six weeks or more of "accommodation" for childbirth, which can be expanded if needed—for instance, if a woman gives birth to twins, or to a child with special needs who requires intensive care. Importantly, this accommodation is not leave: recognizing that graduate students depend on their stipends, the new policies specify that women giving birth will not be expected to teach or to meet research deadlines during accommodation periods, but will continue to draw paychecks, be enrolled full time, and maintain their library privileges. Students on pregnancy/ childbirth accommodation retain their (absolutely vital) health insurance, continue to attend courses they are enrolled in, stay in student housing, and are still full-time students.

These kinds of accommodations can make the difference between a "lucky" ABD like me, with a husband whose full-time job can pay for rent, child care, and living expenses during "leave," and ABDs who are less rich but no less richly deserving. And even graduate students who can afford

---

1. See Cass Cliatt, "University Expands Family-Friendly Policies for Graduate Students," News@Princeton (April 3, 2007), http://www.princeton.edu/main/news/archive /S17/52/12A01/index.xml (accessed April 24, 2007); Michael Peña, "New Childbirth Policy for Female Graduate Students," Stanford Report (January 27, 2006), http://news-service.stanford.edu/news/2006/february1/mom-020106.html (accessed April 24, 2007); "Childbirth Accommodation Policy for Women Graduate Students at Stanford University," Stanford Graduate Student Handbook, http://www.stanford.edu/dept/DoR /GSH/childbirth.html#pre_post (accessed April 24, 2007); Angela A. Sun, "Harvard Lags in Grad Parent Aid," Harvard Crimson (April 12, 2007), http://www.thecrimson.com /article.aspx?ref=518193 (accessed April 24, 2007); "Doctoral Student Family-Friendly Policies," University of Pennsylvania Office of Graduate Studies, http://www.upenn .edu/grad/familyfriendly.htm (accessed April 24, 2007).

to take leave would doubtless find it easier to juggle a new baby with a dissertation if they didn't also have to fiddle around with figuring out library privileges, trying to finish a semester's teaching before going into labor, managing shifting health insurance plans, and begging friends and professors to keep them apprised of official department goings-on while they're off the e-mail list. Policies like these offer not only vital material support—reading them, one thinks, "Of course, it's so obvious! Why hasn't anyone done this before?"—while reducing the tremendous stresses grad students inevitably endure.

It's important, then, to note that one of the greatest features of these new policies is that they kick in automatically. Women in graduate school won't have to worry that somehow "asking" for accommodation will stigmatize them if a clear, thorough, and well-publicized policy makes it plain that the university is staking part of its reputation on supporting *all* its graduate students. We all know about the sources of grad student anxiety: completing course work, exams, and dissertations in accordance with departmental schedules; paying the rent and traveling to conferences for important lines on the CV, all on a grad student stipend; finding a job, and worrying whether one's partner will be willing and able to follow. When you add children to the mix, time and money become tighter, and stress seems to increase exponentially. Knowing that your department and university have your back must surely be as good as—maybe even better than—being able to rely on friends and family to help out once in a while. After all, even the most supportive friends may not really understand your dissertation topic, and sympathetic family members have an unnerving habit of occasionally suggesting that maybe you're doing too much, aiming too high. But with your corner of the academic world behind you—as they should be; you wouldn't have gotten this far if they didn't believe in your work—the message is yes, you can be both an aspiring professor and a person.

In my case, the stress got worse, not better, when I was lucky enough to land that coveted first job. I moved not only across the country, but to a new one (Canada). I knew no one there except the people who had hired me, and I had to get used to both new courses and a new curriculum. Suddenly there was committee work—lots of it—and the structures of undergraduate and graduate education in Canada were slightly different than back home. We had to pay for my work permit and decide whether to get one for my husband (no); there was a complex and expensive process of applying for permanent residency status; our credit history couldn't cross the border and there was a lot of paperwork to make sure our furniture and car could.

We all needed new cold-weather clothes and had to take the exchange rate into account when budgeting for trips to American conferences and American relatives.

By the third year in my new job, I had published in the top journal in my subfield, given invited talks in both Canada and the United States, appeared on panels with some of the best people in my discipline, created new graduate and undergraduate courses, initiated a pilot writing program for my department, and was serving on the academic vice president's advisory committee for undergraduate curricular innovation. I was also gravely ill. After five years of overcoming the odds, surrounded by caring friends and colleagues but without real institutional backing, the anxiety I'd coped with in grad school had deepened into a heavily medicated depression, complete with suicidal thoughts, a marriage in crisis, and the conviction that for the time being I could no longer do it all. Barely able to force myself to show up and teach, I hid in my office between classes and collapsed into bed as soon as I got home. On some days I shamefacedly called in sick; once I sent my husband in with a video camera to record student presentations.

So in the end, after making it through graduate school, I couldn't keep going. My husband once again found a job that paid twice what I could earn, I took a year of leave, and we moved again. After seven months, I no longer think about killing myself, my marriage is much better, my son loves our new home, my writing is going well. And I've resigned my tenure-track job.

As graduate programs and faculty policies catch up with reality and start accommodating parents, I hope fewer stories will end up like mine. Above all, I hope that they help graduate student–parents stop feeling like they need to remain "in the closet," as one woman describes it.[2] Material support is vital; without it, good intentions are just lip service. But while talk may be cheap, discourse still matters. As academics, we know this. The subtext of unacknowledged motherhood clearly reads "mommies not allowed." We can sneak past the warning as long as we keep a low profile, but pregnancy and babies are hard to hide. As long as we're supposed to hide them, parents in graduate school will suffer and sometimes buckle under the pressure; and even men and women who want children, but don't yet have them, will spend a certain amount of time thinking "When should I have kids?" rather than thinking about their research.

2. Joan C. Williams, "Singing the Grad-School Baby Blues," *Chronicle of Higher Education* (April 20, 2004), http://chronicle.com/jobs/news/2004/04/2004042001c/careers.html (accessed April 24, 2007).

Even though right now the policies at Princeton, Stanford, and Penn will only help a few grad student moms directly, they've helped create awareness—and a sense of entitlement—beyond those three institutions. What these policies do is support students. What they show is that motherhood is part of grad school, and that supporting graduate students means supporting grad student mamas.

Momifesto

Affirmations for the Academic Mother

CYNTHIA KUHN, JOSIE MILLS, CHRISTY ROWE,
and ERIN WEBSTER GARETT

As graduate students in a rigorous PhD program, we often marveled at the professors raising young children amid the intense demands of academia. Such conversations took place in private, however, as anything outside of publishing and landing a job was considered frivolous for serious doctoral candidates. We all had babies within the first few years of joining faculties (at a state college, a community college, a private university, and a state university, respectively) and found that sharing our unsettling Dr. Mom experiences in phone conversations, e-mails, or the occasional meeting helped us to process the multifaceted challenges faced by the academic mother.[1] The medieval structures and traditionally juvenile attitudes toward women in the higher education system have not been completely dislodged; they just appear in more covert but equally insidious ways. Motherhood is constructed as All Body—our own and/or our baby's—while scholarly work is rendered All Mind. This is an impossible theoretical dialectic to negotiate, and establishing realistic expectations is crucial for anyone considering (or reflecting upon) maternity in light of myriad obstacles erected by academic culture. We hope the following list might be useful in that regard.

Ten Things We Wish Someone Had Told Us

1. You are strong enough to handle any disturbing assumption regarding maternity before, during, and after your pregnancy—know that it reveals more about the system than it does about you.

---

1. We are not claiming that it is more difficult in our field than in anyone else's. Also, we focus on our experiences as married, heterosexual, biological mothers here, but fathers—as well as adoptive, single, same-sex, step-, and foster parents—also face the stress of sleep deprivation, the work of balancing a new family dynamic with existing job duties, the inevitable financial tangles, the need for institutional compassion, et cetera.

The notions that only an unorganized person would get knocked up and that pregnancy makes women irrational and impossible to deal with are fostered by the higher education system, which is often hostile to feminism and is decidedly antiparent (there is no day care on my campus, for example, and hysterical laughter at the very thought). The default assumption seems to be that faculty members have wives at home who take care of distractions like reproduction. On my campus, suggestions for family-friendly practices such as paid parental leave, designated private nursing areas, day care, and health-care coverage for infertility issues are dismissed out of hand as unnecessary. Which brings me to the whopper: birth or miscarriage is to be scheduled at the convenience of the school, preferably on holidays. You may not want to tell your department chair you are expecting until after the second or third ultrasound, as going back and revealing a miscarriage can be both nerve-wracking and violating. I learned this the hard way.[2]

People may assume all you want to talk about (or are capable of talking about) is your child. In meeting after meeting, the dean would ask other colleagues about their writing projects while she just asked me, "How's the baby?" I felt like she assumed that I was no longer in the same professional realm; I was (only) a mother.

To some onlookers, I waited too long to have children and now am reaping the appropriate punishment for that selfishness (three miscarriages so far). The most vocal detractor has been a sister-in-law who so much as said that maybe this was God's way of saying I shouldn't have another child because I can't handle what I have. When I was pregnant at thirty-three and had gained more than the ideal amount of weight, a doctor told me that my body would have a harder time snapping back and that *this* is what I got for putting my career before my fertility. Thus, according to the larger culture, I am of "advanced maternal age," too old to be trying to have more babies.[3]

2. Anything beyond a so-called normal pregnancy elevates the intensity of what is already an emotionally and physically complex time. Among the four of us, there were several pregnancy losses, symphysis, and preeclampsia necessitating bed rest (and postdelivery: postpartum depression, a broken tailbone, reconstruction of the pelvic floor, and hyperlactation). Online forums specific to the problem, and therapy, proved to be extremely useful resources in these cases.

3. We all finished the PhD before having children and went through our pregnancies at what was labeled "advanced maternal age." The resulting treatment and testing, while important, can be stressful—especially given the reams of pregnancy literature that figures the older mother as a creaky, failing machine who, if struck by complications, should just consider herself lucky that she was able to get pregnant in the first place.

Meanwhile, in my department, I am considered a *young* professor—and *motherhood* is viewed as a code word for "occupational interference."

When I told my chair that I was pregnant, the response was, "You do know how that happens, don't you?" While I was reeling from that, he said, "Oh, I thought you were going to tell me that you'd gotten a job at Cornell"—so I felt troublesome in having become pregnant and also less acceptable for only having become pregnant, rather than landing a prestigious job.

2. You are maternally beautiful, even if you feel more like a spectacle than at any other time in your life.

Your expectant body will be inscribed by colleagues, students, friends, and family. Those notations may seem disparaging or embarrassing even when they probably aren't.

It was difficult not to feel self-conscious standing in front of classes with my belly bursting out of whatever ridiculous ensemble I'd created in an earnest effort to look polished ("Do you think they'd notice I'm enormous if I add this scarf?"). Simply acquiring a professional maternity wardrobe can be hard on a junior faculty or adjunct salary; you might try eBay, where postpartum women often sell gently used work clothes in lots, and baby oriented consignment stores.

You may be shocked at how pregnancy can pull everyone's attention to your body. My pregnant waddle and growing belly prompted unsolicited commentaries: some good-natured, some funny, but all rather unnerving. (And imagine the awkwardness of interviewing for a new faculty position while eight and a half months pregnant—talk about an elephant in the room!)

COLLEAGUE 1: *"You are getting so big!"*
COLLEAGUE 2: *"It's good, though, that you only have one chin. I never understood why pregnant women gain weight in their faces—the baby is in their stomach, for goodness' sake!"*

3. You do not have to hide the physical tolls connected to motherhood.

Both before and immediately after the baby's arrival, concentrating on anything more taxing than watching popsicles melt can be a major endeavor.

Trying to facilitate a sophisticated class discussion while battling severe sleep deprivation, as well as the mommy fog evinced by the odd disappearance of available words in your brain, is not for the fainthearted. (I was up front about the maternal haze, and my students were completely understanding and patient when I'd momentarily forget easy words like *metaphor* or *endnote*.) Know that this situation is temporary and will be resolved when pregnancy hormones subside and your child begins to sleep through the night.

Teaching with pregnancy maladies (i.e., stabbing backache, burning, tender feet, overpowering nausea or heartburn, etc.) is disconcerting, to say the least.[4] Your body may seem not only fragile but also unreliable: Will I throw up in front of my students? Will I faint? Will the baby ever stop kicking my lungs so I can breathe again? If anything does happen, you can't control it and it is not your fault, so try not to worry about it.

You can request accommodations, but receiving them may take resolve. I qualified for temporary disability privileges but was given unsuitable classrooms at the far end of campus and had to organize a room swap on my own; I also had to obtain a Department of Motor Vehicles handicapped tag before I was allowed to park anywhere near my office or where I was teaching.

I gave birth to my first child during the last week of classes, so I had hundreds of essays, exams, and videotaped oral presentations to be graded within two weeks while dealing with a newborn, breastfeeding, and recovering from birth. When my second child was due in the summer, faculty members commented on how well I'd "timed things."

4. You may have more options for maternity leave than it appears.

No one in your college may seem to know, or to care, how maternity leave actually works. Even though I had applied formally for leave and had made a million calls during the preceding nine months, I was on the phone with a human resources representative the morning after giving birth, begging her to put the arrangements in writing so that my doctor,

---

4. For morning sickness, we recommend cinnamon gum, ginger ale, hard candy, and motion sickness wristbands. If all else fails, your doctor can actually prescribe antinausea medication (do not underestimate the benefits of the latter even if you don't like to medicate—it can really take the edge off). And since it is worse when you are tired—naps, naps, naps.

my chair, and my dean were all on the same page. It would be a good idea to secure such a letter before going to the hospital.

Currently, you are federally entitled to twelve weeks of (unpaid) leave by the Family and Medical Leave Act, during which they cannot fire you. Your college may also offer paid maternity leave (typically six weeks for vaginal delivery and eight weeks for caesarean, though it will vary), but paid and unpaid leave will run concurrently, so twelve weeks of leave is all that you are guaranteed.[5]

Inquire about substitute possibilities: babies—how shocking!—have been known to arrive during a term. I was told that I had to take the whole semester off if I took any leave at all, which was both financially impossible and untrue; I later heard about a dean's fund for partial-semester-replacement faculty. I did not take leave, which is most strenuously *not* recommended.

Stay on the good side of your department chair, who can make life as easy or as difficult as she or he likes—and know your human resources contact person, as she or he will be able to reign in an out-of-control chair if it comes to that.

Be prepared: no matter how much leave you are allowed, it will feel entirely insufficient, even though your college may act as though they are doing you a great favor by granting you *any* leave in the first place. Nota bene: there are some countries where paid maternity leave can be between one and two years in duration. Fight for as much as you can get.

My chair said, "You won't breastfeed in the classroom, will you?" I was so horrified by the idea that I just stammered and backed out of the room.

5. You have the right to breastfeed.

Since motherhood is not supposed to have an impact on your job performance, no one takes it into account when scheduling long events. Ergo, committees do not care if you need a break for your lactating body. (Unless, of course, you are shooting milk across the room. In that case, they care very much for you to Go Away and Deal with Yourself, as you've just made an exhibition of the exact thing everyone has agreed not to mention.)

5. If you experience complications during birth and your doctor requires that you have more healing time, your college may approve an extended leave.

You might want to request that your classes aren't scheduled back to back. Often while I was teaching, my breasts would become progressively more engorged: painfully hard, burning hot, and visibly leaky. And someone would always knock on my office door when I was pumping, desperate to fill the bottle so I could achieve two hours of sleep in a row that night. Of course, it was pointed out to me that my door was closed too much: "We want to let students know that we're available."

You will quickly learn the value of a private space. The door to my office would not lock, and occasionally a student or a colleague would barge in as I sat at my desk like a dairy cow. A sign declaring "breast pumping in progress" would have been the obvious solution, but I could never make myself display it.

I was informed that, because of staffing shortages, I should be able to return to work full speed ahead within two weeks of my C-section. As it happened, I miscarried and had a D and C over spring break. I never missed a day of work.

6. You can be dedicated both to your profession and to your family despite those in your department, college, and universe who act as if you can only devote yourself to one or the other.

Some colleagues will be surprisingly supportive while others will be irritated, embarrassed, or both by anything having to do with your being "in the family way." Individuals without children are likely to be your greatest detractors and to see any accommodations for parenting as preferential treatment.

Scheduling our own hours is an invaluable benefit of our positions (the other day-care moms envy me). However, I must toil through all of the "breaks"—and, often, between midnight and 5:00 A.M.—to complete my work. It's impossible to do anything on the computer when the kids are awake; I may miss an entire departmental debate that takes place via e-mail, appearing undedicated to some because I don't immediately contribute outside of standard working hours.

You may confront mommy tracking. On my first day back from leave, a professor beckoned me over and said, conspiratorially, "The reappointment committee agreed that you really need to be working on a book, *if you are at all interested in tenure*," the application for which was years in the future (as if I had wandered off into the wilds of motherhood and no one trusted my desire or ability to fulfill any other obligations).

When I requested classes that ended by 5:30 P.M., so I could make it to day care before they closed, my chair, obviously annoyed, said "I'll try, but don't expect us to keep doing that for you until your kids go to kindergarten or anything."

7. Your identities and behaviors may become über-fragmented, and that is, though complicated, perfectly acceptable.

One role slides into the space carved out for the other, like when I'm playing Buzz Lightyear with my son and thinking about how to introduce postmodernism in my lecture, or when a project goes something like this: start writing, give a bottle, return to writing, find a toy, write a little, change a diaper, write more, give a hug, and—then—finish the sentence I started an hour ago.

Once I took our baby (who had a small fever and couldn't go to day care) to school until my husband could pick him up. While my students toiled over their midterms, my son babbled, cooed, squealed, and noisily hurled every toy I handed him onto the floor. I finally resorted to pacing in the corridor, watching the class through the window in the door, until the exam was over. I've also tried to attend meetings with a baby on my arm, and the rule of nature seems to be that the more hushed and still the rest of the room is, the louder and more wiggly the baby inevitably becomes.

I used to be a morning person, teaching very early courses and accomplishing more by 10:00 A.M. than many people do all day. Now I barely screech into work by that time; just after the click of the car-seat buckle, I am likely to hear "I pooped," which takes us back inside to all the temptations that made it so hard to get out the door the first time.

Once when I was particularly upset by a rough morning and day care drop-off, a colleague-mother said to me, "At our family reunion, my boys talked and talked about how deserted they felt when I sent them to preschool. You see, it stays with them forever."

8. Your decision to utilize day care is not shameful.

I often feel at odds with mothers in the department who stayed home to raise their children and then pursued careers later in life. You can't win with them: you're a bad worker for leaving campus early to get to your kids, but you're a bad mom for leaving your kids in (gasp) day care. It also seems strange that those who had to break through the gender hierarchy now punish younger versions of themselves, as if they resent that we have methods—albeit not perfect—for tackling career and family simultaneously. Obviously, they don't look behind the curtain at the tremendous physical and emotional tolls involved.

The only advice, such as it was, I received from an older female faculty member was that I better get used to leaving my child in day care for gradually longer periods of time if I ever wanted to be academically successful—definitely not what I wanted to hear during my first guilt-filled week back from maternity leave.

My female colleagues with grown children offered much-appreciated empathy. One even told me how, in the 1970s, she placed her baby in a crib in the corner of her classroom and office—and while I think that's wonderful, it is not an option at my school. I worry that teaching despite the fact that my paycheck barely covers the cost of day care prioritizes the desire for a career over the well-being of my children. Yet I also worry that staying at home would be self-centric, given the sacrifices my family and I made in order for me to get a PhD in the first place. Someone suggested that continuing to work outside the home is actually investing in a better future for my family, but it's hard to believe that in the daily chaos.

People kept saying: "X was a professor, then had a baby and decided to leave because it was too much work," and "If you decide not to come back after your maternity leave, we would understand." I was never sure if that meant they wanted me to leave or to stay.

9. You do not have to pretend that it is easy to be both professor and mother.

It's hard not to feel guilty that you are not doing the research and writing projects you planned to do; that you *are* doing the research and writing projects you planned to do; that you can no longer spend the entire weekend prepping and grading; that you do sometimes spend the entire weekend prepping and grading; that you are no longer as available for school events; that you are not available enough for family events; that you are happy in the maternal sphere; that you are happy in the career world; that you are exhausted from all the happiness.

I always smile and shrug when people ask me how I manage both roles. Most of the time I feel like a failure on both fronts.

Expect the inevitable clash of schedules, and know that reasonable people will work with you when these occur (early morning meetings or evening departmental activities can be particularly difficult for parents, adding more chaos to the daily pandemonium). If you are lucky enough to be in a department where a majority of the faculty members has children, you may find that meetings usually end by 5:00 P.M. so that everyone can race to the day-care provider or after-school activity; if not, then you will need to regularly remind your colleagues that you have scheduling constraints.

I heard through the grapevine that one of my colleagues said, about me: "How can she apply for tenure if she's pregnant?"

10. You can promote motherhood professionally—and it is a political statement.

Motherhood is an ongoing subject in my formal projects, ranging from my papers on maternal representations in literature to my poems, all of which I document as part of my professional development requirement.

As cochairs of a recent women's caucus conference panel, we selected the topic of motherhood in art and popular culture. After receiving so many proposals that it was possible to create three panels (a historical first, we were told, demonstrating the interest in the subject), we received a complaint that caucus members felt excluded by the topic (even though the focus was on critical interpretations, not mothering). Interestingly, the Q&A following the panel on motherhood in film *did* turn into a passionate dialogue about how mothers have been marginalized, even punished, in various ways in the academic realm.

Before I came back to work after having my first child, I was terrified I'd seem soft—even that I'd accidentally refer to myself as "Mommy" in front of my students—and I wanted to be seen as a professional again. The longer I've been balancing both worlds, the less afraid I am of blending the two.

Bonus Item: Kindnesses will find their way to you.

Since my baby was due mid-term and I could not afford to take maternity leave, my chair agreed to my proposal that I teach online and weekend classes in lieu of a regular on-campus schedule. Then several of my colleagues cheerfully agreed to cover one Saturday class each, so that I could have some healing time at home.

An adjunct at my school brought me all her son's hand-me-downs when my child was born.

I discovered, in my office, an adorable gift for the baby, with a card from the whole department.

A colleague has repeatedly watched my son while I sat in on meetings for which I couldn't find day care.

Many people seemed supportive of my pregnancies as well as eager to hear news once my children arrived.

We wouldn't trade parenting for anything; however, we are consistently surprised by our determination to stay in the academic game when we receive numerous messages that motherhood is unwelcome. Although an intricate juggling act is required, teaching and mothering can complement each other on many levels. You may find, for example, that maternity leads to an ability to *hyper*-multitask, and the skills from your academic training will be useful in mastering new maternal discourse—for example, "swaddle," "colic," "solids." (You've made it when you hear, "There's a snake in my boot," or "Swiper, no swiping!" and you *get* it.)

With the help of projects like this one, we hope to make life a little easier for the academic mothers to come (which requires reconfiguring the entire patriarchal power regime, but that is a topic for another essay). In sum, we recommend knowing your rights, anticipating challenges, drawing appropriate boundaries, and holding your head up—mothering is crucial to the existence of the species, after all. You are doing incredibly important work that should be celebrated more explicitly in *and* out of academe.

In Dreams Begin Possibilities—

Or, Anybody Have Time for a Change?

JUDITH SANDERS

A friend and I were watching her plump, luscious twin toddlers laugh themselves silly as they learned to roll downhill. She confided that she was pregnant with her third child, so she was leaving her job. "They'll never be like this again," she said of her girls, who somehow kept rolling sideways, "but I can always go back to work."

She is not an academic.

All the recent talk about exit and entrance ramps in women's careers does not yet apply to women in the academy. We cannot leave and then come back ten years later with out-of-date references and no recent publications. We wouldn't even get so much as an interview.

Mothers with PhDs know the musical chairs situation all too well: too many qualified candidates for too few jobs; more and more work piled on those chosen few who do land positions, as strained institutions try to squeeze the most out of each employee. Yes, women have made enormous progress in obtaining access to education and the professions over the last thirty years. But in the academy, the career path originally developed for men-with-wives hasn't changed to accommodate us in more than token ways: an iota of occasional, usually begrudged, maternity leave of a pathetically brief duration, often unpaid, and occasionally a year's slowing of the tenure clock. (In one friend's recent tenure hearing, her male colleagues held her request for such a slowdown against her—claiming that it showed she "wasn't serious.")

The sociologist Arlie Hochschild observes that the feminist revolution stalls as soon as one has a baby. Academia's no ivory-tower exception. Even this far into the second wave, nothing's been done to fix the fact that our prime childbearing years coincide with the years in which we are supposed to move all around the country for postdocs and visiting positions, brave the job market, prepare new courses, publish our dissertations, and get tenure. Consequently, we have a low birthrate, and the quality of our lives if we do have children suffers in a way that seems anachronistic—and unnecessary.

We've all looked around our departments and observed how few of us have children; statistics in a recent article in *Academe* confirm our anecdotal evidence.[1] A few of us have one child, but far fewer have two, and these women are usually incredibly energetic, gifted, and determined souls, some of whom have unusual support systems—a competent grandma nearby, a stay-at-home husband, or a trust fund. Or a capacity to live without sleep. Most of us mortal souls cannot pull it off. And any of us who falls into unusual circumstances, such as having a sick or special needs child, is, like the Cat in the Hat juggling his rake and fish and cake, doomed to fall off the ball.

So most of us still face a devil's choice of children or career, or both with the attendant stress and chaos. This situation is not good—not for us personally, much less for our children, nor for our profession, as it's an open secret that being mothers makes us better teachers. There is no better teacher training, in fact, than learning viscerally that every student is someone's beloved child—or damn well ought to be. There is no more convincing introduction to the value of distinct learning styles, or intensive seminar in gender and development, or effective boot camp for training in efficiency and multitasking. And of course the profound, transformative experience of perpetuating life, that universal essential activity, enriches our scholarship. But all that hard-won knowledge is excluded as if it were a betrayal of our commitment to the life of the mind, when the real cause for the exclusion is persistent sexism, a dismissive belittlement of everything that smacks of the maternal, perhaps because of its threatening pull into regression.

Whether from observation or experience, we know the personal costs of choosing both. We know that those of us who are parents-with-professorships often have households that teeter on the brink of meltdown because no one has time—and because we've all been indoctrinated into devaluing domesticity. We don't like to admit it, but we all know children of dual-career families who spend too much time in day care or in front of a screen, or whose problems get swept under the family rug. Or we must hire out our domestic work and child care to poorer or third-world

1. Mary Ann Mason and Marc Goulden, "Do Babies Matter? The Effect of Family Formation on the Lifelong Careers of Academic Men and Women," *Academe* 88, no. 6 (2002): 21–27. Available at http://www.aaup.org/publications.

women, many of whom have left their own children at home so they can care for ours—that is, we must participate in a system whose ethics are highly dubious. All our sacrifice, the sweatshop work hours at the expense of family life, might make sense if we lived in a poor country, but we live in a fabulously rich one. It's a question not of necessity, but of choices, priorities, values.

We have been so cooperative with the male model that makes us work hardest during our childbearing and child-rearing years because we run scared. The tight job market makes us scared that we'll lose our livelihoods, a prospect that's worrisome enough for couples now that it takes two salaries to maintain a family's toehold in the middle class, and downright terrifying for single parents. Since many of us don't feel we have a choice about whether to earn wages, few of us dare rock the boat. But we are also scared that the boys will kick us out, so we still play by their rules.

As some of us gain power in the profession, as we rise to become chairs and deans and presidents and policy-makers, perhaps we'll be able to overcome such fears and use our power to make the conditions of academic employment more accommodating to the realities of women's—of people's—lives. Perhaps we'll be able to stop perpetuating this fearful, immature erasure of the caretaking that is the major work of our middle adulthood.

To improve our lives as mamas with PhDs, we need two things:

1. Dignified part-time positions—not exploitive adjunct ones that pay Wal-Mart wages—that both men and women can choose when they have to take care of small children, aging parents, sick family members, or even themselves—whenever the caretaking work of life interferes with our availability to the marketplace. Men cannot participate equally in child care and housework unless they can work less, too.

2. More flexible career paths—a willingness to allow people to proceed in the profession even if they have taken time away from it.

Both of these changes depend on a change in the health-care system, linking insurance to citizenship rather than employment, as is the case in every other industrialized country. If our employers were paying only for our labor rather than our health care, they might be more willing to distribute that labor among more workers—including those of us who must or choose to work part time and those who are returning from having devoted ourselves to other aspects of life. I don't even mention here the need for affordable quality day care, part or full time, provided by workers who are trained, treated, and paid as dignified professionals, in day-care centers that are part of the life of the campus—that goes without saying.

But I don't stress that here for a different reason: I'm talking about options that enable us to work less when we need to, not more.

In addition to these changes in the structure of employment, we need to shift attitudes so that raising children is deemed a dignified, worthwhile use of an educated person's time, a serious training worthy of including on a CV and earning respect in an interview. (Imagine—it's hard, but try—a search committee saying, "Terrific, she's raised children: Excellent qualification!") We need to change the culture of our profession to honor the realities of intermittent caretaking work. The profession would be the richer for it. Perhaps some of the conditions that often make our jobs unsatisfying would diminish were we able to lead more balanced lives. Possibly there'd be less politicking and petty judgmentalism if our colleagues had more perspective because they had fuller lives outside the office; perhaps academic writing would be less sterile and earn a wider readership; perhaps some of our students would be less frustratingly indifferent if they'd had parents who had been able to spend more time with them.

What with budget cuts, the tight job market, and existential worries about the humanities' relevance, not to mention general political gloom, it's a difficult time even to daydream of mundane policy changes, but in dreams, as Delmore Schwartz didn't quite say, begin possibilities.

Working what Arlie Hochschild calls "the second shift"—coming home to parent and manage a household after a full day at work—barely leaves us time for mental activity beyond rehearsing our list of things to do, but sometimes during enforced moments of leisure (like being stuck in traffic or waiting for the kids to finish up at the playground) I do find I have a dream, as doubtless others do, as well. I have a dream that one day, academics—both men and women—will be able to take time to go up to the mountain top—or just the hill in the local park, or even a slope on campus—and cherish watching their toddlers roll down, confident that their careers aren't rolling downhill with them. I have a dream that academics will take the wisdom they gain from fostering their children's development back to their intellectual work, and feel confident that their community admires them for doing so. I have a dream that the stalled revolution will jump-start one day, that all women and men, whatever their cultural and economic backgrounds, will be empowered to give the best of themselves to both love and work. Maybe those folks in my dream will even have the time to look up from their toddlers for a moment, take a breath, and enjoy the view.

Contributors

Susan Bassow earned a PhD from Harvard University in 1995; her dissertation on climate change and its impacts on forests led to an American Association for the Advancement of Science Fellowship in Washington, D.C., where she worked (before and throughout her first pregnancy) for the Environmental Protection Agency and President Clinton's White House Office of Science and Technology Policy. Currently, she serves on the Board of Trustees for the Thorne Ecological Institute, organizes science and math programs for the local elementary school, and cares full time for her daughters, ages six and nine. In a typical week, she and her family explore nearby fields and ponds, hike in the mountains, feed butterflies, and promote science and math education.

Leah Bradshaw is a political theorist at Brock University in Canada. She wrote a doctoral thesis, then a book, on Hannah Arendt, to whom she remains indebted for Arendt's example of how to live, love, and think. Recent work has been on the relationship between emotions and judgment, narrative and philosophy, classical notions of love, and empire and polis. She has three children, all of whom call her "Mom," and one mother who insists on calling her "Doctor."

After enjoying years of great travel while studying the evolution of a large group of South American butterflies, **Dana Campbell** finished her PhD from Harvard University just as her first daughter was born. Despite an attractive postdoc offer to work in the exciting new field of "evo-devo," she chose instead to stay at home with her baby. She is still "at home" full time, now with two daughters and a bunch of interesting projects, which include building an interactive animal database for kids, writing a science/psychology activity book for parents of young children, and developing a

Web site for nontraditional academics. Dana and her family live just out-side of Washington, D.C., and spend summers in the beautiful San Juan Islands of Washington State.

Jennifer Cognard-Black's teaching at St. Mary's College of Maryland is akin to the multitasking she engages to be both a professor and a mother. Her courses range from fiction writing to Victorian literature to a class on the literatures of food, "Books That Cook." Her publications include a book on female literary friendships across the Atlantic, *Narrative in the Professional Age* (Routledge) and a coedited collection of letters by Victorian women writers, *Kindred Hands* (University of Iowa Press). Under the pseu-donym J. Annie MacLeod, she also publishes short stories, and, most re-cently, she's written an article for *Ms. Magazine* on plastic surgery. Jennifer is most proud of her daughter, Katharine—her truth and her light.

Nicole Cooley has published two books of poetry with Louisiana State Uni-versity Press, *Resurrection* (winner of the 1995 Walt Whitman Award) and *The Afflicted Girls,* and a novel, *Judy Garland, Ginger Love* (HarperCollins). Her writing on mothering has appeared in the anthologies *Toddler, Liter-ary Mama: Reading for the Maternally Inclined,* and Fence Books' recent collection, *Not For Mothers Only.* She is an associate professor of English and creative writing at Queens College–The City University of New York, where she directs the new MFA program. She lives in New Jersey with her husband and two daughters, Meridian and Arcadia.

Martha Ellis Crone lives in Upper Arlington, Ohio, with her husband and three daughters. She was one of the first two students to earn a BPhil from the University of Pittsburgh's Honors College and she also holds a PhD in Political Science from The Ohio State University. Currently a freelance writer and editor, she is working on her first novel, *Entanglements,* about a university student dealing with an unexpected pregnancy. When she's not writing, she can usually be found driving a Nissan minivan in circles around her suburban town, picking up and dropping off progeny and lis-tening to audiobooks.

Angelica Duran is an associate professor of English and comparative liter-ature at Purdue University. Born and educated in California (University of California, Berkeley, BA and MA in English; Stanford University PhD in English), she nevertheless and thoroughly enjoys living in the U.S.

Midwest during the school year with her husband, Sean, daughter, Jacqueline, and son, Paul. In the summer, the family travels nationally and internationally, most recently to Argentina, Costa Rica, Spain, Thailand, and, of course, the extended family's center in Oaxaca, Mexico.

Rosemarie Emanuele has a PhD in economics from Boston College. There, with the assistance of a grant from the Center on Philanthropy at Indiana University, she began research into volunteer labor and the economics of nonprofit organizations. She currently teaches in the mathematics department at Ursuline College in Pepper Pike, Ohio, where she can often be heard talking about economics or her daughter with equal enthusiasm. Her research has appeared in several economics journals, as well as in interdisciplinary journals studying the nonprofit sector.

Elrena Evans holds an MFA from The Pennsylvania State University and writes for numerous mama-centric publications, including a monthly column for *Literary Mama* (http://literarymama.com). Her work also appears in the anthologies *Twentysomething Essays by Twentysomething Writers* (Random House) and *How to Fit a Car Seat on a Camel* (Seal Press). Although *Pat the Bunny* fits perfectly on her bookshelf next to *Power/Knowledge*, she still hasn't decided about finishing the PhD. She had no complications with her second pregnancy, and lives in Pennsylvania with her husband, daughter, and son. Her Web site is http://www.elrenaevans.com.

Della Fenster submitted her dissertation in mathematics to the University of Virginia balancing her eighteen month old daughter, Hannah, on her hip. Hannah is now fourteen and has two younger brothers, Colin and Casey. Della is currently an associate professor of mathematics at the University of Richmond. She enjoys teaching across the mathematics curriculum as well as the university core course that focuses on great literature. She also recently worked with an undergraduate student to create a travel course to Vienna. Her research has appeared in notable journals with long names, while her personal essays have found an occasional home in *Skirt! Magazine*. She makes an effort to strike a careful balance between dark chocolate and exercise.

Leslie Leyland Fields is the author of five books, among them *Surviving the Island of Grace* (Thomas Dunne) and *Surprise Child: Finding Hope in Unexpected Pregnancy* (Waterbrook). She lives on Kodiak Island, Alaska, with her husband and six children, and teaches creative nonfiction in Seattle Pacific University's MFA program. Her next book, forthcoming from Waterbrook, will expose ten parenting myths (out of a field of, say, fifty-seven), among them "Loving Your Child Is Natural and Instinctive" and "Parenting Is Intense for Only a Season." Her two Web sites are Leslie Leyland Fields (http://www.leslie-leyland-fields.com) and Surprise Child (http://www.surprisechild.com).

Caroline Grant spent nearly three years writing a dissertation that about seven people read (including her mom). Now she is senior editor of *Literary Mama* (http://literarymama.com), where she also writes a monthly movie column for a broad audience (still including her mom). She holds a PhD in comparative literature from the University of California, Berkeley, and has taught at Berkeley, Stanford University, and the San Francisco Art Institute. She lives in San Francisco with her husband and two sons, a life she writes about on her blog, Food for Thought (http://foodthought.org).

Elisabeth Rose Gruner is an associate professor of English and women, gender, and sexuality studies at the University of Richmond. Her research on children's literature has appeared in *The Lion and the Unicorn* and *Children's Literature*, while her work on Victorian literature has appeared in *Tulsa Studies in Women's Literature*, *SIGNS: Journal of Women in Culture and Society*, and the *Journal of English and Germanic Philology*. Although her tenure case made the *Chronicle of Higher Education*, she has managed to combine professing and parenting reasonably successfully, most recently by becoming a columnist for *Literary Mama* (http://literarymama.com). Her essay "Mama Mentor" appeared in *A Cup of Comfort for Teachers*, and her nonacademic writing has also been published in *Brain, Child: The Magazine for Thinking Mothers*, *Toddler* (Seal Press), and *Literary Mama*.

Jessica Smartt Gullion is a medical sociologist who conducts research on lay perception of medical knowledge. She is currently working in an applied setting outside of the academy, and teaches a class as an adjunct professor. Her writings on motherhood have appeared in the *Journal of the Association for Research on Mothering* and on Mothers Movement Online (http://www.mothersmovement.org). She would like to note that none of the individuals mentioned in her essay currently work at that university.

Lisa Harper is an adjunct professor of writing in the MFAW program at the University of San Francisco. She received her BA in English/creative writing from Princeton University, her MA in English/creative writing and her PhD in English from the University of California, Davis. Her non-fiction writing has appeared in *Gastronomica, Literary Mama, Lost Magazine, Princeton Alumni Weekly, Fortnight Magazine,* and *The Irish News.* Her academic writing has appeared in *The Emily Dickinson Journal, Literary Couplings: Writing Couples, Collaborators, and the Construction of Authorship,* and *Switchback.* She lives in the San Francisco Bay Area with her husband, daughter, and son.

After receiving a PhD from the University of Florida and then spending five years at the University of Montana–Western, **Aeron Haynie** is now happily ensconced (and tenured) at the University of Wisconsin–Green Bay where she actually gets paid to teach Dickens and develop cool interdisciplinary courses like "The Culture of Food." She's been published in such places as the *Victorian Institute Journal, Literary Mama, Radical Teacher,* and *Free Verse.*

Sonya Huber is an assistant professor at Georgia Southern University in the Department of Writing and Linguistics, where she teaches creative writing and composition. Her first book, *Opa Nobody* (University of Nebraska Press), presents a portrait of her anti-Nazi activist grandfather in fiction and memoir. Her work has appeared in *Fourth Genre, Literary Mama, Passages North,* the *Chronicle of Higher Education,* and anthologies from Seal Press, University of Arizona Press, and Prometheus Books. She lives in Statesboro, Georgia, with her son, Ivan, and husband, Donny Humes. She should never have worried about having a quiet and judgmental Gerber baby, because instead she got a skateboarding, air-guitar-playing, story-telling ball of pure independence.

Amy Hudock is a single mom who lives outside of Charleston, South Carolina, where she and her daughter ride horses, swim at the neighborhood pool, and fish at the waterfront park. She holds a PhD in American literature and women's studies, and is the chair of the Humanities Department at a private college preparatory school. She is the editor-in-chief of *Literary Mama* (http://literarymama.com), coeditor of *Literary Mama: Reading for the Maternally Inclined* (Seal Press), and author of essays that have appeared in *Skirt! Magazine, ePregnancy, Philosophical Mother, Pregnancy and Baby, Single State of the Union,* and *A Cup of Comfort for Single Mothers.* She blogs at Single Mothering: Southern Style (http://singlemotheringsouthern style.blogspot.com).

Megan Pincus Kajitani made it almost to the end of her four-year Javits Fellowship before leaving the PhD path. She came away with an MA in media and cultural studies from the University of Wisconsin–Madison and a job as a career counselor for graduate students at the University of California, San Diego. Now Megan is a freelance writer and editor; her Web site is at http://www.mpk-ink.com. Recent publications include columns in the *Chronicle of Higher Education,* a chapter in *Children and Media in Times of War and Conflict* (Hampton Press), and an essay in *Sunshine/Noir* (CityWorks Press). Motivated by the events described in her *Mama, PhD* essay, she also writes a blog called Having Enough (http://www.having-enough. com). She lives with her husband and daughter in Carlsbad, California.

Julia Spicher Kasdorf is the author of two collections of poetry, *Eve's Striptease* and *Sleeping Preacher,* both from the Pitt Poetry Series (University of Pittsburgh Press), a book of essays, *The Body and the Book* (Johns Hopkins University Press), and a biography, *Fixing Tradition* (Pandora/US). Most recently, with Michael Tyrell she edited *Broken Land: Poems of Brooklyn* (NYU Press). She directs the MFA program at The Pennsylvania State University and lives in Bellefonte, Pennsylvania, where she is raising a child with an artist to whom she is no longer married.

Jean Kazez lives in Dallas, Texas, where she divides her time between writing, teaching, and enjoying life with her husband and two children. She received a PhD in philosophy from the University of Arizona in 1990. She has written about ethics and everyday life in her book, *The Weight of Things: Philosophy and the Good Life* (Blackwell), as well as in essays about altruism, happiness, and the Mommy Wars in *Philosophy Now* and *The Philosopher's Magazine.* She is currently working on a book about animals as well as on essays about the ethical dilemmas confronted by parents. You can find out more at her blog, Jean Kazez (http://www.kazez.blogspot.com).

Natalie Kertes Weaver is a theologian, poet, painter, daughter, wife, and mother. She chairs the Religious Studies Department at Ursuline College in Pepper Pike, Ohio, and teaches a wide range of courses in theology and religion. She has published academic articles and is currently writing a book on the theology of family and marriage (Saint Mary's Press). Natalie holds degrees in classical languages, philosophy, and ethics, and completed her PhD with a dissertation in feminist theology from Loyola University

Chicago. Natalie is married to her college sweetheart, with whom she has one son, and hopes to grow her family after she is tenured.

Cynthia Kuhn lives with her husband and two sons in Colorado, where she is an associate professor of English at Metropolitan State College of Denver. Her writing has appeared in publications such as *McSweeney's Quarterly*, *Literary Mama*, and *Copper Nickel*; she is also the author of *Self-Fashioning in Margaret Atwood's Fiction: Dress, Culture and Identity* (Peter Lang Publishing) and coeditor, with Cindy Carlson, of a forthcoming collection of critical essays, *Styling Texts: Dress and Fashion in Literature* (Cambria Press).

Laura Levitt directs the Jewish Studies Program at Temple University where she teaches courses in religion and women's studies. She lives in Philadelphia with her partner, David, and their two dogs, Moses and Walden. She is the author of *Jews and Feminism: The Ambivalent Search for Home* (Routledge) and, most recently, *American Jewish Loss after the Holocaust* (New York University Press). Her academic writing is eclectic. She often writes in the first person. Laura's students are in many ways her children. This academic family includes a number of PhDs: Tania Oldenhage, Michelle Friedman, Marian Ronan, Deborah Glanzberg-Krainin, Liora Gubkin, and Amy Weigand.

Julia Lisella is an assistant professor of English at Regis College, teaching courses in American literature and poetry writing. She continues to be fascinated by the connections between the working lives of the women writers she studies and teaches and our own lives. She is at work on a book about maternity, modernism, and radical women poets of the 1930s. She is the author of two books of poetry, *Love Song Hiroshima* (Finishing Line Press) and *Terrain* (WordTech Editions).

Jennifer Margulis is a recovering academic who lives in Ashland, Oregon, with her husband and three children: Hesperus (eight), Athena (seven), and Etani (four). Recently a Fulbright Fellow in West Africa, she has eaten fried crickets in Niger, lectured on slavery in Mauritania, appeared live on prime-time TV in France, and performed the cancan in America. An award-winning professional writer, consultant, and photojournalist, she has published in the *New York Times*, *Ms. Magazine*, *Wondertime*, *Parenting*, the *Christian Science Monitor*, and dozens of other magazines and newspapers.

She has also edited or authored four books, including *Toddler: Real-Life Stories of Those Fickle, Irrational, Urgent, Tiny People We Love* (Seal Press).

Alissa McElreath lives in Raleigh, North Carolina, with her husband, two children, a dog, a cat, and a crazy rabbit. She holds an MA in creative writing from the University of Binghamton and an MA in English language and literature from the University of Rochester. Her doctoral work is currently on hold as she juggles full-time teaching, writing, and parenting. She hopes to complete her second novel by the end of next spring and hopefully, will do more with it than leave it to slowly gather dust at the bottom of a drawer.

Josie Mills holds a PhD in English with a specialty in creative writing (poetry) from the University of Denver. Her poetry has appeared in national and international journals including *Talking River Review, Bitterroot, Colorado Lawyer,* and *Mantis, a Journal of Poetry, Criticism, and Translation.* She lives in Denver with her husband and two sons and is a member of the English faculty at Arapahoe Community College in Littleton, Colorado.

Anjalee Deshpande Nadkarni is a playwright-actor-director living in Syracuse, New York. A graduate of the MFA directing program at Northwestern University, she studied under Robert Falls of the Goodman Theatre. Before and after graduate school, she freelanced as an actor-director. Her acting credits include projects filmed in New York, Chicago, London, and Mumbai; her favorites remain the 1996 film *Once We Were Strangers,* which competed at the 1998 Sundance Film Festival, and the 1998 program *The Prodigal Daughter,* which aired in India on D-TV. Anjalee currently teaches at Le Moyne College and continues to write whenever her two-year-old son allows.

Susan O'Doherty is the author of *Getting Unstuck without Coming Unglued: A Woman's Guide to Unblocking Creativity* (Seal Press). Her work has appeared in numerous publications, including *Eureka Literary Magazine, Northwest Review, Apalachee Review, Eclectica,* and *Literary Mama,* and the anthologies *About What Was Lost: Twenty Writers on Miscarriage, Healing, and Hope* (Penguin) and *It's a Boy!* (Seal Press). New stories will appear in *Hospital Drive* and in *Sex for America,* edited by Stephen Elliott. Her story "Passing" was chosen as the New York story for Ballyhoo Stories' ongoing 50 States Project, and will be distributed in chapbook form at bookstores throughout New York State. Her popular advice column for writers, "The Doctor Is In," appears each Friday on M. J. Rose's publishing blog, Buzz, Balls, & Hype (http://mjroseblog.typepad.com/buzz_balls_hype). She lives in Brooklyn with her husband and her thirteen-year-old son, with whom she is unambivalently delighted.

Tedra Osell earned her PhD in English from the University of Washington in 2002, and wrote her dissertation about eighteenth-century pseudony-mous periodical publication in England. She was an assistant professor at the University of Guelph in Ontario for three years before making the difficult decision to give up her position and move home to the West Coast. She has published essays about eighteenth-century pseudonymity in *Eighteenth-Century Studies* and about contemporary pseudonymity in the *Scholar and Feminist Online* and the *Minnesota Review*. She plans to return to teaching at some point, but for now she is a writing mom. Tedra blogs at the Suicide Girls newswire (http://suicidegirls.com/members/Bitch_PhD/news), where she comments on feminist and reproductive rights issues, and at her own blog, Bitch, Ph.D. (http://bitchphd.blogspot.com), where she comments on anything that crosses her mind.

Miriam Peskowitz is the author, with Andrea Buchanan, of *The Daring Book for Girls* (HarperCollins), *The Truth Behind the Mommy Wars* (Seal Press), and two academic works, *Judaism Since Gender*, edited with Laura Levitt (Routledge), and *Spinning Fantasies* (University of California Press). She is the cofounder of MotherTalk (http://www.mother-talk.com), an on-line book review site that connects mothers, bloggers, and authors. Miriam was an award-winning and tenured professor at the University of Florida, a post she left in 1998 when her first child was born and her workplace had no formal family leave policy for professors. She has also taught at Emory University, Temple University, and the Reconstructionist Rabbinical College. She lives in Philadelphia with her husband and two daughters. Her current Web site is http://www.daringbookforgirls.com.

Christy Rowe is a lecturer in literature/humanities at the University of Denver, where her academic interests range from twentieth-century poet-ics, to travel writing, to sci-fi and fantasy studies (with an emphasis on the cyberpunk movement). A travel addict, she's been to four continents and twenty-plus countries. She has published both critical and creative work (mostly poetry) in journals such as *McSweeney's Quarterly*, the *Denver*

Quarterly, Salt Hill, and the *Journal of Imagism.* Currently she lives in Denver with her husband and two daughters and dreams of her next trip to Thailand.

Judith Sanders works as a freelance writer, editor, writing coach—and as a mother. She received a BA in literature from Yale, where she was a member of the pioneering first full class of women; an MA from the Boston University Creative Writing Program; a Fulbright Fellowship for a year of study and teaching in France; and a PhD in English from Tufts University. She has taught writing and literature at Boston University, the Massachusetts Institute of Technology, Tufts, and Bowdoin College. She has published articles and poems in such journals as the *American Scholar* and *Poetica.* She is currently writing a book of short stories and editing an anthology of mothering poems with *Mama, PhD* contributor Julia Lisella.

After much drama and hand-wringing, **Irena Auerbuch Smith** completed her dissertation and obtained a PhD in comparative literature after her first child was born, then went and had two more children in quick succession, which pretty much destroyed her chances of ever getting a "real" job. She currently lives in Palo Alto with her incredibly patient husband, teaches part time in the mornings, and spends the bulk of her afternoons and weekends driving various children to various after-school activities. Her long-term goals include finishing a memoir about growing up as a Russian émigré in the Bay Area, running the Nike Women's Marathon (she's up to twelve miles), and getting her children to school without sprinting the last fifty yards in an attempt to beat the bell.

Sheila Squillante is a writer of poetry and nonfiction whose work has appeared or will be appearing in such journals as *Prairie Schooner, Clackamas Literary Review,* the *Southeast Review, Phoebe, Quarterly West,* and *Glamour,* and at such online spaces as *Literary Mama, Brevity, Unpleasant Event Schedule,* and *TYPO.* She is the associate director of the MFA Program at The Pennsylvania State University, where she also teaches in the English Department. She lives with her husband and their two-year-old son (whom they did not, much to the chagrin of her good-natured class, name Beowulf); they are expecting a daughter in November of 2007.

Rebecca Steinitz has a PhD in English from the University of California, Berkeley. Formerly an associate professor in the English Department at

Ohio Wesleyan University, she is now a writer, editor, and consultant. She has published scholarly articles on Victorian fiction and life writing in *LIT: Literature Interpretation Theory, Studies in the Novel, a/b: Auto/Biography Studies, Victorians Institute Journal,* and the *Communication Review.* Her essays and reviews have appeared in the *New Republic, Utne Reader, Salon, Inside Higher Ed,* the *New York Observer,* the *Boston Globe,* and the *Women's Review of Books,* among other places. She lives in Arlington, Massachusetts, with her husband and two daughters.

Liz Stockwell grew up in Panama where she spent endless hours exploring the jungle and developing a love for tropical biology. After earning a PhD from the University of Washington with a dissertation titled "Wing Morphology and Flight Maneuverability in New World Leaf-nosed Bats," she spent six years in Halifax, Nova Scotia, rediscovering her Canadian roots and teaching at Dalhousie University. She now lives on Burnaby Mountain near Vancouver, British Colombia, where she spends her days with her two young children, teaching them about the joys of playing in the woods, eating wild salmonberries, and searching for banana slugs.

Jean-Anne Sutherland holds a PhD in sociology from the University of Akron, where she completed a dissertation entitled "'What Can I Do Different, What Could Be Better, What Could You Do More?': Guilt, Shame, and Mothering." As an assistant professor of sociology at the University of North Carolina Wilmington, she continues her research on mothering, guilt, and shame. She is thrilled to be living close to the shore with her daughter, Savannah, and their dachshund, Reggie.

Jamie Warner earned her PhD in political science in 2001 from The Pennsylvania State University, and teaches political theory at Marshall University in Huntington, West Virginia. Her research centers on nontraditional forms of political participation and communication, especially those involving political humor and parody, which makes her research a lot of fun. Her work has appeared in *Popular Communication* and *Women & Politics,* and she's currently working on a book titled *Political Culture Jamming: Politics, Parody, and Truth in the American Public Sphere.* She lives in the woods with her lovely husband, George, where they are growing their first real garden, trying to make cheese, and still debating whether or not to have children.

Erin Webster Garrett holds a PhD in literary studies from the University of Denver and is currently an associate professor of English and women's studies at Radford University. She has written extensively on working mother extraordinaire Mary Shelley, and credits her successful application for tenure to the recent publication of her first book on the subject, *The Literary Career of Novelist Mary Shelley after 1822*. She credits her continued sanity to the births of her children, Walker Bowman, who agreeably arrived on the last day of classes following her first year as an assistant professor, and Katherine Abigail, who arrived three weeks before Erin learned of having been awarded tenure. She currently lives in Virginia with her husband and two children.

Jennifer Eyre White has an MS in electrical engineering from the University of California, Los Angeles. She lives in the San Francisco Bay Area with her (second) husband and three kids. Her daughter Riley (now twelve) swears that she will attend UCLA some day and revisit those hallways and bathrooms that were once her second home. Jennifer still works part-time as an engineering analyst, but somewhere along the line she became a writer, too. She's published in *EE Times, Institute of Electrical and Electronics Engineers Spectrum*, the *International Journal of Vehicle Systems Dynamics, Wondertime*, the Cup of Comfort series (Adams Media), and *Literary Mama: Reading for the Maternally Inclined* (Seal Press), among other places. She writes about the chaos and alarmingly high decibel level of life with three kids on her Web site, Having Three Kids (http://www.Having ThreeKids.com).